(63-18018)   12-10-63

Ancient Peoples and Places

THE BALTS

General Editor

DR GLYN DANIEL

Ancient Peoples and Places

THE BALTS

Marija Gimbutas

79 PHOTOGRAPHS
47 LINE DRAWINGS
11 MAPS

FREDERICK A. PRAEGER
Publisher
New York

Ancient Peoples and Places
GENERAL EDITOR: DR GLYN DANIEL

BOOKS THAT MATTER *Published in the United States of America*
in 1963 by Frederick A. Praeger, Inc.
Publisher, 64 University Place
New York 3, N.Y.
All rights reserved
Library of Congress Catalog Card Number: 63-18018
Printed in Great Britain

CONTENTS

LIST OF ILLUSTRATIONS   6

FOREWORD   11

INTRODUCTION   13

I   LINGUISTIC AND HISTORIC BACKGROUND   21

II   THEIR ORIGINS   37

III   THE BRONZE AND THE EARLY IRON AGE OF THE MARITIME BALTS   54

IV   THE BRONZE AND THE EARLY IRON AGE OF THE EASTERN BALTS   91

V   THE 'GOLDEN AGE'   109

VI   THE BALTIC 'MIDDLE IRON AGE'   141

VII   THE BALTS BEFORE THE DAWN OF HISTORY   155

VIII   RELIGION   179

NOTES   205

BIBLIOGRAPHY   214

SOURCES OF ILLUSTRATIONS   224

THE PLATES   227

NOTES ON THE PLATES   269

INDEX   277

ILLUSTRATIONS

PLATES   1 Ancient Prussians: bronze relief
          2 Corded and pinched pottery from Finland
          3 Grave goods of Battle-Axe culture
        4, 5 Bronze pin and axe
          6 Bronze flanged axe
          7 Bronze axe with semicircular edge
          8 Late Bronze Age socketed axe
          9 Late Bronze Age spearhead
         10 Urn with necklace design
         11 Face-urn with amber bead ear-rings
         12 Face on an urn from Poland
         13 Urn with engraved horse. Stela with sun symbol
       14, 15 Urn with symbolic scene
         16 Sheepskin coat from Masuria
         17 Hill-fort, southern Lithuania
         18 Man's grave goods, western Lithuania
         19 Necklaces from central and eastern Lithuania
         20 Fretworked belt separator
         21 Fretworked fibula
         22 Woman's grave goods, western Lithuania
         23 Woman's grave goods from double grave
         24 Woman's grave goods from double grave
         25 Double grave, Kaunas, Lithuania
         26 Elk in silver-plated bronze
       27, 28 Silver-plated bronze fibulae
         29 Gold-plated plaques
         30 Silver-plated plaque
         31 Details of horse's head gear

6

PLATES 32 Bronze fibula with enamel incrustation
33 Bronze fibula with enamel inlay
34 Pendants with enamel inlay
35, 36 Bronze pendants with enamel incrustation
37, 38 Fibulae with enamel inlay
39, 40 Fibulae with enamel inlay
41 Bronze bracelet with enamel inlay
42 Bronze bracelets with enamel inlay
43 Enamelled ornaments from central Russia
44 Silver fibula and enamelled plaque
45 Chest ornament from woman's grave
46 Chest ornament
47 Silver bow-fibula
48 Silver bracelet
49 Silver necklace
50 Silver neck-ring
51 Snake-headed silver fibula
52-54 Axe, spearhead and shield umbo
55 Man's grave goods, western Lithuania
56 Silver-coated bronze pendant and bronze pin
57 Woman's grave goods, central Lithuania
58 Woman's chest ornament
59 Bronze necklace
60 Silver neck-ring
61 Bronze horseshoe fibula
62 Horseshoe fibula
63 Massive bronze bracelet
64 Man's bracelet
65 Kerchief (reconstruction). Ornament of bronze rings
66 Parts of leather belts. Belt with bronze plates

7

PLATES 67 Instruments for girdle-twisting

68, 69 Swords of Viking type

70 Horse's bridle

71, 72 Details of horses' graves

73, 74 Silver-plated iron bridle

75, 76 Silver-plated iron stirrup

77, 78 Hill fort, western Lithuania

79 Roof poles topped with sun and moon symbols

FIGURES 1 *Map: Baltic tribes and provinces c. A.D. 1200, p. 23*

2 *Map: area of the Baltic river names, pp. 30–31*

3 *Map: expansion of Kurgan culture, p. 39*

4 *Map: distribution of physical types, p. 47*

5 *Proto-Baltic variant of Corded pottery, p. 50*

6 *Reconstruction and plan of house, p. 51*

7 *Stratified barrow, Samland, p. 53*

8 *Map: principal amber routes, p. 58*

9 *Snake-headed stone hoe, p. 60*

10 *Map: distribution of Baltic culture in Bronze Age, p. 63*

11 *Map: distribution of stone hoes and bronze artifacts, p. 64*

12 *Classical Baltic Late Bronze Age barrow, p. 67*

13 *Ornaments from Samland, p. 70*

14 *Ornaments from Samland, p. 71*

15 *Barrow in western Lithuania, p. 72*

16 *Temple ornaments and pendants, p. 73*

17 *House-urn, p. 74*

18 *Face-urns, p. 75*

19 *Necklace from Face-urn period, p. 76*

20 *Solar motifs on face-urn lids, p. 77*

21 *Engravings on face-urns, p. 78*

FIGURES   22   *Bone comb, p. 80*

23   *Plan of fortified village, northern Poland (ancient Prussia), p. 81*

24   *Map: Baltic Early Iron Age groups, p. 83*

25   *Pot-covered urn grave, p. 84*

26   *Urns in stone cists, p. 85*

27   *Barrow containing large stone cist, p. 87*

28   *Geometrically decorated Prussian urns, p. 88*

29   *Urns from Samland, p. 89*

30   *Early Bronze Age Fat'janovo pot, p. 93*

31   *Late Bronze Age and Iron Age pots, p. 96*

32   *Plans of houses, eastern Baltic hill-fort village, p. 104*

33   *Eastern Baltic Early Iron Age hill-fort, p. 105*

34   *Pins from Early Iron Age hill-fort, p. 106*

35   *Weapons and utensils from Eastern Baltic fortified villages, p. 107*

36   *Map: Baltic lands in Roman period, pp. 110–11*

37   *Warrior's grave in tree-trunk coffin, p. 112*

38   *Sudovian farmer's grave, p. 115*

39   *Iron scythe from Latvia, p. 116*

40   *Female head and neck ornaments, p. 127*

41   *Bronze fibulae with cast pin, p. 128*

42   *Bronze fibula with chains, p. 129*

43   *Chest ornaments, p. 130*

44   *Fretworked belt parts, p. 131*

45   *Neck-ring with pendants, p. 133*

46   *Bronze fibula shaped to resemble animal, p. 135*

47   *Bronze fibula with silver-plated foot, p. 146*

48   *Star and sun motifs on fibulae, p. 146*

49   *Owl-head fibula, p. 147*

50   *Map: The Balts after the Slavic expansion, p. 151*

FIGURES 51 *Silver-plated crossbow fibula, p. 156*

52 *Bronze necklace with pendants, p. 160*

53 *Ornamented bracelets, p. 161*

54 *Iron knife in bronze scabbard, p. 162*

55 *Gold-plated ornament on horse bridle, p. 165*

56 *Plan of Jersika hill-fort, p. 170*

57 *Map: Lithuanian empire, fourteenth–fifteenth centuries A.D.,
   pp. 174–5*

58 *Plan of Baltic sanctuary with temple, p. 181*

Foreword

THIS BOOK WAS WRITTEN at Stanford, California, at the Center for Advanced Study in the Behavioral Sciences, located on a hill overlooking broad expanses in all directions. At certain moments here I have visualized the hills and slopes shrouded with green oaks as seen from the castle hill of Gediminas in Vilnius, my native city in the heart of the Baltic lands, from which I am separated by almost twenty years. The Californian sand dunes, at Carmel, remind me of the pure white sands of Palanga, where I used to collect handfuls of amber; and the sunsets in the Pacific, of the peacefully sinking sun as it disappeared into the Baltic Sea, beyond where, to the west, my forefathers thought was the cosmic tree, the axis of the world, holding up the arch of the sky.

I am deeply grateful therefore to the Center for such inspiring working conditions, the delightful atmosphere, and for all the assistance made available to me. I would also like to express appreciation to my many Lithuanian, Lettish, Polish and Russian colleagues for invaluable information they supplied and the illustrations and books they procured, particularly to Drs J. Antoniewicz, V. Ginters, Ju. V. Kukharenko, R. Rimantienė, and A. Spekke. For technical help, editing and typing, I am deeply indebted to Miss M. Gallaher and to my daughter Danutė.

M.G.

| Dates | General Chronological Table | |
	East Baltic Area	Central Europe
c. 1200 A.D.	Beginning of history	
c. 850 A.D.	Late Iron Age	Medieval period
c. 400 A.D.	Middle Iron Age	Migration period
c. 100 A.D.	'Golden Age' (or 'old Iron Age')	Roman period
c. 400 B.C.	Early Iron Age	La Tène
800/700 B.C.		Hallstatt
c. 1100 B.C.	Late Bronze Age	Late Urnfield period
c. 1250 B.C.	Classical Baltic Bronze Age	Early Urnfield period
1450/1400 B.C.	'Trzciniec' Early Bronze Age 'Iwno'	Tumulus period
c. 1600 B.C.		Late Únětice
c. 1800 B.C.	Chalcolithic	Early and Classical Únětice
c. 2200 B.C.	Formation of individual Kurgan groups Coming of the Kurgan (Corded, Battle-axe) culture	

Introduction

IN THE LANDS occupied by the ancient Balts the geography was of many kinds. A long stretch of the Baltic Sea with wind-blown dunes and white sand beaches, embellished with tiny bits of glittering amber, lay to the west. Along the sea shore and along the larger rivers discharging into the sea—the Vistula, Nemunas (Niemen, Memel), Daugava (Düna, Dvina), and their tributaries—were lowlands and the most fertile lands covered with alluvial deposits. Through the ages, the sea coast and these larger rivers were the means by which the Balts were able to communicate with central and western Europe. Farther east, eastern East Prussia (present Masuria in northern Poland), eastern Lithuania and eastern Latvia were surrounded by the moraine belt left over from the last ice age, with many lakes, rocks and a sandy soil; and beyond it to the east were the up-lands, called Byelo-Russia, the Smolensk–Moscow and central Russian ridges, intersected by the valleys of the upper Dnieper and its tributaries and by the river system of the upper Volga basin. To the south, in present southern Byelo-Russia, these uplands were—as they still are—girdled by the swampy area of the Pripet River basin. There are no high mountains in this whole area; the highest points reach only 200 or 300 metres above sea-level.

The lands along the Baltic Sea belong to the central European climatic zone. Then, to the east, begins the transitional zone between oceanic and continental climate, and all the eastern parts combine the continental climate with rather cold winters and warm summers. The period encompassed in this book falls within the limits of the Sub-Boreal and Sub-Atlantic climatic zones. The Sub-Boreal climate, c. 3000–c. 500 B.C., was somewhat warmer and less humid than the Sub-Atlantic, which persists to the present day. The vegetation was as varied as the climate in the transitional zone between central and northern Europe. There is a great variety of forests, deciduous and coniferous. At present, pine and spruce predominate, but earlier, in the Sub-Boreal period and before many regions were cleared and turned into arable land, forests consisted mainly of leaf-bearing trees—oaks, linden, maple, elm, poplar, hornbeam, aspen, birch, ash, hazel, willow. Forest fauna was rich and not quite nordic. Hares, squirrels, badgers, martens, beavers, lynx, boars, wolves, bears, aurochs, bison, wild horses, and elks lived on into the Sub-Atlantic. Only the wild horse disappeared during the Late Iron Age. Aurochs persisted in early historic times, and bison were to be found in the large expanses of virgin forests of present-day northern Poland and southern Lithuania up to the eighteenth century. Forests were full of large grouse and partridges, and in the warm season wild ducks and geese flocked to the swampy regions. All these animals and birds in addition to fish, mushrooms, nuts, honey, and berries formed a great part of the food supply of the farmer living on the high banks of rivers and around lakes near the forests.

The scenery in these lands is most beautiful in late spring and early summer, when the ears form on the fresh green shoots of the rye, flax blossoms in a soft blue, and the morning lark trills above field and meadow. At this season too is heard the song of the nightingale, the call of the cuckoo, and the music of many other birds and insects. Storks with their nests atop farmers' houses are also inseparable from the landscape. In some remote villages, in the middle of the network of lakes and at the edges of large forests, far from the trade routes and towns, lived people who up to quite recently were not much concerned about the outer world. So completely absorbed were they by the life-bringing natural forces, the rotation of the year's seasons, and by their work in the fields, that their way of life, their language, beliefs, and customs remained little changed down the ages. Seen from a distance, their low houses with thatched roofs look like mushrooms harmonizing with the landscape; but one has only to visit the homesteads themselves to see how much love and care was invested in the decoration of doors, window shutters, corner projections, porches, gables, colonnades in front of storehouses, dower chests, spindle wheels, washing-beetles, and other furnishings. Houses were surrounded by a variety of flowers and large trees, usually linden, maple, elm or oak. For about 190 days of the year cattle, sheep, goats, and pigs, collected from the whole village, were kept in pastures and guarded by an old shepherd, who made music on a buck's horn, and shepherd children, who played flutes and quaint wooden pipes; horses were pastured overnight. In the fields, around fires, as well as by the mother's spindle wheel and loom during long winter evenings, folk-songs and tales flourished and were transmitted from generation to generation. Collective field labours were followed by songs, sung in rotation by several voices, and with refrains which harmonized with the rhythm of harvesting, and flax and hemp plucking and drying. From lullabies and wedding songs to songs of lamentation during wakes, man's life was inseparable from *daina*, 'the song' (in the folkloristic archives of Lithuania and Latvia there are about 500,000 collected songs, leading us to wonder how many more may have disappeared in past ages and with the lost Baltic territories). The Balts sang ceaselessly, as though singing were as necessary and as easy as breathing. And their songs for all occasions reflect these people's feeling of kinship with mother earth and her many creatures, and appreciation of her manifold gifts.

One could supplement enormously the evidence of prehistoric monuments by using the folklore and ethnographic material preserved in the most archaic villages, where passing ages have not changed the mode of life from that of prehistoric times. However, the scope of the present book requires us to focus our attention on actual archaeological finds. I shall, nevertheless, in speaking of origin, distribution, and religion, make some use of the linguistic and folkloristic data. The Baltic area is exceptional among the lands inhabited by people of Indo-European origin in that the language and folklore have survived in a remarkably pure state, and ancient cultural traits have not been adulterated or destroyed by the many expansions and migrations of prehistoric and early historic periods, as was the case in most areas of central, western, and southern Europe. The main objects of our attention will be hill-forts and cemeteries, the basic monuments of Baltic prehistory. The many hill-forts jutting out on river banks and lake shores have given the Baltic regions the richly deserved name, 'the land of hill-forts'. They are either sites of communal villages dating from the Chalcolithic, Bronze and Early Iron Ages, or castle-hills, the acropolises of the later Iron Age. However, archaeological finds that have accumulated in the course of the last hundred years come not so much from hill-forts, as from barrow and flat-grave cemeteries. While the systematically excavated hill-top villages or hill-forts do not total more than a hundred, the cemeteries number many more than a thousand.

First signs of interest in archaeological finds in the Baltic lands date back to the seventeenth and eighteenth centuries. The period of romanticism and growing nationalism at the beginning of the nineteenth century greatly increased the search for national antiquities; historians, poets, and writers kept their own private collections. Organized archaeological research owes its inception to a number of historic and antiquarian societies and committees founded in the thirties and forties of the nineteenth century: 'Gesellschaft für Geschichte und Altertumskunde' founded in 1834 in Riga, 'Gelehrte estnische Gesellschaft' in 1838 in Tartu (Dorpat), and 'Altertumsgesellschaft Prussia' in 1844 in Königsberg. Eustach

Tyszkiewicz, who for many years collected archaeological materials and made a series of excavations in Lithuania and Byelo-Russia, published in 1842 a book entitled *A Glimpse of the Sources of Lithuanian Archaeology*. He was well acquainted with the Scandinavian archaeological literature and classified his materials according to Scandinavian standards. In 1855, as a result of his initiative, an 'archaeological Commission' and a museum were established in Vilnius.

In the nineteenth as well as in the twentieth century until the beginning of World War II, archaeological work in East Prussia was in the hands of the 'Prussia Museum' in Königs-berg. It carried out numerous excavations in Samland and elsewhere in East Prussia, and housed the accumulated anti-quities of the ancient Prussians. In the Museum's periodical, *Sitzungsberichte*, current between 1875 and 1940, almost all excavation reports were published. The beginnings of systema-tic archaeological work, of classifications and excavations at the end of the nineteenth century are inseparable from the names of the notable archaeologists, O. Tischler and A. Bezzen-berger. The greater part of Lithuania and Latvia being a province of Imperial Russia, the archaeological work carried out there by Lithuanians, Latvians, Estonians, and Poles was in large part dependent on general trends in archaeological research in Russia. The 'Imperial Archaeological Com-mission of Peterburg', founded in 1859, was a central organ-ization supervising archaeological activities in the whole of Russia including the Baltic provinces. The 'Archaeological Society', founded in 1864 in Moscow, organized Russian Archaeological Congresses in various parts of the country. In 1893, the congress took place in Vilnius, and in 1896 in Riga, focusing attention on antiquities of the Baltic area. After the congress in Riga, a museum was founded there; later, its collec-tions, in independent Latvia, were given over to the State Historic Museum of Riga. Although the attention of Russian archaeologists was in the main focused on southern Russia, particularly on Scythian antiquities, the rich Baltic Iron Age cemeteries and hill/forts were a great attraction. Since the seven/ ties of the last century, the Baltic Iron Age has aroused inter/ national interest. In 1876, O. Montelius read a paper on the Iron Age in the Baltic provinces, Russia and Poland, at the Congress of Anthropology and Archaeology in Budapest; and in 1877, C. Grewingk, professor of geology in the University of Tartu, presented a lecture on the same subject in the Fourth Russian Archaeological Congress in Kazan. Other studies by Grewingk, on the pagan graves in Lithuania, Latvia and Byelo/Russia (1870), and on the archaeology of the Baltic area and Russia (1874), have had a lasting influence on later archaeological research.

Though much important archaeological work was carried out in the Baltic countries and Russia before the first World War, the sources on which this monograph is based come mainly from excavations made between World Wars I and II. During this period, while in Russia the revolution resulted in the liquidation of almost an entire generation of able archaeolo/ gists, in East Prussia, Lithuania and Latvia large/scale excavat/ ions were begun. Finds from hundreds of cemeteries filled the museums, particularly the State Historical Museum in Riga and the Cultural Museum of Vytautas the Great (present Historical Museum) in Kaunas, as well as the 'Prussia Museum', the Danzig and many other provincial museums. This period, too, saw the publication of numerous basic books for the archae/ ology of the East Baltic area. Byelo/Russia and western Greater Russia were for several decades completely neglected until archaeological work was resumed after World War II, and now hill/forts are being explored there with remarkable speed. In the Baltic countries, after the interruption caused by incorporation into the Soviet Union and the loss of key figures in archae/ ological research, the work is again going forward with a new generation of prehistorians. In East Prussia, the situation has changed drastically: the old 'Prussia Museum' no longer exists, its treasures having perished during the war, and only its archives having been transferred to the University of Göttingen in Germany. Northeastern East Prussia, now the Kaliningrad area, is attracting some attention from Soviet archaeologists, while southern and western East Prussia, or Masuria, is being increasingly excavated by Polish prehistorians. Notable results have been achieved during recent decades in the ancient Baltic Sudovian lands in present northern Poland where numerous excavations have been carried out by the Warsaw and Białystok archaeological museums, headed by J. Antoniewicz.

This book is a first attempt to survey the entire prehistoric period from the beginning of the second millennium B.C.— when a branch of the IndoEuropeanspeaking peoples settled and gradually developed its individual cultural features in the area from Pomerania in northern Poland in the west to central Russia in the east—to the thirteenth century A.D., the beginning of history, marked by two major events: the conquest of the ancient Prussians by the Teutonic Order, and the birth of the Lithuanian state.

The Baltic culture was not an isolated island in prehistoric and early historic Europe. In genesis and development it is inseparable from the other IndoEuropean groups. Thus, through the amber trade it was linked with the cultures of central and southern Europe from the time of the Bronze Age; its western branch was closely related with the central European ÚnĕticeTumulusUrnfield and the Germanic or 'Northern Area' cultures. It was not untouched or uninfluenced by the Hallstatt culture, by the westward advance of the Scythians in the eighth and the sixth–fifth centuries B.C., by the eastward flow of the Celts in the third century B.C., and by the movements of Goths from across the Baltic Sea to Pomerania in the first century B.C. and a few centuries later to south

Russia. Its eastern branch was in contact with the Finno-Ugrians in present eastern and northern Russia, with Cimmerians and Scythians north of the Black Sea, and with Slavs, the southern neighbours of the Balts, living north of the Carpathians, throughout the Bronze and Early Iron Ages. Between the second and fifth centuries A.D., due to intensive amber trade with the provinces of the Roman Empire, material standards of the Baltic culture rose tremendously. The East Baltic area became a strong cultural centre, and its influences extended to all of north-eastern Europe. This was the Baltic culture's 'golden age', terminated by the eastern Slav expansion to the Baltic lands in present western Russia—starting at the end of the fourth or during the fifth century A.D. and continuing to the twelfth century and later—and by the ensuing wars of the coastal Baltic tribes with the Scandinavian Vikings in the seventh century. Before the dawn of history the numerous Baltic tribes, ruled by powerful chieftains and landlords, lived through a second 'golden age', assuming a central position in commercial activities between western Europe, Scandinavia, Kievan Rus' and Byzantium.

Lack of general information about their prehistory has in countless instances resulted in the Baltic lands being considered as Germanic and Slavic. Archaeological and linguistic sources tell a different story, however, and they are quite sufficient now to fit a missing link in the mosaics of European ancient history.

CHAPTER I

Linguistic and Historic Background

THE DESIGNATION 'Balt' can have two different mean-
ings, depending upon whether we use it in a geographical
or political sense, or in a linguistic or ethnological sense. The
first embraces the Baltic states—Lithuania, Latvia and Estonia
—on the eastern coasts of the Baltic Sea. Before World War II,
these three states were independent and their population numbered about six million. In 1940, they were incorporated in the
Soviet Union. In this book, however, I shall not be speaking
of the modern Baltic states but of people who belong to one
linguistic group of the Indo-European family, that is, of the
Lithuanians, Latvians, and Old Prussians, along with their
kin tribes, many of which disappeared during the course of
prehistory and history. The Estonians will be excluded since
they are Finno-Ugrians, speaking an entirely different language
from the Indo-European and being of different origin.

The name 'Balts', deriving from the Baltic Sea, *Mare Bal-
ticum*, is a neologism, used since 1845 as a general name for the
people speaking 'Baltic' languages—Old Prussian, Lithuanian,
Lettish, Curonian, Semigallian, and Selian. Of these, only
Lithuanian and Lettish are living languages. Old Prussian
disappeared around 1700 due to German colonization of East
Prussia. Curonian, Semigallian, and Selian disappeared between 1400 and 1600. These were either Lettonized or
Lithuanized. Other eastern Baltic languages or dialects became
extinct in the protohistoric or early historic period and are
not preserved in written sources.

At the beginning of this century, another name for these
languages—'Aistian'—was coming into use. This was taken
from the Roman historian Tacitus, who, in his work *Germania*,
A.D. 98, mentioned *Aestii, gentes Aestiorum*, a people living on

Fig. 1

the eastern shore of the Baltic Sea. He described them as col-
lectors of amber and more energetic cultivators of crops and
fruits than the Germanic people, whom they resembled in
appearance and customs. Perhaps it would have been more
reasonable to apply the name 'Aistians' to the Baltic-speaking
peoples in general, even though it is not known whether
Tacitus used this name to describe all Baltic peoples, or Old
Prussians (the western Balts) alone, or only the amber collec-
tors living on the Baltic Sea coast around Frisches Haff, which
in Lithuanian is still called 'Aismarės' and was called 'Eyst-
meer' by the Anglo-Saxon traveller Wulstan in the ninth
century A.D. There is also a River 'Aista' in western Lithuania. In early historic records the *Aestii* or *Aisti* appear many
times. The Gothic writer Jordanes of the sixth century A.D.
locates the *Aestii*, 'a totally peaceful people', to the east of the
mouth of the Vistula, on the longest stretch of the Baltic sea
coast. Einhard in his *Vita Caroli Magni* of *c.* 830–40 finds
them on the eastern shores of the Baltic Sea, as neighbours of
the Slavs. The name 'Aisti' seems to have had a broader
application than to a single tribe.

The most ancient name for the Balts, or more probably for
eastern Balts, was Herodotus' *Neuri*. Since the prevalent
opinion is that the *Neuri* were Slavs, I shall come back to
Neuri in discussing the eastern Balts in Herodotus' time.

Since the second century A.D., names for separate Prussian
tribes appear: Ptolemy (*c.* A.D. 100–78) knew 'Soudinoi' and
'Galindai', Sudovians and Galindians, which shows that
Prussian tribes had their own individual names from a very
early period. Many centuries later, Sudovians and Galindians
continued to be designated by these same names in the list of
Prussian tribes. In 1326, Dusburg, the annalist of the Teutonic
Order, mentioned ten Prussian tribes, including the Sudovians ('Sudowite') and the Galindians ('Galindite'). The
others were: 'Pomesani', 'Pogesani', 'Varmienses', 'Nattangi',

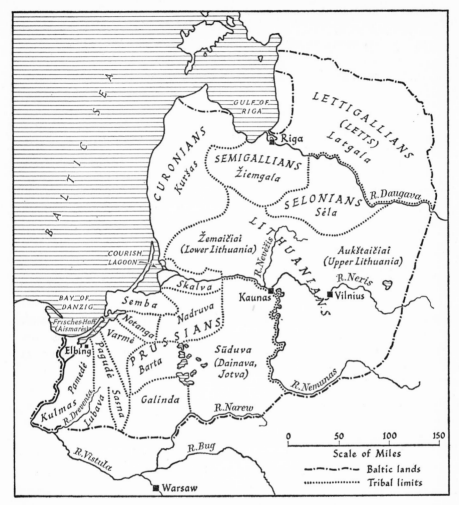

Fig. 1. Baltic tribes and provinces c. A.D. 1200

'Sambite', 'Nadrowite', 'Barthi', and 'Scalowite'. These names
were in Latin form. In present Lithuanian the names of the
Prussian provinces are: Pamedė, Pagudė, Varmė, Notanga,
Semba, Nadruva, Barta, Skalva, Sūduva, and Galinda. There
were two more provinces south of Pagudė and Galinda,

Fig. 1

namely Lubava and Sasna, known from other historic records. Sudovians, the largest Prussian tribe, were also called Jat‑vingians (Jotvingai; Jatwiagi of the Slavic sources).

A general name for the Prussians, that is, the western Balts, comes to light in the ninth century A.D.; this is *Bruzi*, first recorded by a Bavarian geographer some time after 845. It is believed that before the ninth century 'Prussian' was probably the name of one of the western Prussian tribes and was only gradually transferred to other tribes, like the tribal name 'Alle‑magne' for Germany. Around 965 an Arab trader from Spain, Ibrāhīm‑ibn‑Jakūb, who came to the Baltic Sea, spoke of Prussians (*Brûs* or *Burûs*) as having their separate language and being very courageous in wars against the Vikings ('Rus' '). The Curonians, a tribe on the Baltic Sea in the territory of present Lithuania and Latvia, are referred to as *Cori* or *Chori* in the Scandinavian sagas, which mention the wars between the Vikings and Curonia (Kurland) starting in the seventh century A.D. The land of the Semigallians in what is now central Latvia and northern Lithuania is likewise known from the Scandinavian records in connection with the Danish Viking onslaught against 'Semigalia' in 870. Names for other tribes appear considerably later. Those of the Lithuanians and Lettigallians (Letts), living in what is now eastern Lithuania, eastern Latvia and Byelo‑Russia, come into the written records only in the eleventh century.

The Baltic tribes enter into the pages of history one by one between the first centuries of the Christian era and the eleventh century. The earliest historical records are so scarce that the entire first millennium for the Balts is still in a protohistoric stage. Without the archaeological monuments, the way of life and the limits of distribution of these people could not be reconstructed. The tribal names appearing in the early his‑torical records help the identification of archaeologically known cultures, but only in a few cases do these records illuminate the occupation, social structure, customs, appearance, religion, and character of the people.

From Tacitus in the first century, we learn that the Aisti were the only people collecting amber and that they cultivated crops with a patience rarely found among the lazy Germans. In religion and appearance they resembled the Suebi (the Germanic people) but had a different language, more like that of the Bretons (Celtic people). They worshipped the mother goddess and wore boar masks which protected them, and ensured the safety of the worshipper even among his enemies.[1] About 880–90, King Alfred's voyager Wulfstan, who came by sailing boat from Haithabu in Schleswig through the Baltic Sea to the lower Vistula area, the River Elbing and Frisches Haff, described the land of the Aisti (which he called 'Eastland', 'Estum') as very large and containing many towns, each with its own king. They fought many contests among themselves. The king and the richest men drank mare's milk, the poor and the slaves mead. There was no ale brewed among them for there was enough mead.[2] Wulfstan then gives a long description of burial rites and the preservation of the dead by freezing, to which I shall return in the section on religion.

The first Christian missionaries who entered the lands of the ancient Prussians usually referred to them as 'stubborn pagans'. 'Sembi or Prussians are a most humane people (*homines humanissimi*),' wrote Archbishop Adam of Bremen around 1075. 'They go out to help those who are in peril at sea or who are attacked by pirates. Gold and silver they hold in very slight esteem. . . . Many praiseworthy things could be said about these peoples with respect to their morals, if only they had the faith of Christ whose missionaries they cruelly persecute. At their hands Adalbert, the illustrious bishop of the Bohemians, was crowned with martyrdom. Although they share everything else with our people, they prohibit only, to this very day indeed, access to their groves and springs which, they aver, are polluted by the entry of Christians. They take the meat of their draught animals for food and use their milk and blood as drink so freely that they are said to become intoxicated. These men are blue of colour [blue-eyed? Or through tattooing?], ruddy of face, and long-haired. Living, moreover, in inaccessible swamps, they will not endure a master among them.'³ The bronze door of the cathedral in Gniezno in northern Poland dating from the twelfth century depicts scenes of how the first missionary, Bishop Adalbert, comes to Prussia, disputes with the Prussian nobility and is decapitated. The Prussians are shown with spears, swords, and shields. They are beardless but with moustaches, have trimmed hair, and are wearing kilts,

Plate 1   blouses, and bracelets.

The ancient Balts apparently did not have their own writing. As yet no inscriptions have been found on stone or birch bark in native languages. The earliest writings in Old Prussian and Lithuanian date from the fourteenth and sixteenth centuries. All that was recorded earlier about the Baltic tribes was in Greek, Latin, Germanic or Slavic.

Today, the Old Prussian language is known only to linguists who study it from dictionaries published in the fourteenth and sixteenth centuries. The Baltic Prussians were conquered in the thirteenth century by the Teutonic Knights, German-speaking followers of Jesus, and in the course of 400 years the Prussian language disappeared. The crimes and atrocities committed by the conquerors disguised as heralds of the Christian faith are now forgotten. In 1701, 'Prussia' became an independent German monarchy. Since then the name 'Prussian' has passed over to the Germanic people.

The lands occupied by Baltic-speaking people in modern times are about one-sixth of what they were in prehistoric times before the Slavic and Germanic expansions.

Fig. 2   Old Prussian river and place names, although strongly Germanicized, cover the whole area between the Vistula and

Nemunas Rivers.[4] Some names presumed to be Baltic are found even west of the Vistula, in eastern Pomerania.[5] From the archaeological viewpoint there is absolutely no doubt that before the appearance of the Goths in the lower Vistula area and in eastern Pomerania in the first century B.C. these lands belonged to the direct ancestors of the Prussians. In the Bronze Age, before expansion of the central European Lusatian (Lausitz) culture around 1200 B.C., the western Balts seem to have covered the whole of Pomerania to the lower Oder, and what is now eastern Poland to the Bug and upper Pripet basins in the south, since we find here the same culture that was wide-spread in the ancient Prussian lands. The southern extent of the Prussians along the River Bug, a tributary of the Vistula, is indicated by the Prussian river names.[6] The archaeological finds show that present Podlasie in eastern Poland and Polesie in western Byelo-Russia belonged to the Baltic Sudovians until the beginning of history. Only after the long wars with the Russians and Poles during the eleventh–twelfth centuries A.D. did the southern limits of the Sudovian tribe fall back to the River Narew line, and in the thirteenth century they even retreated as far north as the Ostrówka (Osterode)–Olsztyn (Allenstein) line.[7]

Baltic river and place names cover the entire area from the Baltic Sea to western Greater Russia. There are many Baltic words borrowed by the Finno-Ugrians and even by the Volga Finns who lived in eastern Russia, and historic records from the eleventh–twelfth centuries mention a warlike Baltic tribe, the Galindians, above the River Protva near Mozhajsk and Gzhatsk, south-west of Moscow. All this points to Baltic peoples having lived in Russia before the expansion of eastern Slavs.

The Baltic elements in the archaeology, ethnography, and language of Byelo-Russia have intrigued scholars since the end of the nineteenth century. The Galindians around Moscow have provided a great puzzle: both the name and the historic records indicate they were neither Slavs nor Finno-Ugrians, Who were they?

In the Laurentian and Hypatian texts of the earliest native Russian chronicle 'Povest Vremennykh Let', the Galindians appear in 1058 and 1147 in the Slavic form *Goljad'*.[8] Linguistically this comes from the Old Russian *Goljadĭ*, the older form of which was **Golędĭ*. These forms correspond to the Proto-Baltic **Galindā*. The etymology of this word is explained by the Lithuanian word *galas*, 'end'. In Old Prussian, *Galindo* was also the name of a tribal district in the southern part of Baltic Prussia. The Prussian Galindians, as we have noted, were mentioned by Ptolemy in his geography. The Galindians of what is now Russia were very probably so named because they were the Baltic tribe farthest to the east. In the eleventh and twelfth centuries they had been surrounded on all sides by the Russians. The Russian dukes fought for centuries before they finally succeeded in defeating them. At which stage the historic records of the warlike Galindians end. Their resistance apparently was crushed, and they could not survive, being pressed by increasing numbers of Slavic peoples. For Baltic history these few recorded fragments are of utmost value: they show that eastern Balts fought against Slavic colonization in present-day Russia for 600 years and, for linguistic and archaeological studies, they are the basis for reconstructing the area of distribution of the early Balts.

Present maps of Byelo-Russia and Russia betray scarcely any Baltic character in river or place names, so Slavonized are these areas now. Yet linguists have succeeded in unravelling the true story. The Lithuanian linguist Būga, in his studies of 1913 and 1924, identified 121 river names in Byelo-Russia as being of Baltic origin.[9] He showed that almost all the names in the upper Dnieper and upper Nemunas basin are undoubtedly of

Baltic character. Some have corresponding forms in river names of Lithuania, Latvia, and East Prussia, and their etymology can be explained through the meaning of the Baltic words. In some instances in Byelo-Russia the same river name is repeated several times; for instance, *Vodva* (one is the right tributary of the River Dnieper, the other is in the district of Mogilev), which comes from the Baltic *Vaduva* and is a fre-quent river name in Lithuania; another is *Luchesa*, which in Baltic is *Laukesa* from the Lithuanian *laūkas*, 'field'. This river name is known in Lithuania (as *Laukesa*), in Latvia (as *Laucesa*), and occurs three times in Byelo-Russia: north and south-east of Smolensk and south of Vitebsk (the tributary of the upper Daugava-Dvina).

To this day river names are the best guides to establishing ancient geographical distributions of peoples. Būga was con-vinced of the earlier Baltic character of present-day Byelo-Russia, and he even developed the theory that the original lands of the Lithuanians must have been north of the River Pripet and in the upper Dnieper basin. In 1932, a German Slavicist, Vasmer, published a number of names, considered by him as Baltic, of rivers in the districts of Smolensk, Tver (Kalinin), Moscow, and Chernigov, thus extending the Baltic limits much farther to the east.[10] In 1962, the Russian linguists Toporov and Trubachev published a study entitled *Linguistic analysis of the hydronims in the upper Dnieper Basin* (see biblio-graphy, 5). They found that more than a thousand of the river names in the upper Dnieper Basin are of Baltic origin, as their etymology and morphology show. This book has produced positive evidence of a prolonged ancient Baltic occupation of present-day Byelo-Russia and the western parts of Greater Russia.

As the Baltic toponymy of the upper Dnieper and upper Volga basins is a far more convincing proof of the Baltic spread over present-day Russian territories than the archaeological

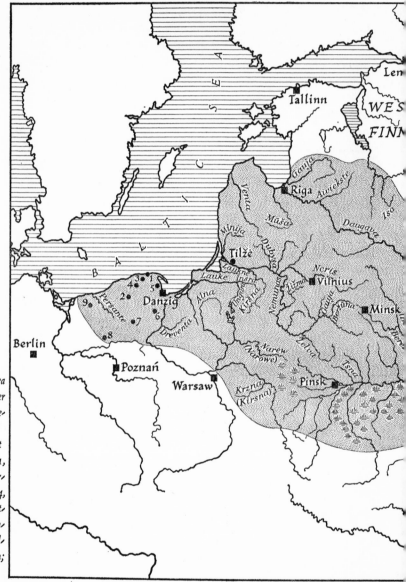

Fig. 2. The area of the Baltic river names. 1-9: Place-names presumed to be Baltic west of R. Vistula. 1, Karwen; 2, Karwen; 3, Saulin; 4, Labehn; 5, Rutzau; 6, Labuhnken; 7, Powalken; 8, Straduhn; 9, Labuhn

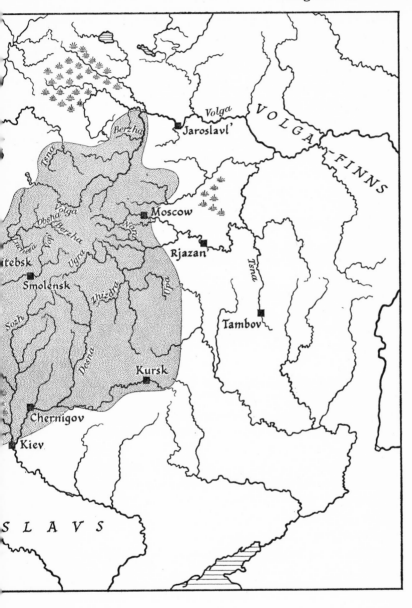

sources, I wish to mention some of the Baltic river names, taking examples from the districts of Smolensk, Tver, Kaluga, Moscow, and Chernigov.

Istra, tributary of the Vorja in the area of Gzhatsk and west, ern tributary of the Moskva (Moscow) river, has exact parallels in Lithuania and East Prussia: the tributary of the Prėglius (Pregel)—*Jstra* or *Insra*, also *Jsrutis*; *Ysra* in the district of Panevėžys—from **In,srā*, the root **ser"sr* meaning 'to flow': *srovė* in Lithuanian means current. The rivers *Berzha* in the area of Beloj and Vjaz'ma and *Berezha* in the district of Tver are connected with the Baltic word for 'birch': Lithuanian *beržas*; and *Obsha*, tributary of the Mezha in the district of Smolensk, is connected with the word for 'aspen,tree': Old Prussian *abse* Lithuanian *apušė*. The *Tolzha* River in the area of Vjaz'ma takes its name from **Tólža*, which has connections with the Lithuanian word *tilžti*, 'to soak, to stand under the water'; the name of the city of *Tilžė* (Tilsit) on the Nemunas River has the same derivation. *Ugra*, western tributary of the Oka, is com, parable to the Lithuanian *Ungurupė*. *Sozh*, tributary of the Dnieper, comes from **Sъža*, the etymology of which is shown by the Old Prussian word *suge*, for 'rain'. *Zhizdra*—tributary of the Oka, and the town of the same name—comes from the Baltic word for 'gravel, grit, coarse sand': the Lithuanian *žvigždras, žvirgždas*. *Upa*, eastern tributary of the Oka, belongs to the series of names in connection with 'river', the Lithuanian *upė*. *Nara*, tributary of the Oka, south of Moscow, appears numerous times in Lithuania and East Prussia: the Lithuanian rivers *Neris, Nerys, Narotis, Narasa, Narupė*, the lakes *Narutis* and *Naročius* and the Old Prussian *Narus, Narys, Naruse, Naruve* (the present *Narew*), all derived from *narus*, 'deep, in which one can submerge', *nerti*, 'to dive, plunge'.

Farthest to the east is the river *Tsna* (*Cna*), tributary of the Oka, south of Kasimov and east of Tambov. This name recurs in Byelo,Russia: a tributary of Usha around Vilejka and a

tributary of Hajna in the district of Borysov, and comes from
Tъsna, Baltic *tusnā*; Old Prussian *tusnan* means 'quiet'. In the
south, river names of Baltic origin reach the district of Chernigov, which is north of Kiev. In this area we find the following river names: *Verepeto*, tributary of the River Desna—in
Lithuanian *verpetas* is 'whirlpool'; and *Titva*, tributary of the
Snov', which flows into the Desna, and which has a corresponding form in Lithuanian: *Tytuva*. *Desna*, the large eastern tributary of the Dnieper, is possibly connected with the
Lithuanian word *dešinė*, 'the right side'.

It is very probable that the name *Volga* goes back to a Baltic
name for this river, derived from *Jilga*, 'long river'. The
Lithuanian *jilgas, ilgas* means 'long', hence *Jilga* is a 'long
river'; certainly this name is very appropriate because the Volga
is quite long.[11] In Lithuania and Latvia there are many rivers
having the name *Ilgoji*, 'the long one', or *Ilgupė*, 'the long river'.

For thousands of years the Finno-Ugrian tribes were neighbours of the Balts and enclosed them on the north and east.
During the earliest period of the relationship between the Baltic
and Finno-Ugrian-speaking peoples there must have been
closer contact than during the later periods. This is reflected in
loan-words from the Baltic in the Finno-Ugrian languages.
There are hundreds of them, known since Vilhelm Thomsen
in 1890 published his excellent study on relationships between
the Finnic and the Baltic languages.[12] The borrowed words
relate to stockbreeding and agriculture, plants and animals, to
many novelties brought by a higher culture, to religion, to
names for family members, parts of the body, colours, time
measuring, and so on. Their meaning and their form prove the
loan-words to be very old, and linguists reckon that they had
been borrowed in the second and first millennia B.C. Many of
these words show that they were borrowed from the proto-
Baltic and not from the modern Latvian or Lithuanian. Baltic
loan-words are found not only in the West Finnic (Estonian,

Livian, and Finnish) languages, but also in the Volga-Finnic languages: Mordvinian, Mari, Mansi, Cheremissian, Ud-murtian, and Komi-Zyrian. In 1957 a Russian linguist, Sere-brennikov, published a study entitled *Traces of an extinct Indo-European language related to the Baltic in the centre of the European part of the U.S.S.R..*[13] He gives a list of words in the Finno-Ugrian languages, which is an extension of Thomsen's list of Baltic loan-words in the Finno-Ugrian languages.

Important evidence as to how far Baltic influence extended into present-day Russia is provided by the fact that many of the Baltic loan-words in the Volga-Finnic languages are not known to the western Finns. They must have been borrowed directly from the eastern Balts who occupied the upper Volga basin and during the Early and Middle Bronze Age steadily penetrated farther and farther to the east. Indeed, about the middle of the second millennium B.C. the Fat'janovo culture, as we shall see below, reached lower Kama, lower Vjatka, and even the Belaja rivers in present Tataria and Bashkiria.

During the Iron Age and in early historic times the imme-diate neighbours of the eastern Balts were the Mari and Mord-vins, the 'Merja' and 'Mordva' of the historic records. The Mari inhabited the districts of Jaroslavl' and Vladimir, and the western part of the district of Kostroma. The Mordvins lived east of the lower Oka. Their distribution area is shown by a considerable number of river names of Finno-Ugrian origin.[14] In the lands of the Mordvins and Mari, river names of Baltic origin are quite rare. Between the towns Rjazan' and Vladimir there were large forests and swamps, which for ages played the role of a natural border between the tribes.

The greatest number of Baltic loan-words in the Finnic languages relate to novelties in the economy: names for domes-tic animals and the ways they were kept and used, for cereal, seeds, tillage, spinning, etc. The borrowed words of course exhibit a much larger variety of novelties brought by the Baltic

Indo-Europeans to the north than do the archaeological remains, since they pertain not only to the material objects, but also to abstract terms, verbs, and adjectives, and to such objects as are not preserved on ancient sites. Among the borrowings which have to do with agriculture are words for cereal, seeds, millet, flax, hemp, chaff, hay, garden or enclosure, harrow, and others. Among the names for domestic animals borrowed from the Balts are those for ram, lamb, he-goat, young pig, and goose. The Baltic word for steed, stallion, horse (Lithuanian *žirgas*, Prussian *sirgis*, Lettish *zirgs*) in Finno-Ugrian means ox (Finnish *härkä*, Estonian *härg*, Lyvian *ärga*, Vepsian *härg*). The Finnish word for yoke, *juhta*, comes from the Lithuanian *junkta-s*, *jungti*, 'to yoke'. Also borrowed were the word for hurdle, an open stall for sheep (Lithuanian *gardas*; Mordvinian *karda, kardo*), and a word for shepherd.

A group of borrowings for spinning, whorl, wool, ripple, heddles, cord shows that a flax and wool industry was introduced by the Balts. Alcoholic beverages were transmitted by the Balts, as borrowed words for ale and mead show. Also, in connection with honey and mead, such words as those for wax, wasp, and hornet were taken over from the Balts.

Borrowed from the Baltic are names for axe, cap, shoe, beaker, ladle, handle, hook, basket, sieve, knife, spade, broom, bridge, boat, sails, oar, wheel, sledge, wall, post, pole, rod, shaft, steam-bath. Even musical instruments such as the *kanklės* (Lithuanian), the zither, were transmitted. The whole list of names for colours is found to be of Baltic origin—yellow, green, black, dark, bluish grey—and names for adjectives— wide, narrow, empty, quiet, old, secret, brave (gallant). The word for love or desire must have been borrowed in an early period since it is found in western Finnic and Volga-Finnic languages (Lithuanian *meilė*, 'love', *mielas*, 'dear'; Finnish *mieli*, Erza-Mordvin *mel'*, Udmurtian *myl*). Very intimate relations between the Balts and the Finno-Ugrians are shown by borrowed names for the parts of the body: neck, back, hollow of the knee, navel, and beard. Of Baltic origin are not only the name for neighbour, but also names for members of the family, sister, daughter, daughter-in-law, son-in-law, and cousin, which suggest frequent intermarriages between the Balts and the Finno-Ugrians. Contacts in the religious sphere are wit-nessed by the borrowing of names for sky (*taivas* from the Baltic *deivas*) and the god of the air, the Thunder (Lithuanian *Perkūnas*, Latvian *Perkonis*; Finnish *perkele*, Estonian *pergel*).

The great numbers of loan-words and the whole series of terms in connection with food-producing economy and tech-nology indicate that the Balts were the carriers of civilization towards the north-east of Europe inhabited by the Finno-Ugrian hunters and fishers. The Finno-Ugrians living in the neighbourhood of the Balts became to a certain degree Indo-Europeanized. In the course of millennia, particularly during the Early Iron Age and the first centuries A.D., the Finno-Ugrian culture in the upper Volga basin and north of the River Daugava-Dvina was adapted to food-production and even the habitat pattern—arranging villages on hills and the building of rectangular houses—was taken over from the Balts. Archaeological finds demonstrate how for centuries bronze and iron tools and ornaments were exported from the Baltic to the Finno-Ugrian lands. From the second to the fifth centuries A.D., the western Finnic, the Mari, and Mordvin areas were flooded with or strongly influenced by ornaments typical of the Baltic culture. Where the long history of Baltic-Finno-Ugrian relations is concerned, language and archaeological sources go hand in hand; and as regards the spread of the Balts in what is now Russia proper, Baltic loan-words in Volga-Finnic languages are witnesses of incontestable value.

CHAPTER II

Their Origins

'Dievas davė dantis; Dievas duos duonos' (Lithuanian)
'Devas adadāt datas; Devas dāt (or dadāt) dhānās' (Sanskrit)
'Deus dedit dentes; Deus dabit panem' (Latin)
('God gave the teeth; God will give bread').

NEW HORIZONS for the explanation of Baltic origins opened with the discovery of Sanskrit in the eighteenth century. Lithuanian and Sanskrit words were compared even before Franz Bopp established in 1816 the foundations for comparative linguistics of the Indo-European language. Similarities between these two have been frequently mentioned as examples for illustration of the widespread dissemination of the Indo-European languages and of their very close interrelationships. As the most archaic of all living Indo-European languages, Lithuanian strongly attracted those studying comparative linguistics. A. Schleicher published his grammar of the Lithuanian language in 1856, and a year later the *Handbuch der litauischen Sprache*; Lithuanian, too, played an important role in his compendium of the comparative grammar of the Indo-European languages of 1861, as it did in other works by prominent linguists such as K. Brugmann, A. Meillet, F. de Saussure, and A. Leskien.

Sanskrit and Baltic are the two linguistic poles between which the languages of the Indo-European homelands are 'found'. Along with the comparative grammars there have appeared volumes of comparative Indo-European antiquarian studies. Reconstruction of the prehistoric eras of Indo-European nations was attempted by using language as the key. These homelands were sought in a temperate zone, because of the existence of names for the four seasons, within an area where there are no tropical or subtropical flora and fauna, and inland from the sea or ocean, since there is no common word for sea. The continental part of Europe and the central part of Asia as probable locations more or less agreed with these language conditions. But within these broad limits individual views varied considerably. O. Schrader (1901), for example, favoured the north Pontic area, while Feist (1913) regarded central Asia as the startingpoint of the IndoEuropean prehistoric migrations, holding the Tokharians in central Asia as likely remnants of the early centre of the IndoEuropeans.

Some linguists, because of the very archaic character of the Lithuanian and Old Prussian languages, believed and still believe that the homelands must be in Lithuania or near it, somewhere between the Baltic Sea and western Russia, or even in a small area between the Vistula and Nemunas. On the other hand, the great accumulation of archaeological finds in eastern Europe and western Asia, and the reconstruction of prehistoric cultures in eastern Europe, Central Asia, and southern Siberia, indicate movements of people from the Eurasiatic steppes into Europe and Asia Minor and the assimilation or disappearance of local Neolithic and Chalcolithic cultures in Europe at the end of the third and beginning of the second millennium B.C.

Fig. 3　In 2300–2200 B.C., the first signs of expansion of an entirely new culture from the steppe zone north of the Black Sea and beyond the Volga can be traced in the Balkans, in the Aegean area and western Anatolia, and soon thereafter in central and Baltic Europe. The Kurgan Pitgrave people (*kurgan* is the Russian word for barrow) from the Volga and the south Siberian steppes and Kazakhstan were ceaselessly advancing westwards. They possessed vehicles, a specialized knowledge of animal husbandry, farmed on a small scale, and had wellorganized small patriarchal communities. The utilization of the vehicle and the stratification of society into warrior and labouring classes were important factors which gave impetus to their

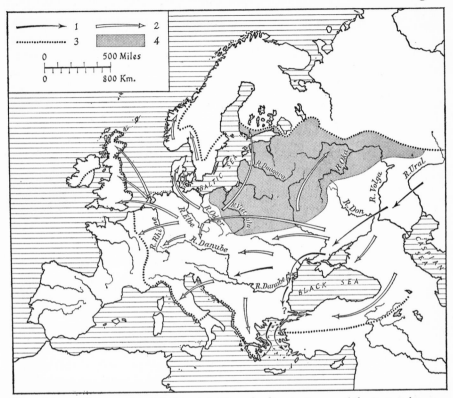

Fig. 3. The tentative expansion of the Eurasiatic 'Kurgan' culture to Europe and the Proto-Baltic area. 1, expansion not later than c. 2300–2200 B.C.; 2, expansion before and around 2100 B.C. (chronology not yet fixed by Carbon 14 dating. The arrows in the Caucasus and Anatolia may indicate an earlier period, c. 2300 B.C.); 3, the area occupied or influenced by the 'Kurgan' (Corded, Battle-Axe) people; 4, the proto-Baltic area during the first half of the second millennium B.C. (unchanged limits in the west until c. 1200 B.C.). The southern limits almost coincide with the limits between the forest and forest-steppe zones in eastern Europe.

mobility and aggressiveness. This type of social structure and economy contrasted with that of the local European Neolithic agricultural people who lived in large communities and apparently in a matriarchal system. The Kurgan people must have established themselves as overlords. Such European Neolithic cultures as the Painted Pottery culture in the Balkans, the Funnel-Beaker culture in central and north-western Europe and the food-gathering culture in the East Baltic area and central Russia were overpowered, but it took at least several hundred years before the old cultures disintegrated or were assimilated.

The archaeological elements of the Kurgan culture fully confirm the picture drawn from shared words in the Indo-European languages. I shall mention here only a few examples pertaining to economy and social structure, stressing pertinent words in the Baltic languages.

Farming was not unknown to the Kurgan people. Pots filled with millet or wheat grains were found in graves and in habitation sites. There is a common Indo-European name for cereals: Sanskrit *yávah*, Avestan *yavo*, Lithuanian *javaĩ*, Irish *eorna*; for grains: Old Prussian *syrne*, Lithuanian *žirnis* (now come to mean 'pea'), Old Slavic *zrŭno*, Gothic *kaurn*, Old Irish *kaurn*, Latin *granum*; and for wheat or spelt: Lithuanian *pūrai*, Old Indic *pūros*, Greek πυζός, and Old Bulgarian *pyro*. Words for the seed (Lithuanian *sėmuo*, Latin *sēmen*) and sowing (Lithuanian *sėti*, Old Slavic *sěti*, Gothic *saian*, Old Irish *sil*) are early Indo-European. All Kurgan habitation sites and graves show that stockbreeding was a main preoccupation and a most important source of food. Sheep, goat, cattle, dog, and horse bones are abundant, and language sources reflect this as the names of all the domestic animals are preserved. Stock was called: Sanskrit *pāçu*, *paçuh*, Latin *pecu*, *pecus*, Old High German *fihu*, Lithuanian *pekus*, Old Prussian *pecku*. The words are connected with the words for money (Latin *pecunia*, Gothic *faihu*, and Old Prussian *pecku*), indicating that cattle played a great role in commerce. There are common names for cow and bull (Sanskrit *gauh*, Avestan *gāuš*, Armenian *kov*, Lettish *gůws*, Greek βοῦς, Latin *bōs*, Old Slavic *govędo*), for sheep (Sanskrit *ávih*, Lithuanian *avìs*, Greek ονς, Latin *ovis*, Irish *oi*, Old

Slavic *ovĭnŭ*, etc.); for goat and he-goat (Sanskrit *aiaḥ*, *ajā*, Lithuanian *ožỹs*, *ožkà*, Armenian *ayc*, Greek αἴς); for dog (Vedic *ç(u)vá*, Lithuanian *šuva* or *šũ*, Avestan *sūnō* (in geni-tive); and for horse (Sanskrit *açvaḥ*, fem. *açvā*, Lithuanian *ašvà*, Avestan *aspō*, Old Persian *asa*). There is no doubt that the meat of domesticated animals and other animal products con-stituted a basic food supply for the Kurgan people as well as for the later Indo-Europeans. The word for meat is the same in many Indo-European languages: Lithuanian *mėsa*, Old Slavic *męso*, Tokharian *misa*, Armenian *mis*, Gothic *mims*. A meal of meat with a kind of gravy was apparently widely used, as suggested by the common word: Latin *iūs*, Lithuanian *jūšė*, Old Slavic *juxá*, Sanskrit *yuḥ*.

The Kurgan people became acquainted with metal several centuries before the end of the third millennium B.C. They acquired their metallurgical knowledge from the local Near Eastern, Transcaucasian, Anatolian, and Transylvanian peoples. Soon thereafter they became eager metallurgists and played a big role in the introduction of the Bronze Age in Europe and in exploring the copper resources of the central European mountains.

The existence of vehicles is shown by actual finds in the Kurgan culture and by words. Nearly all Indo-European languages have the root *veĝh* to designate vehicle.

What we know archaeologically about the habitat and social structure of the Kurgan culture is in full agreement with the linguistic data. The Kurgan people arranged their fortified hill settlements on high river banks. Their earliest acropolises date from the Chalcolithic period and continue throughout the later prehistoric and historic periods in all Indo-European groups. Lithuanian *pilis*, Lettish *pils*, or Old Prussian *pil* correspond with the Greek πολις, Old Indic *pūr*, *puriś*, and Sanskrit *pūḥ*, meaning acropolis, castle, town. There is also the name for a regular village with the root *wik̂*, *weik̂os*, *wes*, and another word for a house group: Lithuanian *kaimas*, *kiemas*, Old Prussian *caymis*, Gothic *haims*, Greek κωμη. The village had its chief: Lithuanian *vëšpatis*, Sanskrit *viç-pátih*, Avestan *vis-patiš*. Houses of the Kurgan culture were small, rectangular wooden structures, comprising one room or one room with a porch, having wattle-and-daub walls and a pitched roof supported by a row of vertical posts. The type and structure of the house is perfectly rendered in words. Thus, for house there is Old Indic *dámas*, Latin *domus*, Greek δόμος, Old Bulgarian *domъ*, Lithuanian *namas*; also for a small house or 'klete': Lithuanian *klėtis*, Lettish *klēts*, Old Prussian *clenan*, Old Bulgarian *klětъ*, Gothic *hleipra*, Greek μλιδια, which is related to the Latin *clivus*, 'hill', and the Greek μλτύς, 'slope'. The root **wei* for 'to twine' (Lithuanian *vyti*, Old Indic *vayati*, Latin *vieo*) is related to the name for wall (Old Icelandic *veggr*, Gothic *waddjus*), and there are common words for post, door, thatched roof, and other parts and activities connected with the building of the house.

The division into warrior and labouring classes as shown by language is confirmed by Kurgan graves: there are on the one hand very many quite poor graves equipped merely with a flint knife or a pot, on the other hand some outstanding, richly furnished graves which very probably belonged to chieftains. Graves also indicate the superior family status of the man, who seemed to have unrestricted property rights over his wife and children. The frequent double graves of a man and a woman indicate the custom of self-immolation by the widow. The wife must follow to death her deceased husband—a custom which continued among Hindus in India (suttee) into the present century, and in Lithuania is recorded in the thirteenth and fourteenth centuries A.D.

Linguists no longer speak of the unity of the Indo-European mother tongue; even in its early stages before becoming widely disseminated it probably comprised at least a number of dialects. Archaeology seems to support this hypothesis, since before the Kurgan people appeared in the Balkans, Anatolia, central and northern Europe, there was much mixing of cul/tures north of the Black Sea. The impetus came from the lower Volga area and east of the Caspian Sea, and there must have been a kind of chain movement. The various Indo/European groups that formed in Europe after the expansion were at the start closely related to the mother culture of the Indo/Iranian bloc and to the ancestral culture of the Tokharians as shown by language relationships between Sanskrit and Greek, Armenian, Slavic, and Baltic on the one hand, and between Tokharian and Greek, Thracian, Illyrian, Slavic, and Baltic on the other. Due to a wide dispersal over the European continent and to a considerable mixing with the local European cultures, the Kurgan culture in Europe resolved into a number of separate groups. The nuclear units of later Slavs, Balts, Germanic peoples, and others appear in the first centuries of the second millennium B.C.

The beginnings of many Indo/European groups in Europe were more or less simultaneous. Rather than attribute the curious similarity between the Lithuanian and Sanskrit to late migrations, we prefer to think that over 4,000 years ago the forefathers of the Balts and of the Old Indian peoples lived in the Eurasian steppes. The Balts preserved archaic forms, living a secluded life in the forests, removed from major routes of many subsequent migrations.

How did the immediate forebears of the Balts reach the shores of the Baltic Sea and what are now Byelo/Russia and Greater Russia? The movement of the Kurgan people pro/ceeded from the lower Dnieper basin in the direction of central Europe and up to the Baltic Sea. One branch settled along the eastern coasts of the Baltic, extending as far as south/western Finland in the north. Another group, bringing with them the same cultural elements, pushed from the middle Dnieper to the upper Dnieper, the upper Volga, and the Oka river area in central Russia.

Between Denmark and Lithuania, in Germany, Czecho-slovakia, and Poland, the new settlers found long-established Neolithic farmers. In the east Baltic area and forested central Russia, they found hunter-fishers, the so-called Comb-marked and Pitted-ware people. A process of hybridization and mutual influences over several hundreds of years can be traced archaeologically. The complex of finds which is known in archaeological terminology as the 'Globular Amphora' cul-ture is a hybrid one, composed of Funnel-Beaker and Kurgan elements, with a predominance of the latter, and in the course of several centuries the Funnel-Beaker culture disintegrated. From the early second millennium B.C., all over the former Funnel-Beaker territory and even in the areas north of it, in southern Sweden and southern Norway and in the whole eastern Baltic area, we find a rather uniform culture usually called the Corded-Ware or Battle-Axe culture. It is actually a variant of the Kurgan culture which developed local features by borrow-ing elements from the Funnel-Beaker population, and was influenced by the Bell-Beaker folk, who reached central Europe from south-west somewhat later than the Kurgan people. The pottery decorated by cord impressions, and stone battle-axes with perforations, were typical objects of this cul-ture. Both are of eastern origin: decoration of pots by cord impression was frequent on pots of the Kurgan culture in the south Russian steppes; the stone battle-axes were an imitation of Caucasian copper axes. There is an astonishing similarity of cultural elements all over central Europe, and the southern and eastern Baltic coasts. This unmistakably shows the routes of the Kurgan dispersal over the Baltic shores.

The Kurgan settlements and graves typified by corded pot-tery and battle-axes in the lands originally occupied by hunter-fishers (the Comb-marked Pitted-Ware culture) contrast markedly with those of the older settlers, and archaeologists in this case cannot be mistaken when they maintain that new people arrived and settled among the hunter-fishers. There is evidence that many sites of the food-producers and of the hunter-fishers were contemporaneous.

The same picture of the spread of a new culture is seen in the upper Volga basin, where the Kurgan sites are classified as the Fat'janovo culture (named after the cemetery at Fat'janovo near Jaroslavl'). As in the East Baltic area, so in Greater Russia the newcomers spread along the rivers and established their small villages on high river banks, whereas the local hunter-fishers continued to live on lake shores or the lower banks of rivers. The Kurgan people occupied the central Russian upland area and did not spread into northern Russia. To the north they can be traced as far as the shores of Lake Ladoga and southern Finland, but they did not survive there for long. In these northern regions they either were assimilated by local people after several centuries, or what was left of them retreated southward. From the middle of the second millennium B.C. the approximate northern limit of the culture of Kurgan origin ran along northern Latvia to the upper Volga. The food-producers stayed in the more favourable climatic zone. This more or less coincides with the area of the deciduous forests, not differing very much from the original Indo-European homeland area which according to the linguistic evidence must have been in the deciduous tree zone, where oaks and apple trees grew, and where squirrels, hares, beavers, wolves, bears, and elks inhabited the forests. The oak and beaver zone extends in the north to the southern part of Scandinavia, and its boundary runs along the Gulf of Finland and south of Lakes Ladoga and Onega. The northern limit of apple trees runs somewhat south of the oak limit, approximately from the Gulf of Finland and northern Estonia to the upper Volga basin. That the ancient Balts lived in the area of deciduous forests is shown by the common names for oak, apple, birch, linden, ash, maple, and elm in all Baltic languages. But they did not have common names for beech, yew, and ivy, which are confined to a more southern region of deciduous forests and are known in the Slavic languages. This is one of the linguistic indications that ancient Balts lived north of the ancient Slavs. All Baltic languages had common names for squirrel, marten, bison, aurochs, and elk.

Physical type as shown by excavated skeletons also confirms the intrusion of new people into the East Baltic area and central Russia. Skulls from graves of the Kurgan (Corded, Boat-Axe, Fat'janovo) culture differ considerably in measurement from those in the graves or settlements of the hunter-fishers of the Comb-marked and Pitted-Ware culture. Those from the graves of the Kurgan culture were long and Europoid; those from the hunter-fisher sites were of medium length or short, with wide face, flat nose, and high eye-sockets. The latter traits are generally similar to those of the Finno-Ugrian peoples of western Siberia. Furthermore, the skulls from hunter-fisher sites in Estonia have shown a certain mixed type presumed to be derived from a combination of Europoid and Mongoloid elements. Their appearance is close to that of the present Manti, Chanti, Samoyeds, and Lapps, all of which belong to the Uralic race. The Europoid skulls from the graves of the new-comers in the East Baltic area almost exactly correspond to those known from northern Poland (former East Prussia), which again indicates diffusion along the coasts of the Baltic Sea. The skulls from the Fat'janovo graves are also very similar, and about the same type is found in the Kurgan graves of the steppe area along the lower Dnieper. The mixture of the two racial types must have started immediately, since we know several Kurgan (so-called 'Boat-Axe') graves from Estonia in which skulls with Mongoloid traits appeared.[1]

Fig. 4

Whether the Kurgan people who settled in the East Baltic

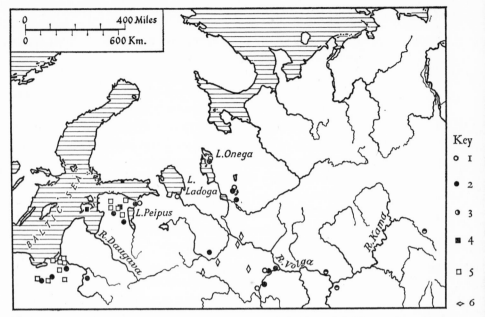

Key

o   1
●   2
◑   3
◼   4
□   5
◇   6

Fig. 4. Physical types in the East Baltic area and Russia at end of Neolithic–Chalcolithic period. 1–3, long-headed, Europoid: in the Corded (Battle-Axe) graves (1), Comb-marked Pottery sites (2), Fat'janovo graves (3); 4–5, short-headed with Mongoloid traits: in Comb-marked Pottery sites (4), Corded (Battle-Axe) graves (5), and east Russian-middle Ural sites (6)

area and in forested Russia spoke a separate language from the other Indo-European groups, archaeological finds cannot tell us. Culturally they were very closely related to the other Kurgan people who occupied central and north-western Europe. During several centuries after 2000 B.C. cultural differences developed among the Kurgan groups, making it possible to define the limits of their distribution. We do not know if the language differentiation followed similar paths, but there is no doubt that it must have been influenced by such factors as diffusion over a large territory and by close contact with the local, non-Indo-European population.

Having used language sources and early historic records to ascertain where the Baltic tribes lived, we can now follow the

47

development of the earliest culture presumed to have belonged to the direct ancestors of the Baltic peoples.

For several hundred years during post-expansion times, the Kurgan culture of central and northern Europe did not change much. It was still a culture on a Chalcolithic level; that is, it continued to be of a Stone Age character, despite the fact that copper artifacts such as spiral rings for women's hair, daggers and awls were used occasionally. What we find in graves and villages is mostly pots, stone battle-axes, axe-heads, flint arrow-heads, knives and scrapers, bone tools, and perforated animal teeth for necklaces—an inventory which does not differ basic-ally from that found in Kurgan graves of the south Russian steppes dating from around 2000 B.C. and earlier. The period before the true metal age in central Europe, that is to say, before *c*. 1800–1700 B.C., is one of adaptation to local conditions and, to a certain degree, of dividing up into local variants. The indi-vidual styles of corded pottery which developed are about the only criteria for defining the cultural limits between these variants. The differences, although slight, indicate the trend towards development of local tastes. Distinctively localized groups emerged, one north of the Carpathians, another in the heart of central Europe, and yet another in northern Germany and southern Scandinavia, not to mention those farther south and west. East of the River Oder, in Poland, north-western Ukraine (northern Volynia), East Prussia, and Lithuania, another unit was established which has its closest cultural rela-tives farther to the north, in Latvia, Estonia, and south-western Finland, and to the east, in Byelo-Russia and central Russia. The unit has every right to claim a proto-Baltic origin; it was a common root from which the Bronze Age cultures of western and eastern Balts developed.

Fig. 3

Many names have been applied to the specific Corded and Battle-Axe culture between the lower Oder and the upper Vistula rivers, and southern Finland. In the upper Vistula basin it is called 'Złota'; in Volynia, 'Volynian Corded'; in the coastal area of northern Poland (Pomerania), East Prussia, and Lithuania, 'Rzucewo' (in Polish) or 'Haffküstenkultur' (in German), the latter meaning 'the culture which extends along the Baltic bays, the Frisches Haff and Courish Haff.' In the East Baltic area it simply retains the name Boat-Axe cul-ture, since stone or 'battle-axes' are reminiscent of boats, and in Greater Russia it is known as 'Fat'janovo'.[2]

On comparing all the cultural elements, even the style of pottery decoration, of these various groups, one has to acknow-ledge the great similarity between them. Differences are not sufficient to warrant considering them as separate cultures. In such a large area one cannot expect identical pots or identical ornaments; but even so, I find in this whole area a remarkable similarity in tool and pottery making and in decoration motifs, as well as uniformity of graves and burial rites. It is a culture which, after all, does not differ basically from its mother Kur-gan culture. The people kept cattle, pigs, sheep, goats, horses, and dogs. They used carefully prepared, nicely retouched flint sickles to reap their harvests. Wheat and millet grains, as well as stone hoes and saddle querns, point to agricultural occupa-tions. Stone and flint axe-heads were used for forest clearing. Triangular flint arrowheads were basic weapons in hunting forest fauna—bears, wolves, fox, lynx, and hare; and bone harpoons and nets were used for river and sea fishing, particu-larly pike in the rivers and seals (*Phoca groenlandica*) in the Baltic Sea. There were various stone and bone instruments for wood and leather working. From their predecessors, the Funnel-Beaker people, these proto-Balts learned to fashion articles of amber and to mine the best varieties of European flint on the upper Vistula and along the upper Bug in Poland. They made cylindrical amber beads and amber buttons, round or quadrangular, having V perforations. They were capable of making a considerable variety of pots for culinary use and

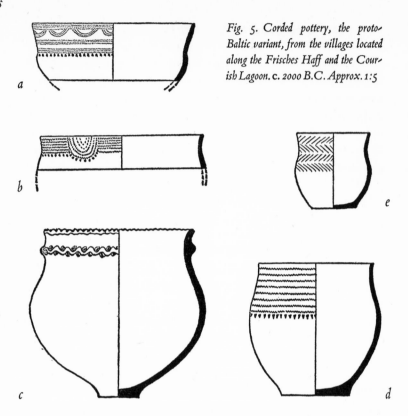

Fig. 5. Corded pottery, the proto-Baltic variant, from the villages located along the Frisches Haff and the Courish Lagoon. c. 2000 B.C. Approx. 1:5

for ritual purposes: beakers, amphorae, globular and wide-mouthed pots, large storage vessels, some with two holes on the side for hanging purposes, boat-shaped dishes, and ladles. The clay moulding was fairly thin, but not particularly well baked. Dishes and some culinary ware excepted, the upper part of pots was always decorated both with horizontal and wavy lines of cord impressions and incisions of diagonal lines forming herring-bone, triangle, and rhomboid patterns. If one looks down at these pots from above, the patterns have the appearance of a radiating sun. The bases of the pots had concavities or simple solar motifs. Sometimes solar motifs are recognizable

Fig. 5

Plates 2, 3

on the sides of pots, incised as semicircles and surrounded with dots.

Such finds come from a number of graves and villages, the best examples having been brought to light during the excava-tions of 1923–36 in Pomerania and East Prussia, west and east of the lower Vistula. The village at Rzucewo, built on dunes along the Baltic sea coast,[3] and the village at Succase (present Suchacz) on the Frisches Haff,[4] are outstandingly preserved and well excavated. Both were inhabited for more than a

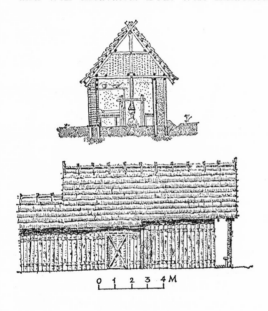

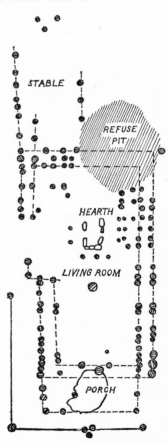

Fig. 6. Reconstruction and plan of a house in the village Succase (Suchacz) on the Frisches Haff. c. 2000 B.C.

hundred years, as several habitation horizons show. Remains of small rectangular houses, 8–12 m. long and 4–5 m. wide, lay one above the other. This stratigraphy indicates that the people established themselves in permanent villages. These were built as a rule on hillocks or dunes, and when the ground was not level the houses were arranged terrace-wise. Such is the case at Rzucewo where houses lie on several terraces which were specially reinforced with stones and timber posts. Succase was a village of twenty houses, placed close to each other at random within a small area. Most of them were one-roomed,

Fig. 6

but they frequently had a small porch at one of the narrow ends. In the main room of each house was a round, hoof-shaped or rectangular hearth, fenced with stones. With a few exceptions, the door was in one of the narrow sides. The plan and reconstruction reproduced here show one of the Succase houses having a large room with a rectangular hearth and a porch. At the north-western end is an added wing, probably a stall for animals. Walls were built of vertical timber posts in two rows, and the space in between the posts was filled with daub. The pitched roof was supported by several thick posts placed along the axis of the house. Near the hearth were timber structures resembling beds or benches. Beneath the entrance of another of the houses was found a human jaw and a necklace of amber beads. This may have been the remains of a human sacrifice performed at the foundation ceremony of the house, and it suggests that amber may have had a special significance in these people's religion.

The deceased were buried in a contracted position lying on their side, men on the right, women on the left, in pits within hut-like structures which had floors paved with flat stones, and timber roofs. The barrow was fenced with timber posts as

Fig. 7

shown in the reconstruction of the stratified burial mound in Kaup in the district of Fischhausen (present Primorsk) in Samland, East Prussia. In this barrow, excavated in the nineteenth century,[5] four graves were found one above the other, the oldest belonging to the Chalcolithic period, and the others to the Bronze Age. Separate graves of cattle and dogs have been found in the cemeteries of the Zĺota group in southern Poland, and in all other graves cattle and sheep or goat bones are frequent.

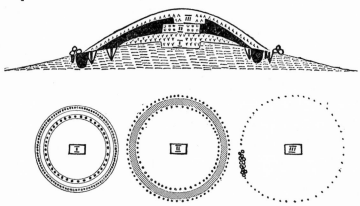

Fig. 7. A stratified barrow (cross-section and plans) from Kaup near Cranz, eastern end of the peninsula of Samland. About 14 m. in diameter. I, c. 2000 B.C.; II, c. seventeenth–sixteenth centuries B.C. III, thirteenth–eleventh (?) centuries B.C. I and II are encircled by two rows of vertical timber posts with a ditch in between. III shows remains of a stone ring

CHAPTER III

The Bronze and the Early Iron Age of the Maritime Balts

AROUND THE EIGHTEENTH CENTURY B.C. the copper industry in the western Carpathian and eastern Alpine zone made remarkable progress, but the metal products of central Europe were not immediately transmitted to the Baltic area. In metallurgy, it remained peripheral, undoubtedly because in the whole region between the Baltic Sea and Russia there are no local sources of copper. The development of the metal culture depended entirely on imports from central Europe to the Baltic Sea area and from the Caucasian and southern Ural metallurgical centres to central Russia.

With the beginning of the European Bronze Age the proto-Baltic sphere became divided into several zones of influence. The western zone, covering eastern Poland, former East Prussia, and western parts of Lithuania and Latvia, was under the influence of the central European metallurgical centre, and throughout the Bronze Age its culture progressed with the same rhythm as in central Europe. In the eastern or continental zone, amid the forests extending from eastern Lithuania and Latvia to the upper Volga basin, the people retained an archaic character, with some influence from their southern neighbours in south Russia. This division continued throughout the remaining prehistoric times: the western Balts, ancestors of the Prussians and Curonians of history, were culturally similar to the people of central Europe—to the culture created by Illyrians and Celts—and to their western neighbours, the Germanic peoples. The eastern Balts were in active contact with the Finno-Ugrians, Cimmerians, proto-Scythians, and early Slavs. Thus the emergence of a vigorous metallurgical centre in

central Europe and of another in the southern Urals caused
some differentiation of the material culture, which during
Chalcolithic times had been much more uniform.

Since there were no copper or gold mines in the Baltic area, AMBER TRADE
what did the Balts barter for metals? What was it that the cen- AND THE
tral Europeans so coveted as to make them want to exchange SPREAD OF
their goods for it? Why are the bronze hoards concentrated METAL
along the Oder and Vistula rivers, and along the Pomeranian
and East Prussian coasts? The answer is: amber, the northern
gold. It was not just the amber that we moderns use for
jewellery; for our forefathers it was a 'substance of the sun',
elektron, as the Greeks called it—an electric, shining substance,
endowed with mystical powers. As precious as gold, it was
sought by both the barbaric north and the civilized south. For
the Baltic area it indeed became a magical 'metal'—*metallum
sudaticum*, or 'exuded metal', as Tacitus called it—a key to prosperity and a basic link with the rising central European culture
and Mycenaean Greece.

There are no written records from the European Bronze Age
era relating to amber, but the fanciful tales and myths mentioning this substance which circulated in Greece and Rome in
classical times may have originated in the Bronze Age. It
is mentioned in Homer's *Odyssey*: the King's palace was resplendent in copper, gold, amber, ivory, and silver, and
Penelope received a necklace of amber and gold, 'like the Sun'.[1]
The connection of amber with the sun appears in the earliest
historic records and the same relationship is certain to have
existed during the whole of the Bronze Age.

Amber is the resin of the pine trees which grew some 60
million years ago on the south coast of Fennoscandia, situated
above the north-western point of the peninsula of Samland
($55°$ N. and $19°$ to $20°$ E.). The shores with 'amber pine'
forests sank beneath the sea, emerged, and then again became
submerged during subsequent geological ages. The resin petrified

in time and huge masses of it were washed up by the sea on what are now the south-eastern shores of the Baltic and on those of western Jutland. It is still found in deep layers in Samland and in Poland. The west of Samland and the north coast of the dune area of Frische Nehrung today supply the greatest quantity of amber. The next most abundant source is the area taking in Kuršių Nerija (Kurische Nehrung) and the Lithuanian and Latvian coasts. Some amber is obtained around the Bay of Danzig and in Pomerania. About 90 per cent of the world's best amber comes from this south-eastern Baltic area.

Until the seventeenth–sixteenth centuries B.C. export of amber had not reached any great intensity. From the shores of the Baltic coasts amber travelled to western, central, and eastern central Europe; even so, amber amulets in the shape of rings with a hole for suspension, and roughly made beads were still quite rare, and amber was not yet shipped in bulk to the south. Metal finds were extremely scarce in the Baltic area. Bone ornaments, such as pins made in imitation of copper pins current in central Europe, were in use.

The beginnings of a transcontinental amber trade and of the Baltic Bronze Age occurred simultaneously. Amber was demanded by the rising central European Únětician culture and by Middle and Late Helladic Greece. When the Úněticians established their commercial relations with the Mycenaeans some time before or around 1600 B.C., the amber trade rapidly reached an amazing volume.

The central Europeans imported amber from the Balts and from the Germanic peoples in Jutland. It is estimated that at least 80 per cent of the graves of classical Únětice contained amber beads. This culture, dating from c. 1650 to 1550 B.C., was already a true Bronze Age culture, producing an enormous quantity of bronze axes, chisels, daggers, halberds, and ornaments. Globular or somewhat flattened spherical amber beads are found in women's and men's graves and in hoards hidden by the travelling Únětician traders. Some huge hoards consist/ ing of luxurious bronze objects—such as metal/hilted daggers, long and narrow double/axes, metal/shafted or wooden/shafted halberds, neck/rings, C/shaped bracelets, pins and hair/rings, gold wires and ear/rings, and including amber beads—are found along the lower Vistula and lower Oder rivers leading to the source of amber. This shows that the amber coasts were already known to central European prospectors and that they brought bronze and gold in exchange for amber from the local inhabitants. They paid for it with the most precious bronzes produced in central Europe and with gold ornaments some of which were imported from sources in Ireland. All over the Baltic coast from Jutland to Lithuania bronze and gold items from this period are being found. One of the metal/hilted halberds was discovered as far north as Veliuona in the district of Kaunas, in Lithuania. In the lower Vistula area, along the East Prussian coasts and particularly in the peninsula of Sam/ land, appear bronze daggers, pins, bracelets, hair/rings, and other typically Únětician artifacts. This peculiar distribution of earliest bronze objects in the East Baltic area can be explained in no other way than by their having been traded for amber.

Amber beads from the Bronze Age are found in a finished state in northern Poland, East Prussia, and Lithuania. That some work was done on them at the source is shown by con/ siderable quantities of finished, half/finished, and broken amber beads found in Juodkrante on Kuršių Nerija (a narrow strip of land between the Baltic Sea and the Courish Lagoon), in western Lithuania. Another indication is that finished amber beads and pendants were exported to the northern East Baltic countries, Latvia, Estonia, and Finland, to north/western Russia, to Sweden and Norway, and even to eastern Russia and the Middle Urals; these beads and pendants found in the north have the same shape as those in the area of their origin.

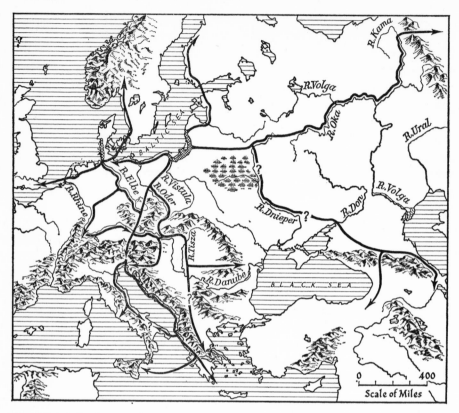

Fig. 8. Principal amber routes during the Bronze Age between 1600 and 1200 B.C. The source areas are indicated by cross-hatching

From the source area the amber was shipped to the Vistula. From the mouth of this river the route went south, but at the bend of the lower Vistula where it comes close to the Noteć (Netze), tributary of the Warta, the main supply turned west/ward, using the Warta and the upper Oder; the amber thus reached Silesia, eastern Germany, Bohemia, Moravia, western Slovakia, and lower Austria—the centre of the Únĕtice culture. From there the amber route continued along the Danube and the Tisza to the Balkans. One branch went down to Italy. Greece may have been reached via the Adriatic Sea or its coasts (as is suggested by amber beads in western Greece) and also via the central Balkans.

Fig. 8

In Greece amber beads appear throughout the Mycenaean period, starting with the earliest group of shaft-graves in Mycenae. Large numbers of spherical flattened beads and spacer beads came from the shaft-graves excavated by Schliemann and dated to the period 1580–1510 B.C., and also from a more recently excavated grave circle at Mycenae, dating from a somewhat earlier period. A great many flattened spherical amber beads and spacers are also known from various *tholos* tombs of the fifteenth and fourteenth centuries B.C.

The Baltic amber has a high succinic acid content, from 3 to 8 per cent, which distinguishes it from the amber from other sources. As early as 1885 amber beads from the Mycenaean shaft-graves were chemically analysed and proved to be of Baltic origin.[2] Since then many analyses of subsequently discovered beads in Greece and Italy have shown the same results.

Inter-regional amber trade resulted in some peculiar objects from distant lands reaching the Baltic coasts. Thus, for instance, a statuette representing a Hittite deity of the air or lightning god was discovered in Šernai near Klaipėda in Lithuania.[3] It must have come from Syria or Anatolia via Greece in the thirteenth century B.C., since almost the same kind of figurines have been found in Mycenae and Tiryns.

While gatherers of amber enjoyed the imported bronzes, the rest of the Baltic population could not afford to have metal tools and ornaments. For a long time metal must have been a luxury. Only flanged axes circulated throughout a larger area. For tilling soil the Balts used stone hoes with a perforation for inserting a haft, which persisted even in the Early Iron Age. A style of hoe developed whose head resembled a snake head. Hence they are called 'snake-headed' hoes, or 'East Baltic' or

AGRICULTURE AND STOCK KEEPING

Fig. 9. Baltic snake-headed hoe of stone from Latvia. 1:4

'Lithuanian' hoes, since they are found only in the Baltic area.[4] Stone, flint, bone, antler, and wood were basic materials for tools and weapons throughout the period which is labelled Early and Middle Bronze Age in central Europe. A unique and most interesting find—an enclosure for accommodating animals in conjunction with a camp site—made recently in northern Poland south of the lake of Biskupin throws light on how the village community sheltered its animals.[5] The enclosure, on an elevation in the middle of flat prairies, was 90 m. in length and 36 to 60 m. in width and surrounded by a ditch, 1·5 m. wide and 1·8 m. deep, and by a small rampart. The fortification had two entrances on the southern side. In the widened parts of the ditch were small huts of the wattle-and-daub type, apparently built for the shepherds. There were also other traces of habitation—fragments of pots, split animal bones, remains of fish, fresh-water mussel shells, tools of flint, antler and bone, pieces of ochre, clay net-sinkers and fragments of a bronze pin. The finds indicate a date around 1500 B.C. Among the animal bones were those of cow, sheep, pig, horse (?), dog, deer, roebuck, and aurochs. The enclosure could have held about 500 head of cattle, sheep, and other animals when they were brought in from pasture to be milked, sheared, or the like. The fortifications protected the cows, pigs, and sheep from the attacks of wild animals.

THE WESTERN BALTS AND THE ÚNĚTICE CULTURE

By following the distribution of Baltic and Únětician pottery types it is possible to draw an approximate line of demarcation between the central European Únětician and the western Baltic cultures. The pottery of these two cultures differed considerably. The Úněticians usually did not decorate their pots, the Balts did so by deep incisions and ridges around the neck: In the fifteenth century B.C. the beakers developed into tulip-shaped pots with several rows of incisions below the neck, and radiating sun motifs in between the incised rows. In northern Poland this pottery is known as 'Iwno' type, named after a cemetery near Szubin.[6] Another criterion for determining the boundaries is the difference in grave structures and grave furnishings. Ůnĕtician graves, under low barrows, were usually of bathtub shape and built of stones. The Baltic ones were contained in timber huts or stone cists having stone pavements for floor, the earthen barrow encircled by timber posts. Inhumed bodies were in treetrunk coffins.

During the Early as well as the Middle Bronze Age, the territory occupied by the Baltic culture had reached its maximal size. In the west, it covered all of Pomerania almost to the mouth of the Oder, and the whole Vistula basin to Silesia in the southwest. During no subsequent age was this culture found so widely; piece by piece it began losing its border lands. At the same time the central European Ůnĕtice culture grew progressively in wealth and power, until its influence reached all of continental Europe. Around 1400 B.C. it expanded to the Middle Danube basin and Transylvania, and its military power controlled a great part of the European continent.

Fig. 10

Throughout the fifteenth and fourteenth centuries B.C. the Baltic culture, while influenced by the central European cultures, did not lose its identity. The grave types and the pottery kept their strong local character, showing that the western Balts in the area of presentday northern and eastern Poland were not occupied or destroyed. The trade in amber did not diminish. About 400 sites showing a very uniform type of pottery, stone, and bronze industry are known from the area between Pomerania in the north and Volynia in the south.[7] The feature common to these hundreds of sites, mostly located on dunes, is the large tulipshaped beaker, plain or with horizontal incisions around the neck. This pottery dating from the fourteenth and thirteenth centuries B.C. is a development of the pottery of preceding centuries. In Polish literature it is known as the 'Trzciniec culture', after a place name in the district of Lublin.

Until the twelfth century, in spite of central European influences, the Baltic cultural bloc continued without major change. It was not until the second vigorous central European expansion, before and around 1200 B.C., that its culture was greatly affected. Then the entire south-western corner of the area in question—central, eastern, and southern Poland—was apparently occupied by the central Europeans.[8]

THE CLASSI-
CAL BALTIC
BRONZE AGE

In the Late Bronze Age the Baltic culture became increasingly resistant to and independent of its influential neighbours. Towards the end of the thirteenth century, between eastern Pomerania and the Bay of Riga and as far as the Warsaw region in the south, it began to develop its own characteristic metal culture. Metal ore was imported in greater amounts and local smiths were sufficiently trained to produce new forms of tools, weapons, and ornaments. Axes, pins, bracelets, and other ornaments took on a local character. Typically Baltic are: the graceful long Baltic battle-axes ornamented with horizontal furrows and striations; working axes with a wide, sometimes semicircular edge; pins with spiral heads, and pins with cylindri-

Plates 4–7
Fig. 11

cal horizontal heads. These are the most characteristic products in bronze between the thirteenth and eleventh centuries. In the early first millennium B.C. local forms of spearheads and socketed

Plates 8, 9

axes were widely used. Imports from central Europe, chiefly from the Lausitz area in what is now eastern Germany, continued and, as before, were concentrated in the lower Vistula area and in Samland, that is, in the places vital to the amber trade.

Fig. 10. Distribution of the Baltic culture, and its neighbours, in the Bronze Age. 1, Baltic Bronze Age culture of the western Balts; 2, Fat'janovo culture (includes 'Bala-novo' variant of the Early Bronze Age and 'Abashevo' of the Middle Bronze Age); 3, Central European Únětice-Tumulus culture; 3a, after the expansion to the middle Danube Plain and Transylvania in the Middle Bronze Age; 4, North Carpathian cul-ture; Bilopotok of the Early Bronze Age, Komarov of the Middle Bronze Age, Vysocko-Bilogrudovka of the Late Bronze Age; 5, North Pontic Bronze Age culture before the Timber-grave expansion; 6, Timber-grave culture (proto-Scythian); 7, Turbino culture

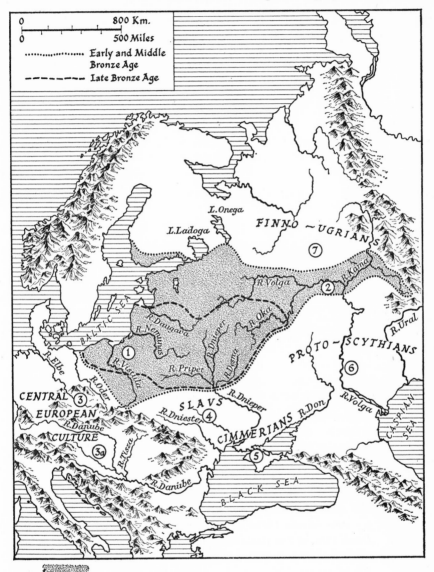

Maximum extent of the Baltic culture during the Bronze Age

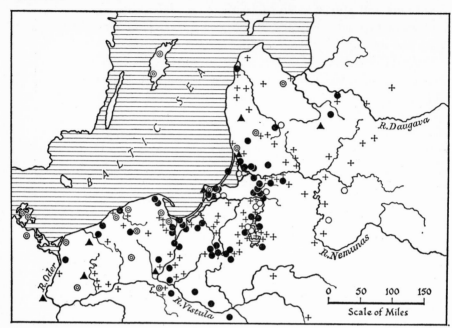

Fig. 11. Distribution of typically Baltic stone and bronze artifacts: 1, flanged axes of the Early Bronze Age; 2, pins with large spiral heads; 3, bronze axes having almost semicircular blades and a concave shaft; 4, battle-axes of 'Nortycken' type; 5, snake-headed hoes

The peninsula of Samland has yielded the greatest number of Late Bronze Age finds. From there come founders' hoards including finished and unfinished bronze specimens and copper ore. One of these huge hoards was discovered at the beginning of this century in Littausdorf near Fischhausen; it contained 118 objects: sickles, spearheads, socketed celts, and bracelets. Some were broken, some defective. The sickle types were much the same as those used by the Lusatians in eastern Germany. This may indicate either that the local smiths travelled or that traders from central Europe reached Samland. Commercial relations were carried on also with the Germanic peoples. In the barrows of Samland were found several of the spearheads and spiked *tutuli* of southern Scandinavian and north-west German type, and Baltic axes appeared in Denmark and southern Sweden.[9]

After the destruction of the Mycenaean culture by the central Europeans, the amber trade seems to have diminished, but not stopped. By the ninth century, amber reappeared in the Near East. On the banks of the River Tigris was found an amber statuette of Assurnasirpal, king of Assyria (885–860 B.C.), about 20 cm. high. It was made of Baltic amber, as shown by chemical tests. Whether the amber for this statuette travelled the eastern route, through Russia and the Caucasus, or through central Europe and the Phoenician trade routes in the Mediterranean, is still a matter for conjecture.

Late Bronze Age burial mounds, known from the coastal area and in particular from Samland, were surrounded by two or three stone rings. These barrows had been built over graves which were covered by a hemispherical stone vault. Graves of the thirteenth century B.C. contained inhumed bodies placed in tree-trunk coffins. Some time in the twelfth century inhumation gave place to cremation, whereafter the western Balts cremated their dead throughout the rest of the Bronze Age and the Iron Age. The custom came from central Europe, as did many other new ideas. As in central Europe, so also in the Baltic area the change was a gradual one; the tomb architecture and grave furnishings remained very much the same. Cremation first appeared in Pomerania and then spread eastward to East Prussia, Lithuania, and southern Latvia.

Fig. 12

Barrows are found in groups, sometimes over a hundred in one place. They constitute the chief source of our knowledge of developments during the Late Bronze Age. Unfortunately we cannot form a complete picture in that we lack a cemetery with all the graves excavated. Cemeteries seem to have been located next to the villages, and barrows were placed at random or in a single row. The larger barrows, up to 3 m. high, were apparently for chieftains or other important members of the community and their families, the smaller ones for the working class. From this particular Bronze Age period some chieftains' graves are known: one comes from the cemetery of Rantau near Fischhausen, in Samland.[10] The inhumed man, who lies in an extended position within the coffin, was placed in the centre of a specially prepared platform of stones. He was equipped with a bronze sword. In the Baltic area swords do not appear in such great numbers as in central Europe, and certainly they were a sign of distinction. There were also in this grave a Baltic battle-axe, amber and blue glass beads, as well as a bronze bracelet and a pin. Comparisons of the sword and other specimens with those current in central Europe imply the thirteenth century B.C. The chieftain's grave was covered by a hemispherical vault of stones, and other people, probably kin to the chieftain for whom the barrow was built, were later

Fig. 12

buried in the vault. The finds of secondary graves were of later type, and in addition, the barrow contained considerably later stone cist graves dating from the end of the Bronze Age to the Early Iron Age. Thus from this barrow we obtain a good sequence of several chronological phases.

In Samland the classical tradition of tomb structure with stone circles and stone vaults was continued for a long period. Similar barrows are found in the whole coastal zone from eastern Pomerania to western Lithuania. In south-western East Prussia and in southern Latvia mausoleum-like cemeteries have been discovered wherein hundreds of graves are compactly placed one above the other. A good example is the Workeim barrow in the district of Lidzbark Warmiński (former Heilsberg).[11] This barrow is only 1·8 m. high and 13 m. in diameter, but it contains about 600 graves. Finds show several successive periods and date the barrow to about 1000–600 B.C. Another 'mausoleum' comes from Rezne south-west of Riga.[12] This one is 2 m. high and contains over

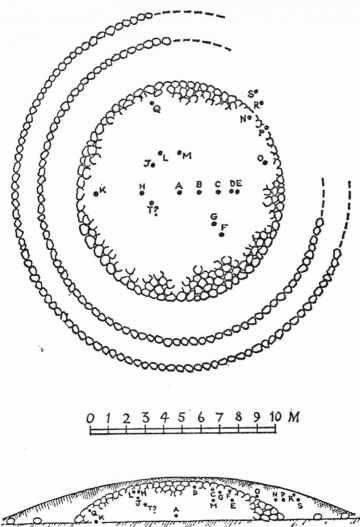

*Fig. 12. Plan and section of a classical Baltic Late Bronze Age barrow, with a central
stone vault and stone circles. Rantau near Fischhausen (now Primorsk), Samland.
A, chieftain's grave, thirteenth century B.C.; B–N, twelfth-century graves; O–S, later
Bronze and Early Iron Age graves*

300 graves dating from the Late Bronze and Early Iron Ages. The earliest burials, dating from approximately the thirteenth and twelfth centuries B.C., were inhumations; then came cremation burials without urns, dating from the end of the second and the beginning of the first millennium B.C. These were succeeded by cremation graves in small stone cists, dating from the end of the Bronze Age and the beginning of the Early Iron Age, which in turn were followed once more by inhuma-tion graves. The same burial mound was used for hundreds of years. It is possible that each was a family or clan burial vault.

Axes, horses, and oxen served as offerings during the funeral rites. In the Rezne barrow alone, the teeth of horses were found in 128 places. Ritual axes were placed not only in the men's graves, but in pots or by the wall of the grave.

THE WESTERN BALTS DURING THE SCYTHIAN AND CELTIC EXPANSIONS
Iron appeared in central Europe in the twelfth century B.C., but not until the eighth century did it revolutionize men's lives; and it was only then that it reached northern Europe. Between the eighth and sixth centuries iron was still extremely rare in the Baltic area, and the general cultural level continued to have almost a pure Bronze Age character. The dividing line at about the end of the eighth century B.C. signifies a change in culture due not so much to technological innovations as to new historical events.

This was the period of the Scythian expansion from the Black Sea area to central Europe. The horsemen who appeared in Rumania, Hungary, and eastern Czechoslovakia, intro-ducing eastern types of horse-gear, oriental animal art, timber graves and inhumation rites, must have been proto-Scythians, the successors of the south Russian Timber-Grave culture of the Bronze Age, who constantly pushed towards the west. Before entering central Europe, they conquered the Cim-merians living along the northern shores of the Black Sea and in the northern Caucasus, and drove them out. As Assyrian and Greek sources inform us, the Cimmerians fled to the Near

East, while the Scythians attained full domination of the northern Black Sea area. There they acquired much of the Caucasian
and Cimmerian cultural legacy and in their spread toward
the west they brought with them Ponto-Caucasian cultural
elements. These oriental influences appreciably changed the
material culture of central Europe.

The Baltic and Germanic cultures in northern Europe
remained untouched by the Scythian incursions, but the new
cultural elements reached them through continuous commercial relations with central Europe. The Lusatian urnfield culture in eastern Germany and Silesia, which during the Bronze
Age had been an integral part of the great central European
cultural realm, still persisted in the first centuries of the Early
Iron Age. The amber trade was not cut off and the Lusatians
continued to be mediators between the amber gatherers and the
Hallstatt culture in the eastern Alpine area and, beginning in
the seventh century, the Etruscans in Italy. Novelties such as
bronze horse-gear comprising bridle-bits, cheek-pieces and
ornamental plates, as well as the initial iron objects, were
transmitted to the Baltic area by the Lusatians. Again, as
during the Bronze Age, hoards and the most richly furnished
graves were concentrated in the source area of amber: in the
peninsula of Samland and on both sides of the lower Vistula.

The period from the eighth to the beginning of the seventh
century B.C. was also for the amber gatherers one of 'oriental-
ization', since in addition to the bronze horse-gear entirely new
forms such as large racquet pins, belt hooks ending in two
spiral plates, and ring- and wheel-shaped pendants appeared;
the prototypes of these objects are to be found in the central
Caucasus. South-eastern influences may have reached the
Baltic area via Hungary and the Vistula. The metal culture of
the western Balts was now remarkably enriched. However, not
all of the bronze ornaments or bronze horse-gear were imported; most of them show local style and local manufacture.

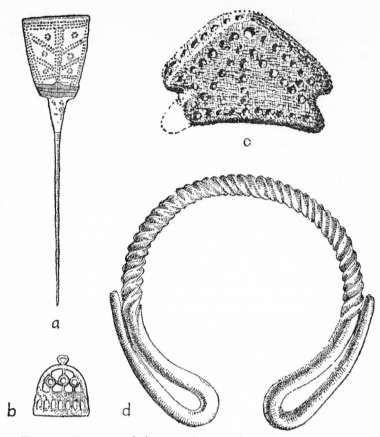

Fig. 13. a, Racquet pin; b, bronze pendant; c, amber pendant; d, neck-ring. From Domnicksruh (a, b) and Trulick (c, d), Samland, c. 750–650 B.C. a, b, d 1:2; c 1:1

Graves and hoards also include bronze forms that are not found either in central Europe or in the Ponto-Caucasian area. The shapes of amber beads and pendants increased in variety: round, rectangular, triangular, rhomboid, some with a tri-angular notch cut into either side and with pitted decoration. Typically Baltic—or, more accurately, Prussian or Sambian—were necklaces with large loop ends, which in the burial mounds of Samland appear together with amber beads, bracelets, pins, and finger-rings.

Fig. 13

Metal finds from the seventh and sixth centuries B.C. in Pomerania, East Prussia, and western Lithuania tell of con/ tinuing contacts with the Lusatians in central Europe and the Germanic peoples. Many hoards from the Baltic coast between the River Oder and Samland contained weapons, horse-gear, and ornaments identical to those of north-western and central Europe. Germanic trumpet-ended bracelets made of gold were found in East Prussia, and from central Europe swords, coloured glass beads, and fine bronze chains. The ornaments favoured by the Balts were pins with large spiral heads, spiral arm-rings made of flat bands ornamented with geometric motifs, and neck-rings made of thin round or flattened copper wire decorated with striations or dots.

Fig. 14

Trading in amber increased remarkably with the Alpine region, the eastern Adriatic coasts, and Italy providing very good markets. Astonishing quantities of amber beads, and pins threaded with amber, are found in the Hallstatt graves, and in the Etruscan graves of central Italy. Amber has frequently been found in graves along the trade routes leading from its source, namely the central European river-ways, the Vistula,

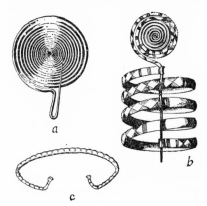

Fig. 14. a, Pin, b, arm-ring, and c, necklace. From the period 650–500 B.C. a, b, near Tilžė (Tilsit), c, Schlakalken, Samland. 1:3

Oder, and Elbe. The demand for amber for making into jewellery had now reached a second peak following that of the Mycenaean/Únětician period in the middle of the second millennium B.C.

Bronze Age tomb architecture continued virtually un/changed except for the new custom of placing the urn in a small stone cist: above the remains of the pyre a circular plat/form of head/sized stones was arranged and encircled by a stone ring, and in the centre was placed the pear/shaped urn, encased in a rectangular stone cist built of thin stone slabs. At the front of the cist a pointed tombstone was sometimes erected under which offerings, such as stone axes, are usually found. The cist was surrounded by a round stone wall built of several layers of stones about the size of a human head, or was solidly covered by a stone vault, the tomb itself being encircled with stone circles and covered by an earth/mound. Similar barrows are encountered between eastern Pomerania and western Lithuania, but the most numerous are known from Samland,

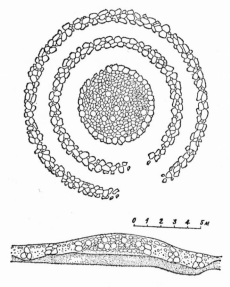

0 1 2 3 4 5m

Fig. 15. Plan and section of barrow having a stone plat/form and three stone circles. Kurmaičiai, western Lithu/ania, sixth–fifth centuries B.C.

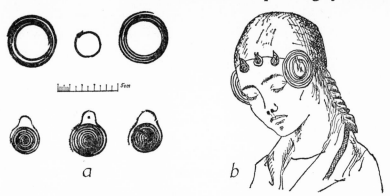

Fig. 16. a, Temple ornaments and spiral pendants originally attached to a woollen cap; b, reconstruction. Kurmaičiai near Kretinga, western Lithuania. Istorinis Muziejus, Kaunas

where at least a dozen were systematically excavated at the end of the nineteenth century.[13] The cemetery excavated in the forest of Drusken (Druskiai), Samland, dating from the seventh–sixth centuries B.C., revealed barrows encircled by from six to eleven or more rings of stones.[14] These barrows, buried as they were for ages under the forest, probably still contain their full quota of stone circles. A barrow revealed during the 1940 excavations in Kurmaičiai in western Lithuania, dating from the sixth–fifth centuries B.C., also shows the popular use of concentric stone circles. The innermost stone ring, 5 m. in diameter, surrounded a round platform paved with stones on which were found an inhumed woman's grave —furnished with temple ornaments and spirals that originally were attached to a knitted woollen cap—and six urn burials.

Around the end of the seventh and in the sixth centuries B.C., in eastern Pomerania and East Prussia the stone cists were enlarged: leading into the central one was a corridorlike structure which had an entrance in the side of the barrow, enabling all successive family urns to be placed under the same roof.

Fig. 15

Fig. 16

Fig. 17. House-urn from eastern Pomerania

Fig. 17

With the increase of commercial activities, cult influences also appeared. The emergence of house-urns is peculiar to the Elbe–Saale region of central Germany, Bohemia, Pomerania, Schleswig-Holstein, Denmark, and southern Sweden. The Pomeranian urns were rectangular and stood on poles, prob-ably in imitation of real houses. Engraved horizontal lines on the front wall may have portrayed the logs of timber houses. The idea of the house-shape very likely stems from Italy, where such urns are known from the eighth century B.C. The central European, Germanic, and Baltic house-urns, which had their own characteristic features, date from a later period, no earlier than the seventh century B.C. In Pomerania the house-urns were not numerous and did not supersede the local type of pear-shaped urns.[15]

Around 600 B.C. there was a new development which also could have come from the south to the north via the amber route, and which had a much more lasting effect on the Baltic culture. This was the appearance of human features on the cover or neck of pear-shaped urns. The portrayal of the human face became so characteristic a trait of the branch distributed over eastern Pomerania and along the lower Vistula in the sixth and fifth centuries, that it gave its name to the Face-Urn culture.[16]

At first the human features were only vaguely marked: two small holes on the neck or cover of the urn to suggest the eyes and a lump between the holes for the nose, with another hole below it for the mouth. The objects found with the urns, particularly swan-neck pins, indicate that they were coeval with the Hallstatt C period (*c.* 650–525 B.C.) in central Europe. These early face-urns, pear-shaped and with a cylindrical neck, were undoubtedly of local manufacture; they are found in typically western Baltic stone cists which housed urns of many members of a family or kin.[17] During the fifth century B.C. face-urns attained a classical shape. The face itself had finely worked features while ornaments, weapons, and symbolic scenes were incised over the neck and belly. Their artistic interest apart, the face-urns have incised upon them many perishable objects that are not found among the archaeological remains. These are

Fig. 18

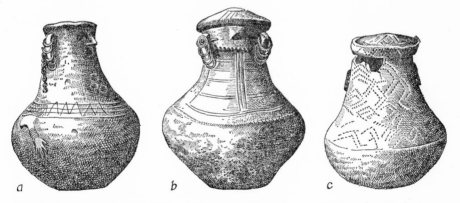

a　　　　　　b　　　　　　c

Fig. 18. Face-urns. Fifth century B.C. a, b, from eastern Pomerania near Danzig; c, from Samland

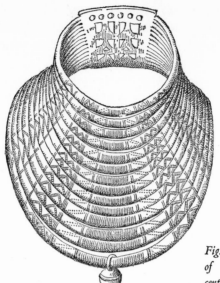

Fig. 19. Necklace from the district of Poznań. Face-urn period, fifth century B.C.

important in reconstructing women's and men's dress, wooden weapons such as shields and spears, wooden wagons, etc., and particularly religious symbols and ritual scenes.

Plate 11

Plate 10

Fig. 19

Some of the urns had ear-rings, made of bronze spirals or of rings on which were suspended glass or amber beads. These were attached to the 'ears'—small handles, with perforations, on each side of the pot's neck. Necklaces were very frequently represented on female urns by joining horizontal and vertical lines, and in the back joint by a 'fretwork' ornament. These were imitations of broad collar-shaped necklaces which are found in graves of Pomerania and East Prussia. Around the neck the urns sometimes had incised points or an incised ridge which represented an amber or glass bead necklace. On the belly were depicted large pins whose heads were made up of concentric circles. It was also quite usual to show a comb on the left or right side of the belly. No doubt those urns richly decorated with ornaments and combs served for female burials.

The symbolic scenes were chiefly confined to the male urns. All urns had lids in the shape of caps which had a hole in the top and which almost always were decorated with a solar emblem.

Fig. 20

The engravings on face‑urns can be clearly divided into two groups. To the first belong the almost naturalistic representa‑ tions of ornaments; to the second, schematized men, horses, wagons, shields, spears, sun discs raised on stelae, fir‑tree motifs, semicircles, and other geometric figures. The most interesting symbolic scenes are found on urns from eastern Pomerania and particularly from the area of Gdańsk (Danzig). Their art is of a peculiar local style as is their symbolic 'script'; most likely they were a product of one tribal unit. Face‑urns in the peninsula of Samland and in western Masuria were most frequently decorated only with geometric patterns and sym‑ bolic scenes, without representations of ornaments.

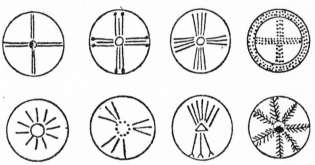

Fig. 20. Solar motifs on face‑ urn lids from eastern Pomerania

The general character of the symbolism on face‑urns is related to that of the Late Bronze–Early Iron Age rock en‑ gravings of southern Scandinavia and of the Camonica Valley in northern Italy, as well as to that on bronze vessels, razors, weapons, and clay figures of that period in the area between Italy and northern Europe.

The most frequent motifs are suns represented in many variations on the lids, or raised high on stelae and accompanied by horses; huge oval shields decorated with lines and dots like the radiating sun and which usually take the central position among other figures; human beings who hold spears and ride horses or four-wheeled wagons drawn by two horses; and two spears separately portrayed. The best examples are on urns from Grabowo and Starogard west of the lower Vistula. Probably the figures pertain to sky and sun deities and their associates, horses, horned animals, axes and spears. The engravings are certainly not realistic representations of hunting scenes or funeral rites.

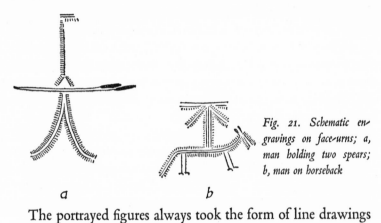

Fig. 21. Schematic engravings on face-urns; a, man holding two spears; b, man on horseback

a   b

The portrayed figures always took the form of line drawings accompanied by dotted lines or diagonal striations. Humans and animals were highly schematized. The men on the Grabowo urn look like gingerbread cookies with outstretched legs and arms, and their heads are circles filled with dots. The men holding spears are elongated beings with long necks, their arms hardly showing; those on horseback or on a wagon usually have no legs, but they are shown with outstretched arms. Although some of the figures look like nothing more than children's drawings, others are charmingly graceful. Urns for distinguished persons were probably decorated by the most eminent artists.

Plate 15

Fig. 21

Face-urns express very well the ancient belief that the deceased continues in his exact image and retains all his charac-teristics. In the art of face-urns we never find a repetition of the same human features, ornaments, or symbols; no two urns are alike. They were made individually according to the dead person's sex, personal qualities, and social status. This last was a matter of great concern; for example, the urn from Grabowo is exceptional and probably belonged to a chieftain, while others were left undecorated.

Another feature of the Grabowo urn is that the symbolic   Plate 15
scenes occupy only about the upper third of the urn, the rest being covered with long vertical lines going down from around the neck and linked with from four to nine diagonal lines. These lines may represent the stitches of an animal-skin cloak. From this and other urns we may guess that chieftains and other distinguished persons wore well-sewn cloaks, and sym-bolic scenes could have been stitched on to them.

The existence of skin cloaks and coats is confirmed by actual finds, preserved in bog burials. From the face-urn period the well-preserved body of a girl of twelve to fourteen years was discovered in 1939 at Dröbnitz, near Ostróda (Osterode) in western Masuria (formerly East Prussia)—possibly a sacrificial burial.[18] The body was wrapped in a coat made of four sheep   Plate 16
skins sewn together, the woolly side against the body. The seams were very finely stitched, and across the top was a turned hem. The patches on the upper and lower parts and the dia-gonal seam across the back show that the coat was mended many times. A bone comb (of the same shape as depicted on face-urns) was attached to the coat by a woollen cord. This bog   *Fig. 22*
burial is of interest since it shows that in addition to the usual cremation of the dead, sacrificial burials in bogs took place, a practice that is also known from the Germanic culture. In the internal organs of the girl were found the remains of meat, fat, peas, wheat flour, and pollens of the blossoms of wild plants.

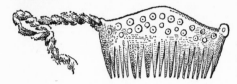

Fig. 22. A bone comb found attached by a woollen cord to the sheepskin coat (see Plate 14) from Dröbnitz bog in Masuria (East Prussia)

While the western Balts lived a rather prosperous life during the Face-Urn period, central Europe suffered new attacks from the Scythians. Traces of the Scythian raids dating to the sixth and fifth centuries are found in western and southern Poland, eastern Germany, Czechoslovakia, and the western Ukraine. Over 50 sites are known having typically Scythian arrow-heads, horse-gear, swords, and ornaments. Many Scythian arrowheads have been found in Lusatian strongholds, indica-ting that the Lusatians were being attacked constantly by the eastern aggressors. The Lusatian strongholds were now in their last stages of survival, and eventually the culture was devas-tated. The Scythians reached the southern borders of the western Baltic lands, but apparently did not succeed in pene-trating farther north. Only a few arrowheads of Scythian type have been found in East Prussia and southern Lithuania, but information is not sufficient yet to draw any inferences. A chain of western Baltic strongholds in northern Poland and in the southern part of East Prussia arose which very probably were built for resisting the southern invaders. Their well-planned fortifications were disposed on the islands and promontories of lakes. The fortified village built on piles on the island of Lake Arys near Pisz (Johannisburg) in East Prussia was encircled by several palisades of wooden stakes.[19] Here the houses were not preserved as they were, by inundation, in the Lusatian stronghold at Biskupin whose defence system was similar.

At present we know of about twenty fortified villages along the lower Vistula, and in Masuria and Samland, which have yielded finds dating from the sixth to the fourth or later cen-turies.[20] All were arranged in strategically well-chosen hills,

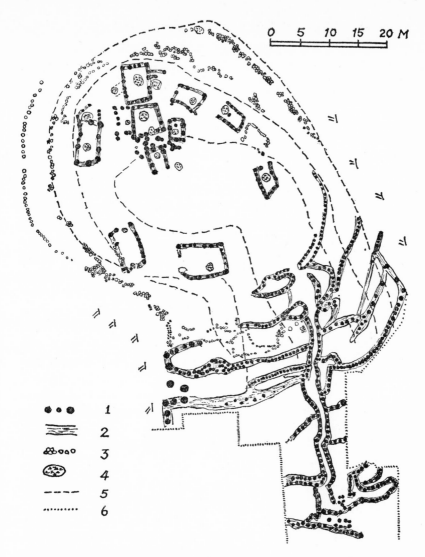

Fig. 23. Plan of a fortified village. Fifth–fourth centuries B.C. Starzykowe Małe, near Susz, northern Poland. 1, traces of timber posts of the houses and of stakes of the palisades; 2, walls (houses) and ditches; 3, stones, 4, hearths; 5, isohypses; 6, limits of the excavated area

surrounded on one or two sides by water. Usually they had earth ramparts 2–3 m. high and about 10 m. wide at the foot, strengthened inside by vertical and horizontal logs, although some had stone walls and additional palisades.

A village of interest, dating from the fifth–fourth centuries and known from the 1929–39 excavations, is located east of the lower Vistula at Starzykowe Małe (former Kl. Stärkenau) near Susz (former Rosenberg).[21] Comprising eight houses and several other structures presumed to be barns and stables, this village was set on the peninsula, fortified by two ramparts of stones and in front by a number of palisades branching off the

Fig. 23

main road which was constructed between two rows of wooden piles. The rectangular houses, which had one room and a hearth, were arranged in concentric circles. One house within the inner circle was distinguished by having a long corridor-like antechamber and several hearths. The latter very likely belonged to the headman of the village. The houses were quite small, some measuring 5 × 3 m., some about 8 × 5 m. From this and other excavated sites we see that villages were small, housing probably from 40 to 60 people. In size the Early Iron Age villages resemble those known from the Chalcolithic period, and in plan and character as defence structures, those of the Late Bronze and Early Iron Age fortified villages of the central European Urnfield peoples.

The Scythian episode in the northern part of central Europe was of short duration. From the fourth century B.C. Scythian traces no longer appear. To what extent the western Baltic tribes helped to hold back the Scythians, future researches will show; but one fact is already clear: the Face-Urn people, probably taking advantage of the breaking up of Lusatian power by the Scythians, expanded southward. The descend-ants of the Face-Urn people occupied the whole Vistula basin in Poland and the part of the western Ukraine reaching the

Fig. 24

upper Dniester in the south.

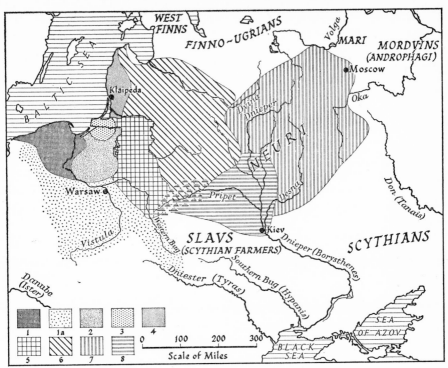

Fig. 24. Baltic groups during the Early Iron Age (c. 600–400 B.C. and later) based on archaeological finds. 1, the 'Face-urn' group of Pomerania and lower Vistula; 1a, the area of expansion of the 'Bell-grave' group, successor of the 'Face-urn' group, in the fourth and third centuries B.C.; 2, the west Masurian group, probably connected with the later Prussian Galindians; 3, the Sembian-Notangian group; 4, the lower Nemunas-western Latvian group connected with the early Curonians (Kurshians); 5, the east Masurian or Sudovian (Jatvingian) group; 6, the Brushed Pottery group ancestral to Lithuanians, Selians, Lettigallians and Semi-gallians; 7, the Plain Pottery culture to be identified with the easternmost Balts; 8, the 'Milograd' group of the seventh–sixth centuries B.C. Location of the Scythian farmers, Neuri and Androphagi based on Herodotus

This expansion around 400–300 B.C. brought changes. The fashionable face-urns gradually lost their human features and developed into much more simplified versions. Only the depiction of a bead necklace around the neck and the sun symbol on the lid remained from the previously rich decoration

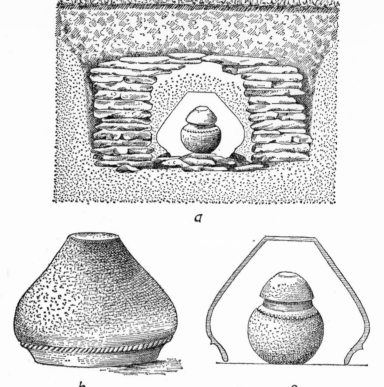

Fig. 25. Pot-covered urn grave from eastern Pomerania. a, grave built of stone slabs; b, pot covering the urn; c, urn

with ornaments and symbolic scenes. In grave pits these simplified pear-shaped urns were covered with a large pot or
sometimes with two or three pots stored one above the other.
In view of this custom, we talk of the 'Bell-Grave' or 'Lamp-
shade-Grave' culture. In the fourth century the pot-covered urn
burials were still placed in stone cists built of stone slabs, but
gradually stone-cist building disappeared and urns with piles
of pots on them were only covered with stones. This change in

Fig. 25

grave type probably came about because of the spread of the Face-Urn people over the territory of the Lusatians who covered their urns with pots. Some scholars are therefore inclined to consider the potcovered urn culture as a continuation of, or resulting from a mixture with, the Lusatian culture. However, it is more logical to suppose that the Lusatians merely influenced the Face-Urn culture. The similarity of the urns of the potcovered urn period to the faceurns is striking whereas there is no genetic relationship to the style of the Lusatian pottery. We can also recognize a very close relationship with the pottery made by other Prussian tribes in East Prussia. The potcovered urn culture is certainly not an 'early east Germanic culture', as Petersen called it in his otherwise valuable study of 1929 describing the graves and finds in the territory of prewar eastern Germany.[22]

Fig. 26

Fig. 26. Urns in stone cists — 'family graves'. Fourth century B.C.; a, from Silesia; b, from eastern Pomerania

The basic monuments of this period are the graves, although traces have been found of over 400 settlements in Poland on river banks, usually on sand dunes, where only pottery sherds and no habitation remains were preserved.[23] Frequently found in graves have been bronze or iron pins with 'sunflower' or small spiral heads, and later types of swan-neck pins; also bracelets made of iron wire, bronze or iron ear-rings, glass beads, and iron razors and knives. Objects imported from the Celtic Early La Tène, such as iron fibulae and belt clasps found in several pot-covered urn burials, suggest that they date from the fourth century B.C. The La Tène fibulae and belt clasps appear in pot-covered urn burials in the upper Dniester area, showing that the southward expansion of the pot-covered urn culture was accomplished by the fourth century.[24]

At the same time, however, traces of the La Tène culture are found in Silesia. Its influence increased during the subsequent period and signs of the Celtic culture of the third century B.C. are found in southern Poland and the western Ukraine. The southern drive of the pot-covered urn people appears to have been stopped by the Celtic expansion eastward. The Middle La Tène (*c.* 300–100 B.C.) graves, settlements, and numerous isolated finds in Silesia, west southern Poland, and the southern parts of the western Ukraine all attest their continuous occupa-tion of the area for at least several centuries. During the third and second centuries B.C. the pot-covered urn burials taper off in southern and central Poland, until they finally disappear about the first century B.C.

Meanwhile, the southern Baltic sea coast east of the River Oder had been gradually infiltrated by the Germanic tribes. In the fourth century B.C., sites of the Germanic Jastorf culture with traits relating them to northern Germany occur in the lower Oder area, and during the third century cemeteries of Jastorf character occur in the east as far as the River Persante (Parsęta) in eastern Pomerania.[25] The Germanic expansion,

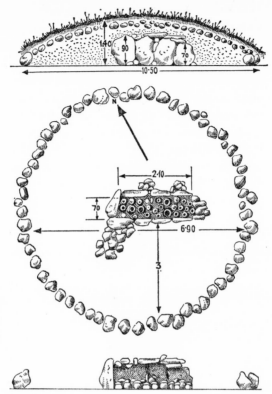

Fig. 27. Barrow encircled and covered by stones with a large stone cist inside housing 27 urns. Grünwalde, near Eylau, East Prussia. Fourth–third centuries B.C.

which caused the complete disappearance of the Lusatian culture in the lower Oder area, reached the borders of the pot-covered urn culture. In the first century B.C., however, cemeteries of the Jastorf culture disappear; instead, eastern Pomerania sees the spread of the so-called 'Oksywia complex', distinguished in its pit-graves by inhumation and, rarely, cremation graves; a characteristic which is held by some scholars to be Gothic, by others Slavic-Venedian. At the time of the birth of Christ and in the first centuries A.D., eastern Pomerania and the lower Vistula area were already occupied by the Goths who came to the Vistula estuary in ships from Scandinavia, probably looking for better lands and a better climate. Their presence is attested by the written records (Pliny, Strabo, Tacitus, Ptolemy) and by their cemeteries and grave goods which differed from those of the Prussians living east of the Goths.[26]

While the strongest tribe of the western Baltic bloc which had manifested itself in face- and pot-covered urn graves disintegrated due to the Celtic and Gothic expansions, the other Baltic tribes were less touched by outside influences and conservatively preserved the local character. The ancestors of the Sembians, Notangians, and Galindians continued throughout

a

b

c

d

e

f

Fig. 28. a–d, Geometrically decorated Prussian urns from the fourth–third centuries B.C.; e, urn with 'eyes'; f, pot within a dish filled with uncremated bird bones

the entire Early Iron Age to build stone cists in which they placed urns of a family or kin, covering them with an earth barrow secured by a stone pavement from above and stone rings around. A classical example of barrows of the fourth or third centuries B.C. comes from Grünwalde (Zielenica) in the former district of Eylau (now Bagratinovsk), south of the *Fig. 27* peninsula of Samland. Prussian tribes skilfully decorated their pottery with geometric motifs: dotted lines forming rhombs, *Fig. 28* triangles, zig-zags and other patterns. In addition to the geo-metric decoration, the Prussian urns of the fourth and third centuries B.C. preserved some features of the earlier face-urns:

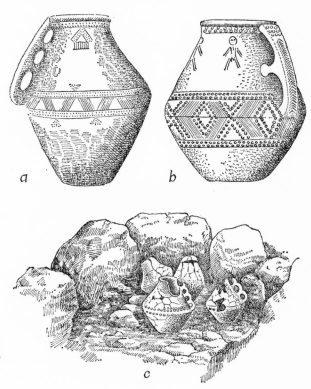

a

b

Fig. 29. Urns (a, b) and urns standing in a stone-cist family grave (c), from the third–second centuries B.C. Samland

c

Fig. 29

lids in the shape of head-caps, a hole in the cap and two in the neck for the eyes. Engravings of human figures and of houses sometimes occur on the urns from Samland. Usual finds, in addition to pottery, were iron needles, awls, lunular razors, glass and white faience beads. Middle and Late La Tène fibulae were imported and imitated.[27] It is of interest that, in marked contrast to the Celtic and Germanic graves, weapons are extremely rare in these Baltic graves. The inland Prussian tribes seem to have lived a rather peaceful life.

CHAPTER IV

The Bronze and the Early Iron Age of the Eastern Balts

THE CHALCOLITHIC AND BRONZE AGE food-producing culture in forested central Russia has, as we have
seen, been given the name Fat'janovo. Since the discovery of
the Fat'janovo cemetery near Jaroslavl' on the upper Volga in
1903 this culture has been treated as a separate unit. Since
Baltic river names extend through Byelo-Russia and central
Russia and a number of Baltic loan-words are found in the
languages of the Volga Finns, the Fat'janovo very likely was
either an easternmost branch of the proto-Baltic culture or a
very closely related Indo-European group which continued in
central Russia throughout the first three-quarters of the second
millennium B.C.

During the Bronze Age the Fat'janovo people spread eastward along the Volga and its tributaries. Beyond the upper
Volga, Fat'janovo sites are found along the lower Oka, Sura,
lower Vjatka, and lower Kama rivers. In the third quarter of
the second millennium it reached its maximum extension: it
spread along the River Belaja as far as the southern Urals. The
Fat'janovians installed themselves in a narrow strip of land
between the Finno-Ugrian hunter-fishers in eastern central
Russia and the proto-Scythians in southern Russia.

They built their small villages on high river banks, usually
fortifying them with ramparts and ditches on the inland side.
These fortified sites were in marked contrast to those of the
hunter-fishers, who lived in unfortified villages on the low
banks of lakes and rivers. All over the upper Volga and lower
Oka the Fat'janovians lived contemporaneously with the
hunter-fishers, whose culture in central Russia of the early

THE EASTERN
EPISODE:
THE FAT'JAN-
OVO CULTURE

Fig. 10 : 2

second millennium B.C. is known as 'Pitted-Ware' and that of the second quarter of the same millennium as 'Volosovo'. The Fat'janovians farmed in the uplands, kept sheep, goats, cattle, pigs, horses, and dogs. They also hunted and fished quite intensively. Men's graves were equipped with archer's wrist guards made of bone. In children's graves miniature clay wheels were found, so that we may infer the existence of vehicles. Metal artifacts increased in number in the eighteenth–seventeenth centuries, and without any other noticeable altera-tions the culture entered the Bronze Age. Copper axes and spearheads gradually replaced those of stone and flint. An outstanding cemetery which yielded a fairly large number of copper axes, spearheads, tubes, and spirals is the Balanovo, excavated between 1933 and 1937.[1] The Early Bronze Age group of sites in eastern central Russia is named 'Balanovo' after this cemetery, and is regarded by some scholars as an independent culture.

The shapes of metal objects are related to those known from southern Russia, showing that the knowledge of metallurgy came directly from the south with the importation of metal ore from the source area in the southern Urals. Also there are some indications that the Fat'janovians in the upper Volga basin may have had contacts with central Europe. Several sites have yielded peculiar cuff-shaped bracelets that are comparable to the Early Bronze Age Únětician bracelets in central Europe.

Graves with inhumed bodies are found in deep pits within timber hut constructions roofed with logs or planks which were covered by low earth barrows. Burial rites and ornamental motifs on pots reveal animal, fire, and sun cults. Separate graves for a sheep, a goat, or a bear occasionally appear in the cemeteries; these creatures were buried with the same rites as humans, and bones of domestic animals frequently occur in human graves. Charcoal, red ochre, tinder, and pieces of flint are common finds in the graves, sometimes inside pots. Could

Fig. 30. Early Bronze Age Fat'janovo ('Balanovo') pot and base with a solar decoration from the Buj II cemetery on River Vjatka

these be the material remnants of a fire cult? On the base of the pot there was a round concavity, either undecorated or adorned with a radiating sun motif. The neck and shoulders of the pots had designs of zig-zags, cross-hatched lines, vertical or diagonal striations, all skilfully incised, stamped, or impressed. These decorations again indicate sun symbols. Indeed, it is very likely that the people worshipped fire and the sun, like their western relatives and other Indo-European peoples. The sun motifs do not occur on the pottery of the Finno-Ugrian hunter-fishers.

Fig. 30

The Early Bronze Age Fat'janovians competed continu-ously for land with the Finno-Ugrians and with the proto-Scythian Timber-Grave people who pressed the Fat'janovians hard from the south, expanding from south Russia to the north-west as far as the River Oka. The lands occupied by the Fat'janovians became narrower and narrower, but before their complete disappearance from Chuvashia, Tataria, and Bash-kiria, the Fat'janovians penetrated astonishingly far to the east: along the upper Belaja and even into the southern Urals. Other sites were clustered east and north of Kazan. This last stage of the Fat'janovo culture dating from approximately 1500–1300 B.C. is called 'Abashevo', after the cemetery dis-covered in 1925 near the village of Abashevo in the northern part of Chuvashia, east of Kazan.[2] Abashevian sites appeared in the southern Urals probably because these people were seek-ing sources of copper. Their settlements in this area yielded a large amount of copper ore, slag, and tools used for metallur-gical purposes. Metallurgy in the southern Urals flourished and the travelling smiths copiously supplied the whole lower and middle Volga basin with copper ornaments, tools, and weapons. The people now produced not only axes, spearheads, awls, and spirals of copper, but also daggers, knives, sickles, bracelets, and quite complicated ornaments such as pendants, rings, and belts made of copper or silver foil with minutely embossed designs of rosette, concentric circle, and leaf patterns. Excellent craftsmanship characterizes the detailed ornamenta/tion with thin copper wire and copper foil sewn on leather. Fragments of preserved pieces of headgear, sleeves, and shoul/der trappings of leather are richly decorated with lines of tiny copper rings, spirals, semispheres, and rosette motifs. Women's costume was tastefully and lavishly adorned. The Abashevian smiths learned much from southern Ural metallurgists, the so/called Andronovo people, kin to the proto/Scythian Timber/Grave people, and with whom the Abashevians had very close contacts.

The richly ornamented Abashevian pots show a gradual development in form and in ornament from the earlier phase of the Fat'janovo culture in eastern central Russia, and Andro/novo influences. The pots were no longer globular but flat/based and sometimes tulip/shaped or biconical, the surface being well smoothed and burnished. Ornamentation was im/pressed with a dentate tool or incised, forming horizontal, zig/zag, wavy line, triangle, or meander patterns. The burial rites of the Abashevo period were similar to those of the earlier Fat'janovo. The dead were buried in pits under low circular barrows, one or several graves to each barrow. In some Chu/vashian cemeteries graves were found to be surrounded by a rectangular, circular, or elliptical timber fence. Each grave was a solid house construction built of vertical logs and roofed with planks.

We know of no cemeteries or habitation sites from the last centuries of the second millennium B.C. to prove the con/tinuation of the Fat'janovo culture. It seems that in the middle Volga and Belaja river basins it disappeared quite abruptly, due to a renewed expansion of the Timber-Grave culture from the south.

The Bronze Age is still a rather obscure period in the area between eastern Lithuania and Latvia and the Oka river basin in central Russia. From pottery remains in fortified hill-top villages it is seen that during the end of the second and the beginning of the first millennium B.C. a cultural differentia-tion gradually took place, and before the beginning of the Early Iron Age several local groups had been formed. One was the so-called 'Brushed-Pottery' group in eastern Lithu-ania, southern Latvia, and north-western Byelo-Russia;[3] another, closely related to the Brushed-Pottery was the Milo-grad group in southern Byelo-Russia and the northern fringes of the western Ukraine;[4] and a third was the so-called 'Plain Pottery' group occupying the Desna, upper Dnieper, upper Oka, and upper Don basins in central Russia. The last-named group, in the basins of the Desna and upper Don, carries the name 'Bondarikha' for the Late Bronze Age cen-turies, and 'Jukhnovo' for the Early Iron Age and the first centuries A.D.[5]

Fig. 24

In spite of some local differences in the above-mentioned areas, which may represent the distributions of separate tribes, the general level of the culture, the patterns of habitat, pottery, and the bone and stone implements, show a remarkable uni-formity and conservativism all over this territory. Bronze axes and ornaments were quite rare. Pins, awls, needles, and arrow-heads were usually made of bone, although hoards with bronze and silver objects of Late Hallstatt and Early La Tène type are known from the Milograd group. Pottery was hand-made, and very simple in form: beaker- or barrel-shaped and flat-based as in the Brushed and Plain Pottery groups, or rounded-based as in the Milograd. We find incisions and pits upon the upper part of pots and frequently pinched ridges or pinched impressions around the neck. The same forms and decoration

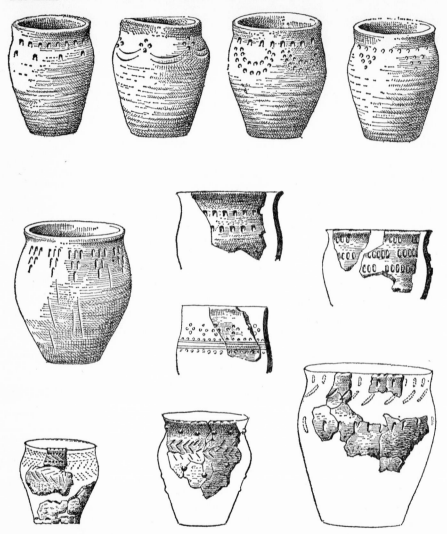

Fig. 31. Late Bronze Age and Iron Age pots from the fortified hill-top villages in the R. Desna, upper Donets and upper Oka Basins, central Russia. Bottom row, Late Bronze Age pots of 'Studenok' type, c. eleventh century B.C.; centre group, Pots of 'Bondarikha' type, end of Bronze Age, c. ninth century B.C.; top row, Pots of 'Jukhnovo' type, Roman period

persist throughout the Late Bronze and Early Iron Ages, and *Fig. 31*
even in the first centuries A.D.

The hill-top village culture in the uplands of eastern Lithuania, eastern Latvia, Byelo-Russia, and western Greater Russia
—as far east as Moscow and the upper Oka and upper Don
basins—lasted throughout several millennia. Its Baltic character is proved by the clear continuity of the cultural remains and
by many river names of Baltic origin which splendidly coincide
with the distribution of the Brushed, Milograd, and Plain
Pottery groups. From the end of the eighth century B.C. onward the earliest written records raise the prehistoric curtain,
throwing some light on historic events in the Cimmerian and
Scythian domains in the Black Sea area; and, from the time
of Herodotus, on the northern neighbours of the Scythians.

At the end of the second millennium the proto-Scythian   HERODOTUS'
Timber-Grave culture moved westward from the lower Volga   'NEURI'
steppes towards the Black Sea coasts, and at the end of the
eighth century B.C. the Scythians succeeded in conquering the
Cimmerians who for over a millennium had occupied the
northern Black Sea coasts. A large proportion of the early
Slavs in the Middle Dnieper basin fell under the rule of the
Scythians, but the Finno-Ugrian tribes and the eastern Balts
living in the forested areas remained outside the orbit of strong
Scythian influence. However, as centuries went by and the
Scythians became involved in war against the invading Persians, the northern tribes were also disturbed. Thanks to these
wars which Herodotus describes in Book IV of his history, we
have the earliest surviving written records concerning the history of eastern Europe at the end of the sixth century B.C.
Allusions to some tribal names may be regarded as references
to the Baltic and Finno-Ugrian tribes. Herodotus, who wrote
around 450 B.C., describes an expedition which the Persian
king Darius undertook against the Scythians in the year 515.
He mentions and approximately locates the seats of 'Neuri',

'Androphagi', 'Melanchlaeni', 'Budini', and other tribes that lived north of Scythia. Although we cannot expect accuracy in Herodotus' geography, his account is of importance. Of the Neuri and their neighbours he writes:

> On the landward side, beginning from the Ister [Danube] Scythia is inclosed by the Agathyrsi first, and then by the Neuri and the Androphagi, and last the Melanchlaeni. (IV, 100)

> So the Ister [Danube] is one of the rivers of Scythia. But the next after it is the Tyras [Dniester], which riseth in a great lake in the north which is the border between Scythia and the land of the Neuri. (IV, 51)

> Beginning from the port of the Borysthenites [at the mouth of the Dnieper], which is in the middle of the whole sea coast of Scythia, the Callipidae, who are half Greek and half Scythian, are the first inhabitants. Beyond them dwell another people, who are called Alizones. . . . But beyond the Alizones dwell the Scythian husbandmen, who sow corn not for food but for sale. And above them dwell the Neuri, and beyond the Neuri towards the north wind the land is uninhabited of men, so far as we know. (IV, 17)

> Across the Borysthenes [the Dnieper], starting from the sea [Black Sea], the first place is Hylaea; and above this dwell Scythian farmers. These Scythian farmers inhabit the land for three days' journey towards the east, extending to the river which hath the name Panticapes [unidentified river], and eleven days' voyage up the Borysthenes towards the north. And the land beyond them is desert for a great space, but after the desert dwell the Androphagi, who are a separate people and in nowise Scythian. And above these the land is truly a desert, and no nation of men liveth there, so far as we know. (IV. 18)[6]

For establishing the location of the Neuri there are several pointers in Herodotus' account. First, that the River Dniester rises in a great lake in the north, which is the border between Scythia and the land of the Neuri. As there is no lake at the sources of the Dniester, one can only guess that by 'great lake' Herodotus possibly meant the Pripet marshes. Hence, the Pripet swamps apparently were the natural border between Scythia and the Neuri. Second, that the Neuri dwell beyond the Scythian farmers who inhabit the land, at the distance of three days' journey toward the east and eleven days' voyage up the Dnieper starting from the place Hylae on the Black Sea. From this it appears that the land of the 'Scythian farmers' was a large area occupying the lower and middle Dnieper basin. From the archaeological point of view, the lands thus assumed to be occupied by the 'Scythian farmers' coincide with the dis/tribution of the so/called 'Chernoleska' culture of the seventh–fifth centuries B.C., which while strongly influenced by the Scythians shows a clear continuity with the preceding culture in Podolia and the middle Dnieper basin, known by the names 'Bilogrudovka' for the Late Bronze Age, 'Komarov' for the Middle Bronze Age, and 'Bilopotok' for the Early Bronze Age. For over a millennium this culture had persisted before the Scythians destroyed it by conquest. There can be no other explanation than that the 'Scythian farmers' and their pre/decessors were the ancient Slavs. The Neuri are considered by Herodotus as a separate people living north of the Scythian farmers, that is, north of the Slavs. The third pointer is that the neighbours of the Neuri were Androphagi, the 'man/eaters', who are identified with the Mordvins living in central Russia east of the lower Oka. The name Androphagi was deciphered at the beginning of this century by Tomashek in his lectures at the University of Vienna; it is a Greek translation of the Iranian name for the Mordvins, 'mardxvār' (*mard*—man; *xvār*—devour).[7] Herodotus describes them as a separate people

and in no way Scythian, while the Neuri 'have Scythian cus/
toms'. This distinction between Neuri and Androphagi may
refer to the difference between the Indo/European and Finno/
Ugrian peoples. Historical accounts concerning the Neuri can
be traced to the fourth century A.D. Roman sources localize
the Neuri in the region where the River Dnieper begins.[8]

There has been a long discussion between Slavic and Baltic
linguists on the question of the nationality of the Neuri; some
maintain that they were Slavs, others Balts. The root *ner/*, *nar/*
nur/ appears in both the Slavic and the Baltic languages.
Linguistic data alone do not answer the question. However, I
wish to stress that river, lake, and village names with the root
ner/ and *nar/* are extremely frequent in the Baltic lands, in
Lithuania and Latvia and in East Prussia, Byelo/Russia, and
the western regions of Greater Russia. The words *ner/ti* and
nar/dyti, meaning 'to dive', to 'submerge', are living words in
the Lithuanian and Latvian languages. Furthermore, the
earliest Russian chronicle of Nestor in the eleventh century
mentions 'Neroma' as a name for the province which was pay/
ing tribute to Rus' and which is presumed to be Latgala or an
area east of present Latvia. It is possibly a survival of the earlier
name for the Baltic tribe used by the Finno/Ugrians, 'Nero/
maa' (*maa* in Finno/Ugric languages means 'land'). From the
archaeological point of view, the culture of eastern Latvia and
the upper Daugava/Dvina basin in Herodotus' time and later
is culturally inseparable from that in the area of Smolensk,
Moscow, Tula, Kaluga, and Brjansk. Here we find the Plain
Pottery group, as is shown on the Early Iron Age map. Even
from Nestor's time, after the Slavic expansion to present/day
Russia, the archaeological finds in the surviving Baltic en/
claves between the upper Dnieper and upper Oka rivers show
a very close relationship to the finds from eastern Latvia. Hence
the links between Herodotus' 'Neuri' and Nestor's 'Neroma'
are not improbable.

Fig. 24

That the Neuri were identified with the Slavs was largely
due to the fact that when, around 1900 and later, linguists tried
to explain 'Neuri' as Slavs, the Baltic culture was too little
known from archaeological sources for it to be supposed that
the Baltic tribes could have lived in Byelo/Russia and the west'
ern regions of Greater Russia, north of the Pripet swamps, in
the upper Dnieper, the Desna, and upper Oka basins. This
area does in fact correspond with the territory of the Neuri
which Herodotus describes as beyond the borders of Scythia,
north of the 'Scythian farmers' (Slavs), and in the neighbour'
hood of the Mordvins (Androphagi). Here we have one of the
strongest arguments, since the eastern Balts and not the Slavs
were the western neighbours of the Mordvins before the Slavic
expansion to present/day Russia, which occurred one thousand
years later. It is therefore highly probable that Herodotus'
Neuri were eastern Balts, although the name itself apparently
is distorted. The eastern Baltic lands could have been called
'Nerava' or 'Neruva', which are typical forms for names of
Baltic provinces. The names for Latvia and Lithuania, ancient
Latuva and *Leituva*, have, for instance, the same suffix and
are believed to have originated from the river names Lata and
Leita.

Except for mentioning that the Neuri have Scythian cus'
toms, Herodotus does not give any other clue as to their way of
life or appearance. He says more, however, about the Finno'
Ugrian peoples, the eastern and northern neighbours of the
Neuri, the Androphagi: that they are the most savage of men,
and have no notion of either law or justice. They are herdsmen
without fixed dwellings, their dress is Scythian, but their
language is peculiar to themselves only. The Melanchlaeni
(who are assumed to be the Volga/Finnic Cheremiss people)
are described as wearing black cloaks; the Budini (possibly
Votyaks) all have blue/grey eyes and red hair. The Budini are
a populous and powerful nation . . . they are pastoral people

who have always lived in this part of the country. Further, Herodotus recounts how the Scythians sought help from the northern nations to counter the Persian attack. The chieftains of the Neuri, Androphagi, Melanchlaeni, Agathyrsi, and Tauri did not agree to be Scythian allies. It is not clear from Herodotus' account how much the lands of the Neuri were affected by the invasions, but he says that the Melanchlaeni, Androphagi, and Neuri offered no resistance to the Scythians and Persians.

So much for Herodotus' story of the Neuri and their neigh-bours. From it we see that the tribes living north of Scythia in a vast region of what is now Russia were known to the Scythians and Persians, and to the Greeks as well.

EARLY IRON AGE HILL-TOP VILLAGES Now we must revert to the archaeological remains in the areas where we do find a continuum of culture in the upper Oka, upper Dnieper, and upper Nemunas basins. Many hundreds of fortified hill-top villages are reported from this region, located on the highest banks and promontories of lakes, by small rivulets or at their confluence with larger rivers. They usually appear in groups at a distance of about 5 km. from one another. As they are situated on the highest spots in the vicinity, it is sometimes possible to see from one hill-fort one or two others. It seems that a group of about five to ten villages belonged to a unit, which may have formed a tribal district. This type of layout of hill-fort groups apparently continued here long after Chalcolithic and Bronze Age times. There are no traces of larger settlements or towns.

Such accumulations of villages are known on the upper Oka and its tributaries Zhizdra, Ugra, Upa, Nara, and others. I purposely enumerate these river names because they are con-sidered to be of Baltic origin. Hill-forts are also grouped on the River Protva south-west of Moscow, and around Smolensk, Vitebsk, Minsk, Homel, and other towns in Byelo-Russia where a number of Baltic river names can be identified; there are many groups in eastern Lithuania and Latvia as well. For the Early Iron Age and for the first centuries A.D. fortified hill-top villages are the basic sources of information. In contrast to the earlier periods and to the area of the western Balts, cemeteries are as yet hardly known here. We are thus better informed about the pattern of settlement and economy than about the burial rites, cults, social stratification, and representa-tive artifacts.

Villages were fortified with ramparts and ditches, and occu-pied an area of some 30–40 × 40–60 m. or more, on which about ten houses were built. The ramparts, 1–2 m. high, were built of stone, earth, or clay. Very often ramparts were of baked clay, and these were interwoven and solidly covered with timber. These were the most durable and still exist. Some of the recently discovered ramparts have 'mysterious openings', which are the subject of many legends. The ditches outside the ram-parts sometimes reach 3–7 m. in depth and 10–15 m. or more in width. In plan the village was of various shapes: oval, elliptical, triangular, or even rectangular, depending on the natural shape of the river bank or the promontory into the lake. Before the houses were built the area was levelled, the lower parts being raised. Ramparts were normally on the inland side which, if not fortified, was accessible to enemies and wild animals. Sometimes ramparts encircled the whole village or protected it from several sides.

Frequently, hill-forts have yielded cultural layers of many periods; some of them were used for millennia. Their character and defence structures changed very slowly. In 1957 a whole village of ten houses dated to the third century B.C. came to light as a result of excavations by T. N. Nikol'skaja at the hill-fort of Nikolo-Lenivets on the bank of the River Ugra, tribu-tary of the Oka.[9] Above-ground, timber houses stood in two rows very close to each other, oriented NE–SW. Between the two rows was a street about 3 m. in width. Houses were

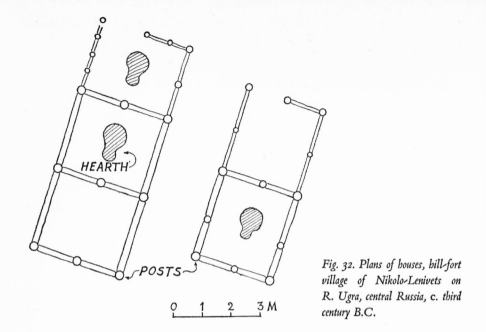

Fig. 32. Plans of houses, hill-fort
village of Nikolo-Lenivets on
R. Ugra, central Russia, c. third
century B.C.

rectangular and of about the same size, either 9 × 3 m. or 6 × 3
m., and most of them had hearths inside. Those without hearths
presumably were for housing livestock, and for barns. The living-
quarters were divided into two or three compartments, each
probably occupied by a family. Houses were built of vertical
Fig. 32   timber posts placed in the corners and at the middle of each
wall; the space between the posts was filled in with horizontal
logs or interwoven twigs, after which the walls were thickly
daubed with clay. The roofs were pitched, and supported by
strong posts in the middle of the house. Floors were tamped
with clay, and open hearths were somewhat below floor level
and surrounded by a clay wall.

Iron sickles and grain impressions on pottery found in many
villages indicate that agriculture was universal. The people
maintained their farms and kept their animals in small areas
beyond the villages, which occasionally were enclosed with
Fig. 33   ramparts as in the hill-fort of Svinukhovo. Grain was kept in

round pits, about 1 m. in diameter. In most of the hill/fort sites over 70 per cent of the animal bones were those of domesticated, and less than 30 per cent those of wild animals. A particular abundance of horse bones, in some cases more than half of all the bones found, may indicate that the horse was used for food. Domestic animals constituted the basic food supply, although wild animals were hunted both for fur and for food. In some sites bones of furred animals such as the fox, hare, squirrel, marten, and beaver predominate; in others, those of bear, roe/deer, and wolf. Fishing was an important subsidiary activity. The presence of small net/sinkers shows that floating nets and seines were used in addition to iron or bone hooks and bone harpoons.

A bronze industry is attested by stone moulds and crucibles. Bracelets, pins, and ornamental plates of bronze or copper were made locally. Hill/forts dated to the period between the fourth

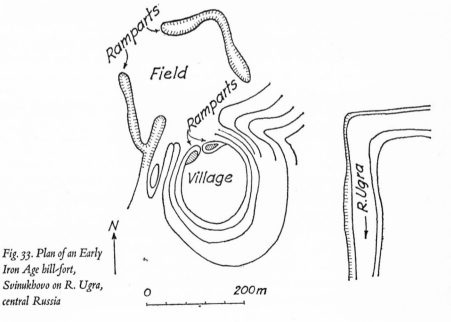

Fig. 33. Plan of an Early Iron Age hill/fort, Svinukhovo on R. Ugra, central Russia

Fig. 34

Fig. 35

and second centuries B.C. have yielded a large number of spiral-headed bronze pins and pins with leaf-shaped, fret-worked heads. Below the leaf were one or two loops apparently for the attachment of chains. Convex plates with several holes were used for attaching to the dress or to belts. Bracelets were embellished with a curving design in relief. The majority of the finds in hill-forts, however, are of bone and ceramic. Bone was used for harpoons, arrowheads, awls, needles, perforators, handles for knives and rods, buttons, children's toys, and disc-shaped whorls; clay, for net-sinkers, variously shaped whorls, horse figurines, toys, and pottery. Pots were thin-walled, made of grey clay tempered with gravel or sand.

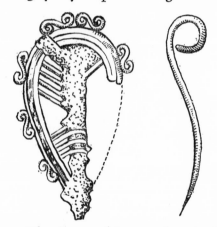

Fig. 34. *Leaf-shaped and spiral-head pins from the hill-fort of Svinukhovo and Nikolo-Lenivets, central Russia. Fourth–third centuries B.C. c. 1:3*

That iron smelting was done in the villages is shown by iron knives, fish-hooks, and sickles, some in unfinished shape or broken, and iron slag and clay ovens. Iron ore was obtained from the local swamps, meadows, lakes, and lake shores which abound in the forested areas of eastern Europe. The ore had to be dug out in the summer, and in the autumn and winter it was washed, dried, heated and reduced to small pieces. After that, the ore was placed in small clay ovens in layers alternating with charcoal, for smelting. Starting somewhere in the middle of the

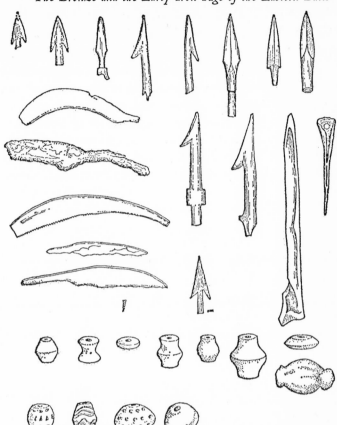

Fig. 35. Bone arrow-heads, harpoons, a pick, a needle, iron sickles and knives, clay whorls and a net sinker from the forti-fied villages in the upper Oka Basin, central Rus-sia. Fourth–third cen-turies B.C.

first millennium B.C., iron production gradually increased, but not before the first centuries A.D. did it replace the tools and weapons of stone and bone.

The changeless life of the eastern Baltic tribes in the Dnieper basin was disturbed in the second century B.C. by the appear-ance of the Zarubincy, assumed to be Slavs (the name 'Zaru-bincy' coming from the cemetery of Zarubinec south of Kiev on the River Dnieper, excavated in 1899).[10] They invaded the lands possessed by the Milograd people along the River Pripet

ZARUBINCY: THE FIRST SLAVIC EXPANSION NORTHWARDS

and up the Dnieper and its tributaries, and the southern territories inhabited by the Plain Pottery people. The Zarubincy
were a peasant folk on a cultural level similar to that of the
eastern Balts, but their archaeological remains contrast in every
detail with those of the older population. Their settlements were
larger and they lived in semi-subterranean huts as opposed to
the small villages and above-ground houses of the Milograd
and Plain-Pottery people. Their urn-fields are in contrast to
the inhumation and cremation graves in pits or in barrows of
the Milograd people. The Zarubinec urns and other pots were
burnished, had a more or less angular profile, frequently
possessed handles, and were decorated with a ridge applied
around the neck. Their prototypes are found in the Vysockoe
and Chernoleska culture of the western Ukraine (Podolia and
southern Volynia) dating from the seventh–fifth centuries B.C.,
and its inheritors during the succeeding centuries. The most
frequent finds in graves were fibulae, derivatives from the
Middle and Late La Tène types of central Europe.

The intrusion of the Zarubincy must be interpreted as the
first Slavic expansion northward from the lands lying in the
immediate neighbourhood. Their movements may have been
prompted by the expansion of the western Baltic tribe, the Pot-
covered Urn-Grave people, in the fourth-third centuries B.C.,
and the subsequent Celtic expansion to eastern Europe. The
Milograd culture persisted alongside the Zarubinec throughout
all the centuries of the occupation, from the second century
B.C. to the second century A.D. A certain revival is discern-
ible around the third–fourth centuries A.D., when Milograd
sites appeared again on the Dnieper as far as Kiev in the south.
Dating from around the third century A.D., finds of the Zarubinec type disappear and by the fourth–fifth centuries are
replaced by another Slavic branch, pushing up the Dnieper
from the south.

CHAPTER V

The 'Golden Age'

THE PERIOD from the second to the fifth century A.D. is the 'golden age' of Baltic culture. Not only were East Prussia and Lithuania now the outposts of active and complex trade with the provinces of the Roman Empire and Free Ger⁄ many, they had also grown through increasing industry and agriculture into a vigorous cultural centre that influenced all of north⁄eastern Europe. Never before had the Balts enjoyed such a wealth and variety of metal products. In the Bronze and Early Iron Ages, bronze objects had been concentrated around the sources of amber and the principal trade routes, and were items of luxury; now, metal production had increased so much that bronze and iron objects were commonly used by all people, even in areas far from the Baltic Sea. Trade routes lead⁄ ing to the north, and east to the Finno⁄Ugrians in the North⁄ east Baltic area, Finland, and northern and eastern Russia, intersected on territory occupied by the Baltic tribes. The Balts thus became the most important transmitters of the metal culture to the north and east, and their zone of influence was geographically the largest in Europe outside of the Roman Empire.

Fig. 36

Fig. 36 (overleaf). Baltic lands in the Roman period, c. A.D. 1–500. 1, Baltic; 2, eastern Slavic (Chernjakovo culture, c. third–fifth centuries A.D.); 3, Zarubincy sites, second century B.C.–second century A.D.; 4, barrows of fourth–fifth centuries presumed to be Krivichian; 5, Finno⁄Ugrian; 6, Gothic cemeteries and their tentative spread to the Black Sea; 7, limits of the Roman Empire; 8, amber route between the area of source and the Roman provinces; 9, principal trade routes of Baltic ornaments; 10, westward expansion of the Huns, late fourth century A.D.

Key   1   2   +3   ▲4   5

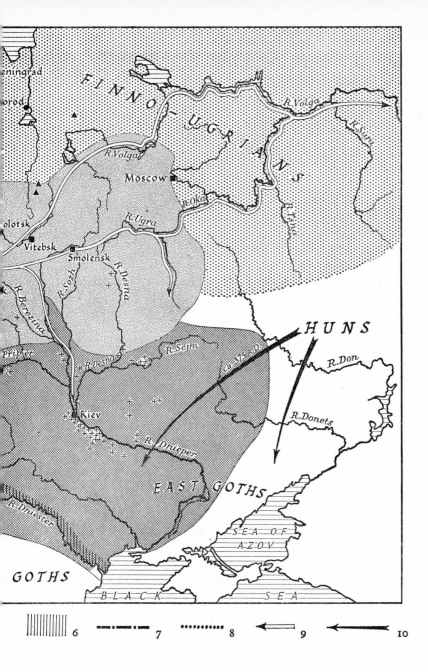

GOTHS
FINNO-UGRIANS
Moscow
HUNS
EAST GOTHS
Kiev
R.Volga
R.Volga
R.Oka
R.Ugra
R.Desna
R.Sozh
R.Berezina
R.Pripet
R.Sejm
R.Desna
R.Dnieper
R.Dniester
R.Don
R.Donets
SEA OF AZOV
BLACK SEA
Smolensk
Vitebsk
olotsk
eningrad
orod
ca.375 AD

6	7	8	9	10

III

GRAVES: CON
TINUITY AND
DISTRIBUTION
Fig. 37

The Baltic tribes, except for the Prussians, abandoned cremation at about the time of the birth of Christ and began to inhume their dead. Separate tribes developed their own distinctive burial rites: some—for instance, Sembians, Semigallians, Letigallians, Lithuanians, and other eastern Baltic tribes—built earth barrows above single or family graves and surrounded them with stone circles. Sudovians built stone barrows; Curonians placed their dead in stone circles or rectangular walls; their neighbours in central Lithuania used flat graves, supporting the treetrunk coffins with stones. The differentiation of local burial rites as from the second century A.D. enables us to follow the borders between the various Baltic tribes, which remained unchanged in this area up till the beginning of history.[1] The continuity of the burial rites which can be observed from almost a thousand cemeteries, some containing hundreds of graves dating from a single century or several, gives basic proof of the stability of the Baltic tribes during the Iron Age. Settlements, in many cases stratified, substantiate a long, undisturbed occupation. There is no evidence of migrations, shifts of population, or invasions of the Baltic lands by foreign peoples. Throughout the 'golden age' the Balts possessed about the same lands as during the Early Iron Age: from the lower Vistula in the west to the basin of the Oka in the east, and from the basin of the DaugavaDvina

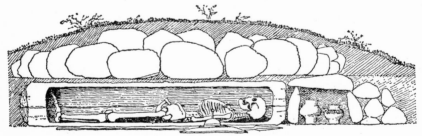

Fig. 37. Warrior's grave in a treetrunk coffin. Shield and spear along the side, pots with provisions behind the head. Second or third century A.D. Cemetery of Wiekau, Samland

in the north (up to the upper Velikaja River in north-western   *Fig. 36*
Russia) to the Pripet swamps in the south. The amazing
increase in finds is due to the growth of population, agriculture,
metal industry and trade, and the accumulation of wealth in
individual hands.

The hill-top village—a typically Baltic settlement pattern   VILLAGES AND
throughout earlier centuries—was not sufficient for the require-   HILL-FORTS
ments of the growing material culture and population. From
the first centuries A.D. onwards, the villages began to extend
downward over the slopes into larger areas sometimes covering
from 10,000 to 20,000 sq. m. While hill-top villages continued
to exist, the more populated areas gave rise to larger villages
which, for their protection, were sited next to a small, fortified
earthwork. Earthworks, though considerably smaller than the
area housing the village community, had higher ramparts and
deeper trenches, and the slopes were terraced and paved with
stones. The ramparts were up to 5 m. high and 20 m. wide,
built of fairly thick, long timber stakes and covered with earth
and stones. Ramparts and wooden palisades sometimes surrounded the whole earthwork. The level area within the fortifications was small, usually not more than 100 sq. m. In several   Plate 17
instances, traces of one or two wooden structures, probably also
for defence, were found within the fortifications. The hill-fort
of the first centuries A.D. is the prototype of the later feudal
castles; the village with scattered farmsteads, of the townlets
which grew beside the castles.

In his *Germania* (A.D. 98), Tacitus mentions that in the cul-   AGRICULTURE
tivation of corn and other fruits of the earth, the Aistians
'labour with more patience than is customary to the laziness
of the Germans'—*Frumenta ceterosque fructus patientius, quam pro
solita Germanorum inertia laborant*. No wonder that the settled
Baltic tribes occupying fertile East Prussian lands were able to
make a better impression on Tacitus concerning their agricultural activities than were the restless Germanic tribes on the

southern Baltic coasts. What do the archaeological finds add to Tacitus' telling statement? When he wrote, the Baltic cul/ ture was still in the stage of the Early Iron Age; the *floruit* of the metal culture started after *c.* A.D. 100. Archaeological data on the agriculture of the second and third centuries A.D. in/ creases: finds of iron axes, hoes, sickles, and scythes from those times in graves and villages are numerous. In 1961, a farmer's grave dating from the second or third century A.D., contain/ ing iron/tanged plough/shares in addition to fragments of iron/ mounting of the wooden parts of the plough, a large sickle ('bush/knife' having an indented blade), knives, axe, chisel, awl, instrument for striking fire, and spear, was discovered in the cemetery of Szwajcaria near Suwalki, which belongs

Fig. 38

to the Sudovian tribe.[2] Iron shares, it is presumed, were attached horizontally or at a slight angle to the wooden plough. The area where this find was made was hilly and forested and the plough was probably used after slash/and/burn to clear it of roots and all other remains. The iron plough/shares from Szwajcaria are the first to be found in the Baltic area and the earliest in all north/eastern Europe. Wooden ploughs made from a tree/top will continue to have been used, as they were in the Middle Ages and later. So apparently were wooden har/ rows, as is shown by the early borrowing of the Baltic word for harrows by the Finno/Ugrian tribes. Iron hoes are found in the heavy clay soil area of the Lielupe/Mūša basin in central Latvia and northern Lithuania. While iron sickles, small and large, of Early Iron Age type continued in use, the scythe made its way from the west to the flatlands of East Prussia, western and central Lithuania, and Latvia. Here it replaced the sickle,

Fig. 39

but in the uplands of eastern Lithuania, Latvia, Byelo/Russia, and central Russia the sickle remained in use. The geo/ graphical distribution of the scythe and the sickle, defined by lowlands and uplands, continued throughout the following centuries. Even today in the sandy highlands and lake areas of

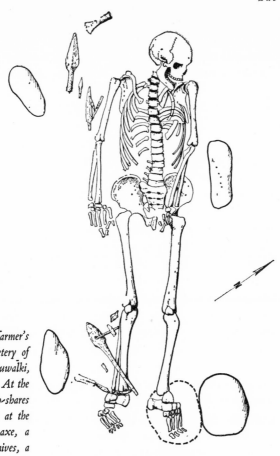

Fig. 38. Sudovian farmer's grave from the cemetery of Szwajcaria near Suwalki, c. A.D. 150–250. At the feet lie iron plough-shares and a shrub knife; at the head, a socketed axe, a spearhead, three knives, a chisel and an awl

the moraine belt the sickle is still being used by Lithuanian, Latvian, and Byelo-Russian women (the scythe, in prehistory and history, was always wielded by men).

In addition to wheat, millet, and barley, known from earlier times, rye and oat grains appeared in the storage pits of villages dating from the second century and later. Wheat, millet, and rye were found in the largest amounts. Among the wheat

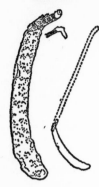

Fig. 39. Iron scythe, c. A.D. 250–350. Maskatuži, south-western Latvia

grains were distinguished the species *Triticum diccocum, spelta, vulgare,* and *compactum,* of which the most common were *diccocum* and *spelta,* as in the Bronze and Early Iron Ages.

The grain storage pits usually appeared in the house area. One of the most interesting 'granaries' from the hill-fort of Gabrieliškiai near Girkalnis in central Lithuania was 2 × 2·5 m. in diameter and 30 cm. deep, paved with stones and apparently lined with birch bark, containing about thirteen gallons of grains of all the above-mentioned species, remains of charred bread, bronze ornaments, an iron spearhead, and six badly worn Roman coins, one of which was of Marcus Aurelius' reign (161–80), while the other five were no longer decipherable.[3] The various grains were found mixed together: it is likely that they were sown thus and that bread was made of mixed grain flour.

Large cemeteries continuing in use at the same place for centuries—they are found to the greatest degree of concentration in the most fertile areas such as Masuria, Samland, Notangia, the clay soil region of the Rivers Pregel (Prėglius) and Inster (Įsrutis), the alluvial depression of the lower Nemunas, the clay soil lowlands of the River Lielupe-Mūša basin and along the lower Daugava—indicate a stable agricultural population that used the same arable lands over a long period. The presence of seeds of the weed *Chenopodium album* found among the grains supports this contention. The seeds of rye-grass (*Bromus secalinus*) found among the rye grains bear witness to fallow fields, indicating the two-field system. Slash-and-burn agriculture was used at the same time, particularly in the hilly and forested areas extending eastward from east Masuria, eastern Lithuania, and eastern Latvia to Byelo-Russia and central Russia. The large iron sickle, an instrument used for cutting shrubs and young trees, was distributed over these same areas. In the less fertile zone of the eastern Baltic lands the grain species appear to have been less numerous. In the villages of the upper Dvina basin, east of Velikie Luki, only the soft-grained *Triticum vulgare* of the wheat family and barley have been found.[4] Flax and hemp were widely spread, as is attested by linen fabrics and hemp cords, although the seeds of flax are not known and hemp grains, being fatty, survived only in exceptional cases.

In the breeding of domestic animals there were no changes from the earlier periods. The eastern Baltic hill-forts show about the same percentage of domestic animal bones as in the Early Iron Age: domestic animal bones to wild animal bones were in the ratio of 70–75 to 25–30 per cent or less, with cattle dominating, followed by sheep, horse, and pig. The Sudovian and Lithuanian sites yielded a considerable number of sylvan horse bones of the tarpan type (*Equus gmelini*), which were also present in the Early Iron Age settlements. In the forested up-lands (the Polotsk, Vitebsk, Smolensk area), the hill-top villages yielded a large number of bones of the local species of small, thin-legged cattle. These animals survive on green fod-der in pastures throughout a considerable part of the year. Bones of swine and boar appear frequently in the Baltic villages.[5]

ANIMAL HUSBANDRY

Iron slag and small vaulted clay ovens for iron smelting were found in many villages, where trained smiths very probably formed a separate class of people, released from farming. Hoards were found to contain smiths' equipment including anvils, hammers, chisels, and files. Iron axes, socketed or per-forated (socketed in the western, with shaft-hole in the eastern zone), hammers, chisels, knives, awls, needles, shears, scythes, sickles, hoes, spearheads, shield buckles, bridle-bits, spurs, and other objects show entirely local forms. Any weapons or tools having common prototypes (chiefly Celtic and Germanic) in central Europe before the birth of Christ attained a purely Baltic character around A.D. 200.

METALLURGY

Besides the iron industry, the manufacture of bronze, brass, silver, and gold greatly increased. At the end of this period steel came into use; socketed axes of the fifth century were made of this metal, attained through a prolonged heating of iron in contact with charcoal. All the processes of metallurgy were used: casting, hammering, riveting, winding, twisting, engraving, incrustation, oxidation.

TRADE The Baltic culture was a link in the chain of the so-called 'barbarian' cultures beyond the imperial frontiers, and its growth certainly owes much to the influence of the Roman Empire and its provinces. Through the increase in trade relations during the second and third centuries, this culture became inseparable from the general cultural pulse of Europe.

Again it was amber that attracted the south and kept alive the long-standing trade routes between the Baltic Sea and the Adriatic. From the classical authors we learn how greatly amber was valued and desired, and from where it was shipped. During the first and second centuries A.D., at least five Greek and Roman authors mention and describe the shores of the Baltic Sea, called in ancient times the 'Northern' or 'Suevian' ocean. These were: Strabo, Pomponius Mela, Pliny the Elder, Tacitus, and Ptolemy. Even earlier, the sources of amber were known to travellers, as Pliny mentions in his account of the journey of Pytheas of Massalia which took place around 320 B.C. Pliny (A.D. 23–79) writes in his *Natural History*:

> Pytheas says that the Gutones, a people in Germany, inhabit the shores of the estuary of the Ocean called Mentonomon, their territory extending a distance of six thousand stadia: that, at one day's sail from this territory, is the Isle of Abalus, upon the shores of which amber is thrown up by waves in spring, it being an excretion of the sea in a concrete form; also, that the inhabitants use this amber by way of fuel, and sell it to their neighbours, the Teutones. Timaeus, too, is of the same belief, but he has given to the island the name of Basilia.[6]

At the end of his long account of falsehoods that have been told about the origin of amber, and calling 'amber—a thing so common, . . . which is imported every day', Pliny states:

> There can be no doubt that amber is a product of
> the islands of the Northern Ocean, and that it is the
> substance called *glaesum* by the Germans; for which
> reason the Romans, when Germanicus Caesar com/
> manded the fleet in those parts, gave to one of these
> islands the name of Glaesaria, which by the barbar/
> ians was known as Austeravia.

The 'amber island', *Glaesaria*, called *Abalus* by Pytheas, *Basilia* by Timaeus, *Balcia* by Xenophon of Lampracus (also mentioned under this name by Pliny in *Natural History*), and *Austeravia* by the barbarians, cannot be anything but the Penin/ sula of Samland. It was taken for an island because the ancient travellers reached it from the west by way of the sea.

Tacitus states clearly who the amber gatherers were: 'On the coast to the right of the Suevian ocean, the Aistians have fixed their habitation . . . [here follows the description of their language, customs, and patient cultivation of crops]; and fur/ thermore they explore the sea for amber, in their language called *Glesum*, and are the only people who gather that curious substance. It is generally found among the shallows, sometimes on the shore.'[7]

About the amber trade and the Roman passion for amber we again hear from Pliny the Elder:

> Amber is imported by the Germans into Panno/
> nia, more particularly; from whence the Veneti
> called by the Greeks Eneti, a people in the vicinity
> of Pannonia, and dwelling on the shores of the
> Adriatic Sea, first brought it to general notice. . . .
> From Carnuntum in Pannonia, to the coasts of
> Germany from which the amber is brought, is a dis/
> tance of about six hundred miles, a fact which has

only very recently been ascertained; and there is still living a member of the equestrian order, who was sent thither by Julianus, the manager of the gladia/ torial exhibitions for the Emperor Nero, to procure a supply of this article. Traversing the coasts of that country and visiting the various markets [*commercia*] there, he brought back amber, in such vast quantities as to admit of the nets, which were used for protect/ ing the podium against the wild beasts, being studded with amber.

The arms, the litters, and all the other apparatus were for one day decorated with nothing but amber, a different kind of display being made each day that these spectacles were exhibited. The largest piece of amber that this personage brought to Rome was thirteen pounds in weight.[8]

Then he describes several kinds of amber:

There are several kinds of amber. The white is the one that has the finest odour, but neither this nor the wax/coloured amber is held in very high esteem. The red amber is more highly valued; and still more so, when it is transparent, without presenting too brilliant and igneous an appearance. For amber, to be of a high quality, should present a brightness like that of fire, and not flakes resembling those of flame. The most highly esteemed amber is that known as the 'Falernian', from its resemblance to the colour of Falernian wine; it is perfectly transparent, and has a softened, transparent brightness. Other kinds, again, are valued for their mellow tints, like the colour of boiled honey in appearance. It ought to be known, however, that any colour can be imparted to amber that may be desired; it is sometimes stained with kid/ suet and root of alkanet; indeed, at the present day, amber is even dyed purple. When a vivifying heat has been imparted to it by rubbing it between the fingers, amber will attract chaff, dry leaves, and thin bark, just in the same way as the magnet attracts iron. Pieces of amber, steeped in oil, burn with a more lasting flame than pith or flax.

So highly valued is it as an object of luxury, that a very diminutive human effigy, made of amber, has been known to sell at a higher price than living men even, in stout and vigorous health.[9]

In addition to Pliny's account of amber imports into the Roman Empire, there are as evidence the amber objects them/selves: a vast number of beads, vases, cosmetic jars, lamps, human effigies, Eros figurines, busts of bacchantes, sculptures of lions, panthers, dogs, goats, tortoises, dolphins, snails, birds, various fruits, and countless other objects. One of the most beautiful collections of amber objects comes from the work/shop at Aquileia, of the first and second centuries A.D.[10]

The amber traffic traversed central Europe and was con/trolled chiefly by the native inhabitants. The principal route from Samland and the mouth of the River Vistula followed the same direction as during the Mycenaean Age: up the lower Vistula to the River Warta, then up its tributary Prosna to the upper Oder in Silesia, thence to Moravia and down the River Morava to the Danube. Through the fortress of Carnuntum at the junction of the Morava with the Danube (the present Pet/ronell near Hainburg in lower Austria), as mentioned by Pliny, the traffic entered Pannonia, the province of the Roman Empire in present/day western Hungary and northern Yugo/slavia. According to Pliny, the Veneti living on the shores of the Adriatic dispersed the amber from Pannonia to Italy. Aquileia, the important point of assembly at the northern coast of the Adriatic, could be reached by good roads through the province of Noricum in present/day Austria.[11] For local trading in amber many other waterways were also used, in

Germany leading to the River Elbe and Bohemia. In later cen‑
turies, in the third and particularly the fourth and fifth, when
Goths had established themselves north of the Black Sea, the
amber trade lent added importance to the Vistula‑western Bug‑
Dniester route. The Dnieper route across Byelo‑Russia and
Lithuania may also have been used. Goths, Sarmatians and
Huns made frequent use of amber for their ornaments, and it is
found as far east as the Kirghizian steppes.

The Baltic people apparently did not themselves carry the
amber to the south in the centuries around the birth of Christ.
They sold it to the Germanic tribes who were then their
immediate neighbours at the mouth of the River Vistula. The
amber was sold in the trade centres, the 'commercia', there, in
Samland, at the mouth of the Nemunas near present Klaipéda
(Memel) or Tilžė (Tilsit), and possibly in Galindia and
Sudovia—places where the greatest quantities of Roman im‑
ports were concentrated. Maintenance of long‑distance trade
routes across Free Germany, far from being an easy task, repre‑
sented a constant struggle with ever‑increasing tolls, and there‑
fore the exploratory journey of the knight of Julianus in
Nero's reign must have been, as Wheeler suggests, an attempt
to simplify and cheapen the process.[12]

In trading with the Germanic tribes for metal, fur was next
in importance to amber. Tacitus mentions that mainland Ger‑
mans were very fond of wearing dress decorated with fur which
they obtained from across the ocean. This waterway may have
been the East Baltic. The many trade routes across the Baltic
coastlands leading to the northern forested zone were very prob‑
ably used for fur traffic. Otherwise it would be difficult to
explain what kept the long‑distance trade routes of north‑
eastern Europe alive. In this trade the Balts must have acted as
mediators between the Finno‑Ugrians and the Germanic
peoples in addition to shipping furs from their own country.
The Finno‑Ugrian habitation sites yielded considerably more

bones of furred animals than the Baltic sites. Also, the Baltic export to the south could have included horses, cattle, skins, goose feathers, honey, wax, and other items that were traded in early historic times.

Roman imports into East Prussia, western and central Lithuania, and into western Latvia are quite impressive: many thousands of Roman coins, in addition to terra sigillata pots, fibulae, glass beads, bronze vessels, oil-lamps, and bronze statuettes. ROMAN IMPORTS As would be expected, the imported items are found around the amber source-areas, particularly in Samland, Masuria, and western Lithuania, at the seashore, and along the river courses. In East Prussia alone we know of some 250 find places, cemeteries, and hoards with Roman coins, certain of the hoards containing hundreds or thousands of silver and bronze coins. For example, the treasure found near Ostróda (Osterode) at Preussisch-Görlitz included 1,134 denarii, and another at Dorotowo (Darethen) in the district of Olsztyn (Allenstein) in Masuria had 6,000 denarii. In many other hoards silver denarii number from 100 to 400.[13] In Lithuania there are now over 60 known places, mostly cemeteries, with a total of about one thousand Roman coins; they are grouped at the seashore and the lower Nemunas, and taper off along its tributaries. In Latvia there are not less than 42 places, also at the sea coast, and some around Riga and along the River Daugava.[14] Further east and north, coins and other imports are scarce. From Byelo-Russia, around Minsk, only a few places containing Roman coins are reported.

The distribution of Roman coins identifies the most active Baltic trade centres and the disseminating commercial arteries within Baltic territory. The great number of coins shows that amber was exchanged for these, more than for jewellery or other items. They must have been greatly valued by the native peoples. There is hardly a known cemetery in Samland or Curonia dating from the third century A.D. where Roman

Plate 18

coins were not found. They were put in the men's graves beside other valued belongings. The Curonians always placed Roman coins behind the head, usually in a birch-bark case, next to the miniature clay pots, an iron axe, a scythe, and two spears. The coins, however, had no value as currency. They were even made into ornaments and, attached to chains, worn as necklaces. Silver denarii were used as material for solid silver fibulae or for silver plates to coat the bronze fibulae, neck-rings, and bracelets. Bronze coins and silver denarii date from the second to fourth centuries A.D., the greatest number being from the period between the reigns of Trajan and Commodus; the latest are from A.D. 375. The majority of the coins come from the Roman provinces, Pannonia and Noricum and, through the agency of the Germanic tribes, from the Rhine-land and central Germany as well. Some could have reached the Baltic coast from the Roman province in southern Russia.

From *c.* A.D. 100 onward and from the same origins, chiefly Pannonia and the Rhineland, come other Roman articles: fluted glass bowls and beakers, bronze vases, situlae and sieves, terra sigillata pots, drinking horns, and series of fibulae, includ-ing the beautiful fretworked winged fibulae, the strongly pro-filed bow fibulae having triangular legs and shields on the bow, which are decorated with rows of small triangles of blue and red enamel, and fretworked and enamelled disc-fibulae.[15] Glass and terra sigillata pots are known only from East Prussia, but some of the ornaments travelled quite a distance from the amber coasts. A bronze vessel made its way to the fourth-century grave of a rich woman, in the suburb of Kaunas. From Kapseda in western Latvia a Roman oil-lamp made of ash-grey clay closely parallels those found in the Crimea and the lower Dnieper region, where they are dated to the second cen-tury B.C. This lamp is one of the few known imports from southern Russia, and if it arrived in the East Baltic before our era, may represent one of the earliest items of Roman import.[16]

Plate 24

Trade with Free Germany and with the provinces of the Roman Empire undoubtedly played a decisive role in the prosperity of the local metal culture. Provincial Roman and Germanic fibulae gave impetus to the rise of new forms. However, the variety of forms in jewellery that emerged between the second and fourth centuries was stimulated not only by these Roman and Germanic examples. Many types go back to the local forms of the Early Iron Age and some reflect remote relationships to the jewellery of the Celtic La Tène. The most telling factor in shaping the 'golden age' was creative vigour. The imported articles were not imitated; forms were not merely borrowed but transformed. The new variants created followed the 'Baltic line'. One can see a certain Baltic art style latent in the Bronze and Early Iron Ages, which during those early times never unfolded entirely; metal was scarce and perishable materials were used. Now, through the combination of native inspiration, southern influences, and the general rise of welfare, the Baltic style came into its own.

In the pages that follow I shall try to survey bronze, silver, glass, and gold ornaments without going into too great detail in their description or chronology. Both points have been well examined by other prehistorians.[17] The chronology can be established by reference to the Roman coins or other imports in graves, the rapidly changing and spreading local forms of ornaments, particularly those of fibulae, and the stratigraphy. However, the dating is approximate, remaining in frames of about 50 years. Roman coins, unfortunately, do not indicate the date of their issue; an appreciable time span must be allowed for their travel to the Baltic lands and for their use by the local people.

Throughout the four centuries forming the 'golden age' we find constantly evolving variations of jewellery types, some styles being short-lived, others lasting through the four or five centuries. This period, which reached its zenith around A.D.

300 when the Balts achieved an especially notable aptitude and individuality in jewellery making, must be treated as a whole, and the illustrations taken to represent the most typical of a multiplicity of ornaments. They are chosen from the central Baltic tribes, chiefly Curonians, Lithuanians and Sudovians.

For the women's head-dress we find circular temple orna-ments made of bronze spirals or bronze plate, one of the most characteristic pieces of Baltic jewellery and worn for centuries *Fig. 16* since the beginning of the Early Iron Age. In the first cen-turies A.D. these ornaments attained their greatest variety of forms. In addition to those made of round wire coiled four or *Fig. 40b* five times, which have prototypes in the fifth century B.C., there came into fashion the plate-shaped ones made of cast bronze decorated with concentric lines in relief or fretwork. *Fig. 40a* Around the edges they were adorned with small rounded 'buttons' or with braided bands and fretworked zig-zags or small circular plates also in concentric design. In the middle was a circular hole with an opening on one side, probably for inserting the girl's braids, as shown in reconstruction. In graves, temple ornaments always appear in pairs, one on each side of the skull. Some remains of hair and woollen cloth on the inner side indicate their attachment to the hair and the woollen cap. Temple ornaments became particularly frequent in the second and third centuries A.D. and persisted until the sixth century. They are found in greatest quantities in western and central Lithuania.

Temple ornaments and simple beret-like woollen caps appear to have been worn by girls and younger unmarried women. Married and rich women's head-dress was more refined. They wore head cloths descending over the shoulders and secured either by woollen caps embellished with small round bronze *Fig. 40c* plates and double spiral pendants or by broad diadem-like bands of a woollen cloth adorned with small, round or rectangular bronze plates. The edges of the head cloth were sometimes

Fig. 40. a, Girl's and woman's head and neck ornaments in central Lithuania of the second century A.D.: bronze temple rings, fibula, and necklaces made of bronze spirals and lunar and solar pendants; b, girl's ornaments of the second century A.D.: temple ornaments, glass bead necklace, fibula, and bronze chain attached to pins; c, Curonian woman's head and neck ornaments, c. A.D. 300. Western Lithuania

adorned with such plates. The richer the woman, the more spectacular was her head-dress.

In all known graves that yielded items of head-dress there also appeared considerable numbers of other ornaments: fibulae, necklaces, neck-rings, bracelets, finger- and toe-rings, and chains attached to pins. In 1951 was found one of the earliest graves to contain the refined head-dress of a woman of rank; this was in Kurmaičiai near Kretinga, western Lithuania, and

Fig. 41. Bronze fibula with cast pin from rich woman's grave in Kurmaičiai, near Kretinga, second century A.D.

is dated to the second century. The woman's broad diadem was adorned in front with two vertical rows of rectangular decorated plates, the fillet with alternating plates of round or rectangular design. The edges of the head cloth, 70 cm. long, were also embellished with rectangular plates. The cloth was fastened on top of the head with a shielded bow fibula; two other fibulae were fastened to the blouse. Two barrel shaped bronze pins connected by a bronze chain fastened on to the woollen cloak. Beyond her head lay a birch bark box filled with ornaments: trumpet ended neck rings, a twisted neck ring with button shaped clasped ends, and a massive round bracelet decorated with a pulley motif. In addition a spool of very well preserved woollen thread was found.

With the second century A.D., Roman imported glass bead necklaces appeared en masse in a variety of colours and shapes. These necklaces are of transparent beads, usually blue or green, spherical, conical or cylindrical, ribbed or fluted. Found, too, were necklaces of enamelled beads, usually of dark red colour alternating with black, yellow, and green, or with white, yellow, brown, or grey. Very prolific were gilt beads, spherical, conical, or pendant like ending in spirals. The largest quantities of beads come from the regions where Roman coins abound, with particular concentration in Masuria and the lower Nemunas basin. In the latter area around A.D. 300 a local glass industry was started, to adorn native types of fibulae and neck rings with blue hemispherical beads. Beads of bronze

Fig. 41

Fig. 40b

Plate 19a

and amber were also produced locally. It is of interest to note that amber beads were extremely rare in the land of amber; they appear in greatest numbers outside the source-area. To the amber gatherers the substance was apparently so common that they yearned for more exotic ornaments. In the villages of Samland amber is usually found in raw or half-finished condition.

Necklaces were also made of bronze-wire spiral beads with lunular or solar pendants attached. Solid or fretworked lunular pendants branching out into three parts at each of the two points, and pendants of wheel or rosette shape, or made of triangular or rectangular plates, were particularly frequent from the second century to about A.D. 400. Pendants were also suspended on chain-holders from neck-rings and chains. Pendants, fretworked chain-holders, and chains made of tiny bronze-wire rings were the most cherished and the most characteristic types of jewellery in the period between A.D. 200 and 400. Chains ending in pendants were attached to fibulae or, more frequently, to a pin or two pins with barrel-shaped, disc-, wheel-, ring-, or rosette-shaped heads, secured to the cloak on both sides of the chest at the shoulders; the pendants covered the whole width of the woman's chest. Usually more than one, they numbered from two to six, suspended on semicircular or rectangular fretworked chain-holders. Used also as pectorals were

Fig. 40a

Plate 19b

Fig. 42

Fig. 43a

Fig. 42. Bronze fibula with chains attached, c. A.D. 200. Pakuonis near Kaunas

a

b

Fig. 43. Chest ornaments. a, made of fretworked plates and pendants suspended on pins. Bronze. 1:3. Labotakiai, district of Klaipéda, western Lithuania. c. A.D. 300; b, made of bronze bars, chain-holders and pendants attached to pins having silver-plated rosette-shaped heads. Aukštakiemis near Klaipéda, western Lithuania. c. A.D. 300. Formerly in Prussia Museum, Königsberg

Fig. 43b

Fig. 44
Plate 20

tubes made of spiralled bronze wire, or striated or ribbed bronze bars spaced with fretworked plates and pendants.

Skilful examples of ornamental openwork in bronze, other than the chain-holders, is seen on belt parts or spacers showing a variety of geometric patterns, and in some cases, schematized human and bird figurines. The most accomplished fretwork ornaments are found at the end of the third and throughout the fourth century. To this period can also be dated the rosette-shaped fibulae and heads of pins coated with silver plate in a concentric ring pattern; such fibulae and pins, often with blue glass beads on top of the central protuberance, being a speciality of the Curonian tribe. The rosette-shaped fibulae, known in a great variety of styles, go back to imported prototypes in the Danubian provinces of the Roman empire, but those made in the Baltic lands attained a purely local character.

Plate 21

Plate 22

Plate 23

In the series of endemic ornaments neck-rings were extremely abundant. The five dominant types are: those with trumpet ends, those with 'button' or conical clasping ends, those with one end spoon-shaped and a hook on the other, twisted and ending in large loops, those with a hook and loop, and those with a circular plate or box on one end and a hook on the other, usually with a wire wound over the ends. These neck-rings were made exclusively of bronze wire, the more refined examples being coated with silver at the ends and decorated with blue glass beads. A handsome collection of neck-rings of four of the above types was found in the previously mentioned rich woman's grave in Veršvai, the suburb of Kaunas, beside the Roman bronze vessel and other ornaments.

Plates 24, 25

The trumpet-ended neck-rings, very frequent in the second and third centuries, go back to the local Early Iron Age and ultimately to the Middle La Tène prototypes in central Europe. Considerable quantities of them were found in Samland,

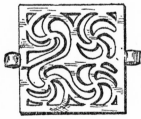

Fig. 44. Fretworked belt parts. Bronze. Fourth century A.D. Stragna, near Priekulė, western Lithuania

Plate 24

Plate 22

Plate 23

Lithuania, and Latvia, tapering off into Estonia and Finland. Neck-rings with button-shaped clasping ends also have their beginnings in the era before the birth of Christ. In the third and fourth centuries A.D. their ends were usually conical. They developed into several variants within the tribal boundaries and were most popular with the Curonians and other tribes in Lithuania and Latvia. Neck-rings with peculiar spoon-shaped ends are native to central and eastern Lithuania, making their appearance around A.D. 300 and lasting until about 600. The latest variants known from eastern Lithuania and Byelo-Russia were quite massive and frequently made of silver. Twisted neck-rings with looped ends were most fashionable in the eastern Baltic lands between central Lithuania and central Russia in the fourth century. Those ending in a hook and a loop or plate, and having ends wound with wire, had been widely distributed throughout the Rhineland, Scandinavia, and central and southern Russia. The Balts, particularly the Prussians, adopted them and developed a number of variants, such as the decoration of ends with rings and ribbing in the third and fourth centuries.

A remarkable series of neck ornaments was achieved through combining pendants and neck-rings with looped and conical ends. Lunular, semicircular, triangular, or rectangular plates with embossed ornament were suspended on twisted or ribbed bars and on fretworked plates from the ends of the neck-rings. To the dangling-plate pendants, solar pendants were added, secured on a wire connecting the loops, the wire spiralling in the centre in lunar pattern. Obviously these pendants were connected with solar and lunar symbolism.

Fig. 45

Both outside influence and the ability to adapt to local style are demonstrated by about a thousand bow-fibulae scattered all over the area from the Vistula to Finland. Among the earliest were the flat-bow type with 'eye' ornament and several variants of strongly profiled fibulae. They reached the western Balts

Fig. 41

Fig. 45. Neck-ring with conical ends and pendants attached. c. A.D. 300. *Pleškučiai near Priekulė, western Lithuania*

through the lower Vistula. In the first centuries A.D. their production was concentrated in the hands of the Prussians, in Samland and in Masuria, whence they spread over Lithuania, Latvia, and the lands of the western Finns. In the third and fourth centuries local variants appeared. The profiled bow-fibulae with horizontal projections at the head, the middle of the bow, and at the foot, developed into a peculiar stepped

Plate 22

fibula type with their centre of production in Masuria. In the third and fourth centuries they were the most frequent fibula types in the coastal region between East Prussia and Finland, with local variants in Curonia and the northern East Baltic area. Second in number only to these were the crossbow fibulae, which became extremely common in the fourth and fifth centuries. After that they branched into many local variants and were in use for five hundred more years. Around A.D. 400, the crossbow fibulae attained their most elegant and bizarre form. Often they were made of silver or, if of bronze, were embellished with striated silver rings placed in groups over the shaft and on the spiral and silver plates in between.

Plate 27

The most beautifully wrought examples of these ornaments adorned a chieftain's chest.

Bands of pointillé, pulley motifs or concentric circles, little suns; horizontal, vertical, or diagonal striations; net pattern, zig-zags, crosses, rhombs, braided motifs, ribbing, and embossing—all of these types of design embellished neck-rings, fibulae, massive or delicate banded bracelets, pendants, horse-trappings, pots, and bone objects. This simple and serene but extremely painstaking and minute decoration characterizes Baltic ornamental art throughout the five centuries, and in later prehistoric times it was still faithfully carried on, with varied combinations of the same motifs. Animal and anthropo-morphic motifs were rare but not unknown. The Prussians

Fig. 46

made fibulae in horned animal shapes and the bands of geo-metric motifs on pottery were interspersed with horse and sun symbols. From the princely grave of Szwajcaria comes a plaque

Plate 26

in the form of a stag. The silver-plated frontispiece of the horse-harness from the same grave was adorned with two highly stylized human heads in addition to pulley, concentric circle and rosette motifs, and incrusted blue glass beads. The tech-

Plate 31

nique and the decoration on this piece of harness indicate local origin.

Fig. 46. Bronze fibula with a leg in the shape of horned animal's head (for the body the popular bow fibula with step-like projections was used). Third century A.D. 2:3

A special achievement in the decoration of ornaments was the use of enamel inlay. The local industry of incrustation started in the second century A.D., soon after the appearance of the first enamelled imports from the Danubian provinces of the Roman empire and from the Rhineland. The enamelled disc-shaped fibulae and the incrustation technique itself show that much was learned from the imported enamelled objects, but promptly the process was adopted by Baltic tribes and enamel was soon applied to ornaments of local style.[18]

The earliest horseshoe-shaped fibulae with red and green enamel inlay are found in the Vilnius and Kaunas areas in Lithuania dating from the second century A.D. To the same century, or around A.D. 200, are dated enamelled disc fibulae from northern Masuria, the land of the ancient Galindians. In these two areas, Galindia and eastern Lithuania, the greatest quantities of enamelled objects are found. Among them the semi-lunar fretworked or solid pendants and horseshoe fibulae decorated with crescentic projections found in eastern Lithuania and eastern Latvia are striking examples of Baltic art of the third to fifth centuries. Enamel inlay was also used for the decoration of neck-rings and bracelets. The earliest enamelled bracelet, dating from the second century A.D., comes from western Lithuania; it has red enamelled squares of a net pattern,

Plates 32, 33

Plates 34-40

Plate 41

the enamelled areas alternating with groups of iron ribs. Other enamelled bracelets were of the broad-band type with projecting ends and broadened in the middle; they had fretwork squares, the solid parts being inlaid with red, orange, white,

Plate 42

and green enamel. These latter date from the fourth century. Flattened parts of neck-rings and bow-fibulae also were appropriate for incrustation. The most masterly examples of enamel decoration were long chains made of many fretworked plates with enamel inlaid squares, circles, crescents, or triangles, apparently used as attachments for drinking horns. Colours of the enamel were dark red, red, green, blue, light blue, orange, and white. These outstanding examples, dating from the fourth century, are from Galindia in southern East Prussia, and there

Plate 43

are very close, even identical, parallels from central Russia[19] and the Kiev area.

In the fourth century Baltic enamelled ornaments were dispersed all over north-eastern Europe: to Estonia and Finland in the north, and thence to Sweden; via eastern Lithuania and the upper Dnieper to the Kiev area and the Ukraine; and along the routes of the Desna, Ugra, Oka, Volga, and Kama rivers to eastern Russia and almost to the Middle Urals.[20] There is no doubt that they spread through the eastern Baltic lands from the hub of their industry. The most important production centre of the enamelled ornaments was most probably in Galindia around the Masurian lakes.

A magnificent collection of enamelled ornaments comes from a hoard hidden in the hill-top village of Moshchiny on the small Popolta river, a tributary of the Ugra, in central Russia. Illustrated here is merely a small part of the fretworked

Plate 43

enamelled plates—the drinking horn attachments, the crescentic pendants with projections used for making bead necklaces and the broad bracelets. In addition, there were numerous neck-rings, glass beads, and ornamental plates. This huge hoard of 85 objects now occupies an entire glass case in the

Historical Museum of Moscow. Sixteen hundred years ago the collection probably belonged to a trader who travelled from Prussian Galindia across eastern Lithuania and Byelo-Russia to Moshchiny. He may have picked up some neck-rings and bracelets in eastern Lithuania, where exact parallels are known. The hoard indicates that Moshchiny was one of the entrepôts of the traffic accessible to the eastern Baltic tribes on the route it took along the River Ugra and the River Oka into the lands of the Volga-Finnic tribes.

With the progress in agriculture, trade, armaments, arts and crafts, a section of the community had become well-to-do. Some unusually ornamented women's graves are known from as early as the second century. In the fourth and fifth centuries the number of graves belonging to the wealthier class increased remarkably, and they contrasted notably with those of the poor. The evidence of social differences is striking in large cemeteries where, among hundreds of graves, only a few are outstanding in wealth. Wealthy women wore all of the available jewellery: bracelets, neck-rings, fibulae, and chains. A woman in the double grave of Veršvai, dating from the fourth century was not only adorned with ornaments but behind her head were additional neck-rings, bracelets, glass beads, chains, and a bronze pot, while the man at her side was equipped with an iron axe and a pin. A woman in a double grave in the cemetery of Upytė in central Lithuania had six bracelets on each arm, a silver necklace, a wheel-shaped silver fibula with chains and pendants, three long chains and a bronze pin, while her dress was adorned with bronze spirals along the edge. The man with her had no grave goods at all. In the fourth and particularly the fifth centuries, silver fibulae, gold plaques, and bronze ornaments plated with silver were the usual attributes of the higher-ranking people. Although men's graves were not resplendent in jewellery, in some chieftain's graves there were fine specimens of silver or gold fibulae and plaques, enamelled

CLASS
SOCIETY

Plate 25

Plate 23

ornaments, drinking horns, swords, shields, spears, and horse bridles.

Magnificent princely burials of the Sudovian tribe dating from the fourth and early fifth centuries were found in the large cemetery of Szwajcaria situated on what is now the Polish–Lithuanian border near Suwałki during the 1956–7 Warsaw archaeological expedition headed by J. Antoniewicz.[21] The chieftains' barrows were the largest in the cemetery, 18 m. in diameter, while other barrows averaged between 8 and 10 m. The chieftain who had ruled during the fourth century lay inhumed upon a sandy platform under the barrow. He was aged about 55, while other people in the same cemetery were younger—between 30 and 40 years of age. He was furnished with an iron sword 85 cm. long, a shield, spears, an axe, iron shears, a bone comb, a pair of pincers, a horse bridle, silver fibulae, silver and gold-plated plaques, and a silver figurine of a stag. The horse head-gear in particular shows the splendid decoration, specially designed for the chieftain's horse: silver-plated frontispiece with blue-glass beads, embossed rosettes and stylized human heads. Only the large iron shears contrasted with the other exquisite princely belongings. They certainly do not indicate that the chieftain used to shear sheep in his lifetime; they were laid close to his face apparently to protect him against the evil powers.

In the centre of a princely barrow in Szwajcaria dating from the beginning of the fifth century a horse lay buried on a layer of sand 2 m. from its cremated master. The horse's legs were contracted, which suggests they were fettered with a rope before the burial. Among the cremated remains of the chieftain lay a sword 94 cm. long, a silver crossbow fibula, a round enamelled plaque with a knob in the middle, amber beads and a pair of iron shears.

The sword was made by the 'patterned steel' technique—in which layers of iron and steel are heated together at a high temperature. For this reason it is presumed to be a Roman import. A similar sword was found at Nydam near Sonderburg, Jutland. Altogether, only three swords of this kind are known in the Baltic territory; two from Szwajcaria and one (1 m. long) from another chieftain's grave at Krikštonys on the River Nemunas in southern Lithuania. All three appear to have belonged to Sudovian chieftains. The disc-shaped plaque decorated with concentric circles of bluish-white and white enamel is an ornament that does not appear among the local enamelled jewellery. It originated in the Rhineland, where it was made in the second half of the third century. Similar plaques were exported to Scandinavia; they probably reached the Sudovian lands in the fourth century and were placed in the chieftain's grave around the beginning of the fifth. This late date is indicated by the silver crossbow fibula current in the fifth century.

The 'golden age' may be considered as having begun with the feudal system, which reached its peak before the dawn of history. The presence of several chieftains' graves within the borders of one tribe speaks for the existence of local districts each ruled by one lord. One district centre of this type was located near the above-mentioned cemetery of Szwajcaria. There was a large settlement and a small hill-fort 1 km. away from the cemetery containing the graves of chieftains of earlier and later periods. Five other contemporary cemeteries were found within a radius of about 5 km. from this centre, but these did not contain any princely graves.[22] The chieftain's grave at Krikštonys in southern Lithuania,[23] which is about 50 km. from Szwajcaria, indicates another seat of a landowner and the centre of another administrative unit. When all the chieftains' graves have been discovered we shall be able to count the districts within the limits of one tribe, but the few known at present already illustrate the manner in which the lands were divided. Approximately the same pattern of tribal administration and ownership of lands by a powerful chieftain is known to us from the beginning of history. The only difference was that in the first centuries A.D. the earthworks and castles were of miniature size, and the towns were in the embryonic stage.

During the 'golden age', the foundations were laid for the economy, for feudalism, the habitation pattern, and art. In the centuries to come, these were to continue and develop further.

CHAPTER VI

The Baltic 'Middle Iron Age'

THE PERIOD from the fifth to the ninth century, or the 'Middle Iron Age', runs parallel to two major events: the Slavic expansion to the lands of the eastern Balts which started around A.D. 400 and the Swedish (Viking) expansion to the East Baltic coasts which started around A.D. 650. How-ever, the bulk of the Baltic tribes resisted the aggressions and further developed their individual culture.

Among the Baltic tribes the Prussians and Curonians con-tinued to play leading roles. As soon as the Goths had left the lower Vistula area, Prussians took it over, firmly established their seats and remained there until the second Germanic invasion, that of the Teutonic Order in the thirteenth century. Sudovians and Lithuanians managed to survive in their former lands. Their ornaments and pottery dating from the time of the 'golden age' to the tenth century are found in present northern Poland as far south as the lower Bug, and the upper Pripet swamps.[1] By the sixth–seventh centuries the Lettigallians had expanded over northern Latvia, which previously had been occupied by the western Finno-Ugrian tribes.

In all the Baltic lands not touched by Slavic expansion we find further development of the culture whose foundations had been laid during the first centuries A.D. The pattern of split-ting up into tribal units remained about the same. Each Baltic tribe had its own types of graves and burial rites. The Prussians cremated their dead and deposited the cremated bones in urns or pits in flat graves. The Sudovians, who in the first four centuries inhumed their dead under stone-covered barrows, started cremation rites in the fifth century. Their stone-covered barrows contained several graves, some of which might belong to one family. The Lithuanians also went over to cremation during the fifth and sixth centuries, but continued to bury the ashes of their dead in earth barrows surrounded by a fence of stones. The Semigallians continued with inhumation, but their family barrows, used in the first centuries, began to dis-appear about the fifth century, giving way to large cemeteries with individual graves. The Curonian inhumation graves were surrounded until the seventh century by rectangular stone fences, one grave adjoining the other in a honeycomb pattern. From the seventh and eighth centuries onward, the fences disappeared and cremation rites infiltrated; at first they were used sporadically, but by the tenth and eleventh centuries universally. Only the Semigallians and Lettigallians kept to inhumation.

At the foot of the hill-forts, villages constantly grew in size, some of them to such an extent that the chroniclers of the ninth century referred to them as 'towns'. Large earthworks on the high banks and promontories of rivers and lakes adjoining the sizeable villages or 'towns' were heavily fortified. An increase in the fortifications, with the use of timber constructions and tamped clay for building of ramparts, can be observed from the fifth century onward. Hill-forts of this kind are known from excavations in the Curonian,[2] Semigallian, Lettigallian and Lithuanian[3] lands. In some earthworks the area encompassed by such fortifications was from one-half to one hectare (about $1\frac{1}{4}$ to $2\frac{1}{2}$ acres).[4]

There are thus clear indications that the feudal castles, as defence posts for the growing towns, had already come into exis-tence in the period from *c.* A.D. 500 to *c.* 800, and subsequently became the centres of larger administrative units. The forma-tion of the feudal system must have been accomplished before the ninth century; in that century it is attested by written records. The Anglo-Saxon traveller Wulfstan, while visiting the Prussian lands in about 880–90, saw many 'towns', each with its king.[5] In his book *Vita sancti Anscharii*, completed in 876,

Rimbert, a disciple of archbishop Ansgar of the Bremen-Hamburg diocese, finds five 'states' in the land of the Curonians: *Regnum vero ipsum quinque habebat civitates.*[6] In describing the wars between the Swedes and Curonians in 855, to which we shall return, Rimbert mentions the two towns 'Saeborg' and 'Apulia' in which, during the war, thousands of warriors were said to have assembled in the hill-forts: 7,000 in Saeborg, 15,000 in Apulia. The numbers must be exaggerated, but that there were sizeable towns from which to recruit many men is evident. These towns themselves have not as yet been uncovered, but traces of settlements around the large earthworks are being found over a large area. In the ninth and successive centuries, the town around the castle of Impiltis near Kretinga in western Lithuania covered at least 50,000 sq. m.

In the lands of the ancient Prussians large trading towns emerged at the latest around A.D. 600. One of these was Truso, south of Frisches Haff and north of Lake Drausensee (ancient Drusine). The name of the town is the earliest known historically in the Baltic Sea area. In Wulfstan's account of his travels, we find the 'town of Truso' located on the River Elbing ('Ilfing') which flows from the lake to the Frisches Haff ('Estmere'). Archaeological finds abound in this area; several settlements and cemeteries have revealed finds dating from the seventh to twelfth centuries. The size and importance of Truso grew particularly during the centuries following.[7] For East Prussia, Truso played the same role as Haithabu for north-western Germany or Slavic Vineta for Pomerania. Another trading centre lay at Wiskiauten (Viskiautai) at the south-western corner of the Courish Lagoon in northern Samland; it was the gateway for the traffic leading to the east via the lower Nemunas basin into the lands of the Curonians, Lithuanians, and other Baltic tribes. Finds from around A.D. 800 reflect the trade with the Vikings, and from the eleventh and twelfth centuries, an intensive local production and exchange.[8]

Although after the fall of the Roman Empire the trade with the south diminished, it did not entirely cease. The amber route continued to be used in the fifth and sixth centuries. Numerous Roman-Byzantine coins and gold solidi are found along the lower Vistula, along the Prussian coasts, and south of the Frisches Haff and the Courish Lagoon. The most recent of the gold solidi are from the reign of Anastasius I, 491–518. In the north, the coins spread as far as Latvia and Estonia. Imported objects from the Gothic kingdom now reached the lands of the Prussians, in particular the Galindians, taking the place of imports from the Roman Empire provinces. The women's graves yielded many Gothic fibulae dating from the fifth century and around A.D. 600. Some show close resem-blance to the Langobardic fibulae in south-western Germany and upper Italy, some to those in southern Russia.[9] In Strob-jehnen, Samland, appeared a golden neck-ring decorated with a hunting scene reminiscent of Scythian art; this neck-ring also must have reached the amber coast via southern Russia.[10]

Archaeological evidence has definitively established the exist-ence of relations between the Ostrogoths and the Prussians over a century or so later, after the death of the Gothic king Ermana-ric. More interesting aspects are revealed by ancient texts relating to the amber route to Italy. At the beginning of the sixth century, the Aistians found a way for their amber to reach Ravenna, the Gothic capital in Italy. We learn about this from the letter of the great Gothic king Theodoric (A.D. 454–526) to the Aistians ('Haesti'), in which he thanks them for gifts of amber, and, basing his knowledge of the substance on Tacitus' accounts, goes on to explain what amber is.[11]

This letter by Theodoric, the last known text mentioning amber, is interesting on several counts. First, that the Central European amber route between East Prussia and Italy, which may have been cut off for a century or so following the fall of the Roman Empire, was reopened. Second, that the Aistians were recognized as important people with whom the Goths ex-changed presents, and sought to maintain good relations in the future. The amber trade initiated in the sixth century probably was disturbed by the western Slavic expansion to Bohemia and Moravia and the subsequent movements of the Germanic tribes westward and southward. Nor do the archae-ological finds show the Balts to have been involved in distant trade from the seventh to ninth centuries.

The objects imported during post-Roman times, including the beautiful Gothic fibulae, did not exert any noticeable influence on the further development of Baltic ornamental art. Up to the seventh and eighth centuries, when some Scandina-vian art elements appeared, it continued the art traditions of the 'golden age', although women's and men's ornaments became progressively less exquisite.

The style of dress remained basically the same. Diadems made of bronze spirals and tubes separated by spacer beads adorned women's heads, neck-rings of glass and amber beads ornamented the neck, and bronze chains attached to bronze or silver fibulae or pins decorated the chest. Woollen caps, pro- Plate 45 fusely decorated with bronze or silver spirals and by pendants, continued to be worn by girls through all the remaining cen-turies of the Iron Age. The crossbow type of fibula was most in evidence. Fibulae were more solid than in the fourth century, and frequently made of silver, decorated with silver rings and Plates 46, 47 gold plates having a net pattern. From these, many variants developed; particularly beautiful were those having semi-circular or star-shaped prongs covered by silver plates em- *Figs. 47, 48* bossed with dots, circles, small suns and stars.

In the sixth and seventh centuries silver ornaments increased to a remarkable extent. Exactly where the raw silver came from, we do not know. It may have followed the Dnieper route, the amber route via central Europe, or come across the Baltic Sea via Sweden. The most characteristic were massive round silver

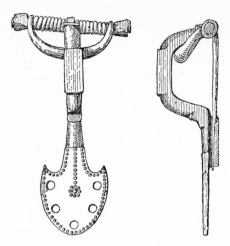

Fig. 47. Bronze fibula with a silver-plated foot. Sixth century. Plavniekkalns, central Latvia. 1:2

Plates 48-50

Plate 51

Fig. 49

bracelets thickening at the ends, and neck-rings made of silver wire with overlapping ends as well as others with overlapping pinched ends. That they were of local make is indicated by the decorations—striations, circles, semicircles, spirals, dots, tiny triangles, and rhombs. Silver cases for drinking-horns were made of silver plates with horizontal bands of embossed ornaments, sometimes portraying rows of schematic human figurines or stags. The Curonians, inspired by examples of Scandinavian art, added some new forms and decorative motifs. Snake-heads appeared on the ends of large crossbow fibulae of the seventh century, since when the schematic snake-head has been a feature of Baltic art right up to the folk art of the twentieth century. The so-called 'owl-head' fibulae, frequent in Curonia in the eighth and ninth centuries, developed through imitation of fibulae with crescent shields and triangular prongs, current in the sixth-seventh centuries in Gotland.

Fig. 48. Star and sun motifs on fibulae (like Fig. 47) from East Prussia

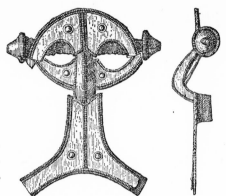

Fig. 49. Owl-head fibula.
Bronze, coated with silver plate.
Ninth century A.D. Lubāna,
Latvia. 1:2

The amount of silver rich people possessed is impressive. Some of the neck-rings were of tremendous size, while one of the necklaces from eastern Lithuania weighed well over two pounds, and another was made of twisted silver wire 130 cm. long—large enough to put around a horse's neck. Wealth was now blunting aesthetic sensibility, and by the seventh or eighth centuries, a certain crudity had entered into their art.

The changing times were also marked by a significant increase in the production of weapons. This progress in armaments and the growing importance of cavalry can be observed particularly in those tribes which were exposed to the attacks of aggressive neighbours. Shields having round iron umbos with hemispherical or conical protuberances in the middle, iron swords about 50 cm. long with a broad one-edged blade and a wooden hilt, iron spearheads with rhomboid or leaf-shaped heads, stirrups, bridle-bits and other parts of horse bridles regularly appear in the Sudovian, Lithuanian and Lettigallian warrior graves. Perhaps the well-equipped cavalry of these tribes stopped the constantly expanding Slav peoples from penetrating into their tribal territories. The Curonians on the Baltic Sea were faced with the mounting danger from Scandinavia, and their graves also reflect this troubled period.

Plates 52-54

Plate 55

Here, too, in warriors' graves we find spurs, horse bridles, spearheads, and shields, as well as scythes, socketed axes, knives and ornaments. The burial of his horse beside the deceased warrior was frequent. In the bog of Tira near Rucava, in western Latvia, a wooden shield was found intact, covered on both sides with leather and having in the centre a hemispherical iron umbo. The shield dates from the beginning or middle of the ninth century; that is, from the period of the fiercest battles between the Curonians and the Danes and Swedes.

Slavic pressure northward was the outward sign of turmoil in southern Russia, and reflected changes in the ethnic configuration. The Hun invasion in A.D. 375 destroyed the power of the Gothic kingdom. As soon as the Slavic tribe of the Antae shook off the supremacy of the Goths, it expanded over the Black Sea coasts from north of the lower Danube to the sea of Azov. Subsequent invasions by the Turko-Tartar peoples, the Bulgars and, particularly, by the Avars who in the first half of the sixth century penetrated as far as the barrier of the dense forests along the River Desna and the upper Oka, culminated in the Slavic advance into the lands of the eastern Balts and the Finno-Ugrians, where least resistance would be encountered.

By A.D. 400, the heavy traffic between the Balts and the Finno-Ugrians, which had reached its peak in the fourth century, was cut off. Some hill-top villages and hill-forts in the Baltic area were deserted; some show levels of destruction caused by fire. Those villages whose remains show habitation to have continued experienced a decadence of material culture. This is the indirect proof of the disaster that befell the eastern Baltic tribes.

The earliest stages of the Slavic expansion northward cannot as yet be established in a satisfactory manner by actual archaeological finds. The number of cemeteries and settlements discovered is as yet too scanty. However, here and there have emerged single barrows and settlements having analogies in the Kiev region, Volynia, and even in the Slavic lands of central Europe, and which cannot be considered as Baltic. It seems that the area between Kiev and Novgorod was occupied in consecutive waves by different tribal groups between the fifth and eighth centuries.

Villages consisting of semi-subterranean houses with clay floors and clay-plastered walls, urn burials in round, conical or elongated barrows, timber structures within the barrows, and crude and polished pottery akin to that in the regions of Kiev, and Volynia, and in Bohemia and Moravia, are distinct elements of the Slavic culture expanding to the lands north of Kiev and Voronezh. A number of cemeteries and settlements of a related character in Volynia, in the middle Dnieper basin, and in the region of the upper Don near Voronezh, dating from the period between the sixth and ninth centuries, are undoubtedly Slavic. They are labelled 'sites of Prague type' in Volynia, 'hill-forts of Romny type' along the lower Desna, on the rivers Sejm, Sula and Vorksla, and 'hill-forts of Borshevo type' on the upper Don and the upper Oka.[12] Some differences in grave types indicate that these sites may have belonged to several eastern Slavic tribes, the Drevljane, Poljane and Vjatichi known from the earliest historic records. The dating of the earliest cemeteries and villages is based entirely on comparisons of their pottery with that known from Bohemia and Moravia, which indicate the sixth and seventh centuries. Whether some of the barrows and hill-fort villages can be dated back to the fifth century[13] remains for future researches to prove. As yet the graves have not yielded any datable metal objects.

Early traces of Slavs in the north are found in the area of Pskov, east of Estonia and Latvia and south of Lake Peipus in the basin of the River Velikaja. Here the long, narrow burial mounds with cremation graves and very sparse grave goods are

Fig. 36:4

identified with the Krivichi tribe. Their dating to the fifth century is based on finds of round and convex ornamental bronze plates, tweezers and bracelets thickening at the ends which have analogies in the Finno-Ugrian stone barrows in Estonia. The earliest Krivichi also appear to have occupied the hill-fort in Pskov, which superseded the Finno-Ugrian layer of the so-called Djakovo type, and the unfortified settlements along the upper Velikaja River, which replaced the Baltic hill-fort villages having plain and brushed pottery. These settlements yielded pottery and metal objects of a type similar to that in the long barrows.[14]

It is strange that the earliest barrows and settlements attributed to this tribe are found so far north and not on the upper Dvina River and in the areas of Smolensk and Polock, where Krivichi are attested from the seventh or eighth centuries to the thirteenth. Obviously, they did not use the Dnieper route in their expansion, but may have come up from the south via the upper reaches of the River Nemunas across the lands of the Baltic Brushed Pottery group. As yet their sites in present western Byelo-Russia cannot be identified archaeologically because of the lack of excavations, but there are some lingual testimonies suggesting that this was the line of the Krivichian spread; namely, early Slavic borrowings from the Baltic (for instance, the river name *Mereč* from the Lithuanian *Merkys*, tributary of the upper Nemunas, considered by linguists to be prior to the ninth century)[15] and relationships between the early Pskov and Polish dialects.[16]

In the present districts of Smolensk and Polotsk the long barrows of Krivichi type date back to the eighth century and later, with the exception of a few assumed to be of an earlier date.[17] Many barrows in these areas have yielded purely Baltic finds of the Lettigallian type. These date from the fifth to twelfth centuries.[18] Even south of Smolensk, Moscow, and Kaluga, along the tributaries of the River Zhizdra and upper

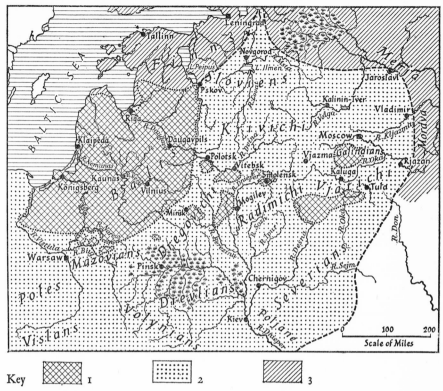

Key [1] [2] [3]

Fig. 50. The Balts after the Slavic expansion. Tenth–twelfth centuries A.D. 1, Balts; 2, Slavs; 3, Finno-Ugrians

Desna, a number of excavated barrow cemeteries and hill-forts of Baltic type have yielded finds related or identical to those in eastern Latvia, and which can be dated up to the twelfth century.[19] The archaeological finds fully confirm a dating up to the twelfth century for the remnants of the Balts west of Moscow, in the area between Smolensk, Kaluga and Brjansk. Moreover, they can be identified with the Galindian tribe known from Laurentius' and Hypatius' versions of the Russian chronicle describing the wars between the Russian dukes and the Galindians on the River Protva in the eleventh and twelfth centuries.

Fig. 50

151

The Slavic expansion did not wipe out the eastern Balts immediately. They persisted in larger and smaller enclaves for many centuries. It is highly probable that before the Slavic Krivichi, Dregovichi and Radimichi came to dominate the upper Dnieper basin, there existed a Baltic population whose culture was particularly closely related to the Lettigallians in eastern Latvia. We see that from the beginning of the Slavic expansion to the formation of the three Slavic states—those of the Novgorod, Rjazan and Kiev Slavs—in the ninth century and even several centuries later, there were considerable num, bers of Balts in present Byelo-Russia and in the west of Greater Russia. The process of Slavonization begun in prehistoric times continued into the nineteenth century. The Byelo-Russians have borrowed many words, most of them of daily usage, from the Lithuanian peasant vocabulary. The ethnography in the districts of Kaluga, Moscow, Smolensk, Vitebsk, Polotsk, and Minsk to the middle of the nineteenth century is highly indica, tive of the Baltic character. Indeed, Slavonized eastern Balts make up much of the population of present Byelo-Russia and a part of Greater Russia.

WARS WITH THE SCANDI- NAVIANS   Contacts with neighbours across the Baltic Sea, in Gotland and Middle Sweden, were before the seventh century occasional and of commercial character. Some Baltic ornaments dating from the fifth and sixth centuries have been found in Gotland. Their origin can be traced to the area of Klaipéda or East Prussia. The statement found in some popular books that the Norsemen were intensively exploring the eastern Baltic shores in the fifth and the sixth centuries, and that in the sixth century a group of them settled at the mouth of the Daugava, is not so far supported by archaeological finds.[20] Not until after A.D. 650 were the Baltic Curonians hit by Swedish expansion. Excavations in Grobin (Grobiṇa) near Liepāja in western Latvia, carried on by Birger Nerman since 1929, have brought to light three cemeteries with cremation graves, weapons, and ornaments of Scandinavian character. Finds from two of the cemeteries had their closest analogies in Gotland, those from the third in the Mälar valley of central Sweden. From the first half of the eighth century onward, traces of Scandinavian colonies appear in several other places: Sauslaukas near Durbe in western Latvia, Apuolė in north-western Lithuania, and in the area of Elbing (Truso). After A.D. 800, the Scandinavian finds again diminish, except for the colony in Grobin which persisted to about 850 and that in Elbing where Scandinavian finds date to about 900.[21]

The Icelandic and Norwegian sagas, recorded in the thir-teenth century though they go back to prehistoric songs, com-memorate the successes of the Swedish kings Ivar vidfamne and Harald hildetand. The first, who died around A.D. 700, is said to have conquered 'Kurland, Saxland and Eisland' and all the countries in the East to Gardarike in Karelia (*Hervarar Saga*). After his death the dynasty came to an end, but his daughter's son Harald hildetand again established Swedish rule in these same lands. Swedish expansion along the eastern Baltic coasts in the period 650–750 is confirmed by archaeo-logically attested colonies. Further events are recorded by Rimbert in *Vita sancti Anscarii,* in which there is a detailed description of the wars waged by Danes and Swedes against the Curonians in the middle of the ninth century.

When Rimbert mentions the Curonians for the first time, he writes: 'A tribe, called Chori, living far from them [Swedes], was earlier subdued by the Swedes, but it was a long time ago, when they revolted and liberated themselves from the yoke.' Then he mentions that at the time when Ansgar visited Sweden for the second time, somewhat after 850, the Danes had under-taken a military expedition by sea to Curonia, but suffered a crushing defeat. Half of the Danes were killed, half their ships were captured, and the Curonians gained a large war booty of gold, silver and weapons. When the Swedish king Olov heard of this disaster, he took a huge army to Curonia. The first surprise attack was aimed at the town of 'Seaborg' (probably in the area of Grobin), which was defended by '7,000 warriors'. They plundered it and burnt it to the ground. Encouraged by this success they disembarked and after five days of hurried march they excitedly fell upon another Curonian town called 'Apulia', but in this town they found '15,000 fighting men'. A furious battle started. Eight days passed without success for either side, and on the ninth day the Swedes were beginning to despair of victory. In their desperation the Swedes even appealed to the Christian God; whereafter they attacked the town with renewed courage, but before the battle started, the Curonians sent messengers and declared themselves ready to submit. As booty they gave to the Swedes gold and weapons which they had taken from the Danes a year earlier, promised to pay taxes, to obey the Swedish king, and handed over 30 men as hostages.[22]

The plateau of the earthwork of Apuolė ('Apulia') was found sown with about 150 iron arrowheads, many of them bent or broken, as one would expect a battlefield to be. The arrowheads are typical of Scandinavia in the ninth and tenth centuries.

But the Curonians were free again soon after. Subsequent Swedish onslaughts on Curonia were unsuccessful. The opposition was too strong for the Norsemen to overcome, and their attempts at colonization of the Baltic coasts in Curonia during the two centuries, from 650 to 850, were only shortlived episodes. For the second half of the ninth and for the tenth century, archaeological finds of Scandinavian type in the Baltic lands are scarce. The Vikings had by this time focused their attention on eastern Slavic and the FinnoUgrian lands north of the Balts.

CHAPTER VII

The Balts before the Dawn of History

SEVERAL CENTURIES before the written records which illumine the birth of the Lithuanian state and the ensuing wars with the Teutonic Knights, the Baltic tribes enjoyed their second 'golden age'. Their lands remained intact, economy and trade progressed, arts and crafts flourished. The coastal tribes, particularly the Curonians, were now on the offensive in the war of piracy with the Scandinavian countries.

The Curonians had become Baltic 'Vikings'; they were the most restless and the richest of all the Balts during this period. That the Curonians were attacking Denmark and that its coasts in winter and in summer had to be guarded against them and other Vikings from the east is attested by the *Heimskringla* of Snorre Sturleson, set down during the reign of the Norwegian King Harald Hardready (1045–66).[1] Snorre Sturleson mentions in his *Ynglinga-saga* that in 1049 under King Svein, and in 1051 under King Magnus, a special sermon against Curonian pirates was introduced in the Danish churches: 'O mighty God, protect us against the Curonians.'[2] From the early thirteenth-century chronicles we learn that it was customary for the Curonians to devastate and plunder the Danish and Swedish kingdoms and to carry away church bells and other objects.[3] CURONIAN-SCANDINAVIAN RELATIONS

It is to be expected that Curonian weapons and ornaments would be found all over the western Baltic Sea coasts to Denmark. That they reached Gotland even before the wars with Denmark is shown by a number of Curonian pins, fibulae and swords dating from the tenth century. These articles have been found in various places along the coasts of Gotland. Some are isolated finds, but some come from graves. In Hugleifs near Silte a woman's grave containing typically Curonian

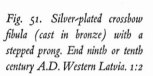

Fig. 51. Silver-plated crossbow fibula (cast in bronze) with a stepped prong. End ninth or tenth century A.D. Western Latvia. 1:2

Fgi. 51

ornaments was discovered, including a fibula similar to the one illustrated on this page. Other Curonian finds on Gotland were pins with triangular or cross-shaped heads, and swords such as are found in great numbers in western Lithuania, particularly around Klaipėda and Kretinga. Whether these isolated finds are merely imports from Curonia or the relics of a Curonian colony on Gotland is difficult to tell, but the grave at Hugleifs certainly proves the presence of some Curonians on the island. Other Baltic finds on Gotland, and in Uppland and Öland in central Sweden, point to commercial relations during the tenth and eleventh centuries. A fragment of a silver neck-ring with saddle-shaped end, which is a widely distributed type in central and eastern parts of Lithuania and Latvia, was found on Gotland (Boters near Gerum) together with Arab, Byzantine, German and Anglo-Saxon coins. Another neck-ring of the same type comes from Öland.[4]

Trade and wars of piracy between the Baltic and Scandinavian Vikings continued intermittently throughout the tenth and eleventh centuries. Rich and well-settled Curonia attracted the rapacious Vikings from Sweden, Denmark, and even from Iceland, but they, in turn, were decoyed by the Curonians who plundered their coasts. Thus the powers were balanced by piratical raids on both sides, and sources do not mention any larger wars. Bands of marauders anything from seven to 30 strong usually carried out such raids, not far from the coast, to facilitate a fast retreat. For this reason, on both sides of the Baltic the settlements are found a considerable distance in from the sea. Almost all the larger Curonian towns and villages were located from 5 to 25 km. from the coast.

A picturesque illustration of Viking raids and a description of the living standard of the Curonian landowners at the begin-ning of the tenth century is presented by the Icelandic *Egils-saga*. In it we find a long account of how Thorolf and Egil harried in Curonia around 925.[5] It is replete with precious fragments illuminating details in the life of a Curonian feudal lord. We read of fights with swords, spears, and arrows, of clothes being thrown over the enemy's weapons, of enemies being captured and held in cellars ('holes') for years or being killed by torture. The feudal lord's castle comprised many houses and barns, surrounded by ramparts ('fences'). Houses were built of great logs of timber, and had chambers on the first floor and stairs leading to attics. The chambers had flat shield-wainscots. The lord slept in the attic, and serving-men made the beds. In the attics were stored weapons and wooden chests full of silver. The lord and his men feasted in a 'hall', which probably was the largest room in one of the buildings. But that is about all that we learn from the Scandinavian narrators, and for the other gleanings we have to return to the graves.

The graves of the Curonians known now from not less than 30 large cemeteries in western Lithuania and western Latvia are extremely rich in grave furnishings and full of silver, bronze and iron. Let us examine one feudal lord's grave from the cemetery of Laiviai near Kretinga in western Lithuania dating from around A.D. 1000: cremated bones were in a man-sized tree-trunk coffin, accompanied by nine fibulae, a leather belt ornamented with bronze and amber beads, three spears, an iron battle-axe with a broad blade and a socketed axe, an iron

instrument for striking fire, a sickle, an iron key and bronze
scales, a saddle and iron bridle-bits; there were in addition
several miniature tools and weapons, which either were symbols of his other possessions or belonged to his servants and
slaves. Women's graves were particularly rich in bronze and
silver ornaments.[6] From what is found in the graves we can
readily visualize how all these goods must have filled up the
treasure chests kept in the landowner's house. Equally rich
graves also appear all over the Baltic coasts from the Vistula in
the south to Latvia and Estonia in the north, and this explains
why the Scandinavians were persistently lurking around the
East Baltic coasts. Commercial activities between the Prussians and Curonians and the Swedes and Danes are indicated
by finds at the trading posts: in Truso (Elbing), Wiskiauten in
Samland, at the mouth of the River Nemunas, in Grobin near
Liepāja, and at the mouth of the River Daugava. In addition
to trading and harrying, the Scandinavian Vikings had
missionary aims, but these seem to have been very secondary
and without consequences. It is recorded that one merchant
swayed by the Danish King Svein Estrithson (†1076) by many
gifts founded a church in Curonia, but it soon became
deserted and forgotten.[7]

ORNAMENTS,
ARTS AND
CRAFTS

Plates 68, 69

From the end of the ninth century onward, the Curonians
and other Baltic tribes enjoyed a truly remarkable enrichment
of their material culture. The influence of Viking art is con-
spicuous where the borrowing of certain motifs such as snake
or animal heads, or the imitation of Viking sword designs, are
concerned. Basically, however, either the forms of ornaments,
tools and weapons were developed from the prototypes of their
own earlier periods or new, exclusively Baltic, forms were
created. In geometric ornamentation a true finesse was achieved
and in jewellery forms, a great variety; but it is equally true
that in over-all style, a clear thread can be seen to run right on
from the 'golden age'.

The love for hanging attachments and for chains secured on large pins or brooches did not diminish. In rich women's graves, the triangular and cross-shaped heads of pins and the chain-holders were coated with silver-plate and adorned with blue beads. Heads of pins in the Curonian area took a particu- Plates 56, 58 lar variety of forms: cross-shaped, having disc ends; triangular with a rosette motif in the middle; and those with spiral heads, fretworked, or with rhomboid heads decorated with a minute geometric ornament in relief. The more delicate ones were used in women's head-dress to secure the head cloth. Also found is a series of bronze or silver neck-rings: the twisted kind with plain ends, with double-looped ends, with a saddle end and a Plate 57 loop or with three cones at one end and an ornamented plate at the other, and those made of flattened wire on which tri- Plates 59, 60 angular or elongated pendants were attached. The latter were *Fig. 52* most characteristic of the Semigallian woman's ornaments. Those with looped and saddle ends are widely spread over Lithuania, Latvia, and the ancient Sudovian lands. In addi- tion to bronze- or silver-plated crossbow fibulae with a step- like prong, there were gigantic crossbow fibulae with snake- head ends and poppy-head ornament on both sides of the bow. These continued in vogue until the eleventh century. After the ninth century, however, the horseshoe fibulae, common to all northern Europe, became the most popular. The earliest, dating from the seventh century, had spiralled ends; in the ninth and tenth centuries they developed into a great variety of forms in the Baltic lands: some with ends that thickened or were flattened, others with poppy-head, animal, star-shaped, rectangular plate or octagonal ends. In men's and boys' graves Plates 61, 62 they appear attached to linen blouses, sometimes from ten to 20 of them covering the whole width of the chest, or are pinned on the garment along the whole length of the body from the neck to the knees. A separate series among the fibulae were made of round or rectangular plates, usually fretworked and

Fig. 52. Bronze necklace with flat overlapping ends and pendants attached. Tenth–eleventh centuries A.D. Aizezari near Sakstagals, Latgale

showing cross, rosette or swastika patterns. The swastika ends were sometimes finished with animal heads reminiscent of the Viking animal whorl. An enormous variety of bracelet forms are encountered, a great many of which were banded and richly decorated geometrically. Characteristic of ancient Prussia and Curonia, as well as the adjacent areas, were those with stylized animal heads in which the Viking influence can be recognized, but their bands were decorated in purely Baltic style; dotted lines, forming rectangles, cross patterns, circles, tiny triangles, or rhombs and striations. Men's bracelets were broad and weighty. On them we find a painstaking geometric decoration in bands of zig-zags and rhombs as if in imitation of woven patterns.

Fig. 53

Plates 63, 64

Similar ornamental motifs were applied everywhere: on all flattened parts of neck-rings, fibulae, bracelets, belts, on the hilts of swords, on the sockets of spears, on bronze-coated leather sheaths for knives, and on horse bridles. Larger surfaces were divided into horizontal or vertical bands. This can be seen for instance on a bronze-coated leather sheath for a knife, a weapon with which a warrior in the tenth and eleventh centuries was usually equipped. Whether these motifs—incised, engraved or embossed on bronze and silver—appeared in woven garments, we do not know, but woollen head-cloths and kerchiefs were embellished with bronze plates. Thanks to this decoration, some woollen kerchiefs woven with the aid of

Fig. 54

Fig. 53. Bracelets with stylized animal-head ends and geometric decoration. Tenth–eleventh centuries A.D. Pryšmantai near Kretinga, western Lithuania

Fig. 54. Iron knife sheathed in a richly decorated bronze scabbard. Turaida, central Latvia, c. eleventh century A.D. 2:3

four heddles and having edges finished with a twisted band were preserved almost intact. They were either solidly covered with rectangular bronze plates and had several rows of spirals along the edges and attached pendants, or decorated with tiny bronze plates forming multiple swastika, triangle and other patterns. These decorated woollen kerchiefs were a part of the national costume of the Semigallian and Lettigallian women. Leather belts were likewise adorned with round, conical or rectangular plates of bronze or of lead coated with silver, and

Plate 65

Plate 66

bronze staples forming bands of zig/zags, triangles, or rhombs. Sometimes, on both sides of the bronze or silver clasp hung tassels of bronze spirals with amber beads at the ends.

Such fragments of linen and woollen garments as were found indicate several weaving techniques. Some were woven with the aid of four heddles; some, three. For the latter, hori/ zontal looms must have been used. Also, during these cen/ turies girdles were made of twisted white and red woollen thread. These are the forerunners of the present girdles, call/ ed *juostos*, a peculiar Baltic ornament used by men and women for tying around, or decorating the edges of, garments. In teen/age girls' graves of the tenth and eleventh centuries, instruments for girdle/weaving are frequently found.

Plate 67

Women's and men's costumes from the last centuries of pre/ history can be almost fully reconstructed. Although each tribe's costumes varied in details and in the application of local sets of bronze ornaments, in general style they were very much the same all over the Baltic area. Girls continued to cover their heads with a woollen cap decorated with bronze plates and pendants; women used a head cloth secured by a diadem or pins. The linen blouse had a high closed neck around which several bronze or silver necklaces, with glass or amber beads, bronze spirals, or pendants, were worn. The blouse was secured at the neck with round or horseshoe fibulae. The woollen skirt reached to below the calf; the woollen apron, the lower part of which was embellished by rows of bronze spirals, being shorter. The kerchief worn over the shoulders was made of a relatively thick woollen cloth. It was secured in front either with a massive bronze or silver/plated fibula or with large pins from which hung one or several chains. On each arm were worn from one to two or six bracelets.

Men were dressed in linen blouses secured with pins, woollen trousers, a long woollen jacket girdled by a leather belt, and a woollen cloak pinned with a massive fibula. The richer the man, the more elaborate was his belt, and instead of bronze he used silver ornaments—necklaces, fibulae, bracelets, and finger-rings. To complete the warrior's equipment there was a knife in a leather sheath coated with bronze or silver plates and attached to the belt, an iron instrument for tinder, as well as helmet, shield, long iron sword, spear, battle-axe, bow and arrows with iron tips, and spurs.

From the chainholders or brooches hung triangular or trapezoid bronze plates, jingle bells, miniatures of horses and water-birds, pincers, combs, and incisors of wild animals. This peculiar assortment of pendants suggests that they were not used for their aesthetic value alone, but had a symbolic significance. They tinkled when the wearer moved or walked, and thus helped to ward off evil spirits.

Our brief survey of ornamental and symbolic art would not be complete without a glance at the artistic skill which went into the decoration of horse harnesses. In their love for the horse, the Balts are on a par with the Scythians. In no other European country—not excluding the Indo-European groups —do we find the horse held in such high esteem down the ages; and this is still borne out by present-day folklore. In no other country but the Lithuania of the eleventh and twelfth centuries do we encounter separate large cemeteries for horses.[8] It was the riding horse, the *žirgas* (this Lithuanian word being connected with *žergti*, to straddle), who was the faithful companion of the warrior, and in full decorative splendour went with him to the grave. The headgear and the leather belts of the harness were solidly covered with lead plates coated with silver and embossed with rosettes, intertwined zig-zags and other motifs. Some more elaborate harness decorations were covered with gold plate in patterns combining animal heads and geometric motifs. On both sides of the horses' head or on the forehead, jingle bells or chains with bronze or silver pendants were suspended from the harness belts. The round

Plate 70

Fig. 55

Plates 71, 72

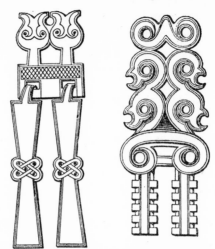

Fig. 55. Ornament (details) on horse bridle. Gold plate. Lake Vilkumuiža, Talsi, western Latvia

or cross-shaped spacers between the leather belts of the harness were of bronze, lead or silver, or iron coated with silver and incrusted with bronze. The bridle-bits and cheek-pieces were usually of iron. The horse belonging to a more im-portant personage had cheek-pieces covered with silver and curved in baroque style, their ends taking the form of stylized animal heads and their edges having incrustations of bronze or embossings. Saddle-cloths were adorned with triangular and rhomboid plates. The iron stirrups were usually covered with silver, the examples from the twelfth century being decorated with highly stylized animal heads and plant motifs. Even horsetails were not left without ornaments: they were encircled by large spiral rings of bronze.

Plates 73, 74

Plates 75, 76

At the dawn of history the arts and crafts had reached their most advanced stage. Metallurgy, leather working, glass and amber industries, and pottery were in the hands of craftsmen who had their workshops in the larger towns, in feudal castles and in the villages. Only weaving, spinning and sewing remained family affairs, and even here the highest-ranking families probably had local seamstresses, spinners and weavers at their beck and call. The potter's wheel, introduced around the tenth century, had gradually replaced the ancient craft of hand-made pottery which in each tribal group had its own distinctive appearance; now it became more uniform, was ornamented with wavy and horizontal bands, and sometimes was marked by the maker's symbol. Also by this time, mill-stones (revolving querns) had replaced the primitive saddle querns.

PROGRESS IN AGRICULTURE Progress is noticeable in all branches of the economy. All tools show a development in form. Iron axes assumed broad edges which in building houses and fortifications and in clearing forests served better than the previous narrow edges. Scythes became longer; sickles were more gracile, taking on a curved point, and some having a dentate edge. Iron plough-shares became more popular. Some time between the ninth and twelfth centuries the two-field system in agriculture appears to have been replaced by the three-field, to judge by the preponderance of winter crop grains over wheat and barley in a number of settlements. Peas and beans were now widely used. Among the domesticated animal bones found, those of pig are second in number only to those of cattle.

CURRENCY AND TRADE Before the tenth century, currency had apparently not yet supplanted the trading of cattle, fur, amber, silver, and other barter goods. These became inconvenient with the new demands of a growing population, towns, trade routes, and stepped-up commerce. Local currency appeared in the form of finger-like silver bars with one flattened side, weighing either 100 or 200 grams. Characteristic of the earliest stages of Lithuanian history, they are found in rich graves together with silver ornaments, or in large hoards, and were in use from the tenth to the beginning of the fifteenth century. The silver bars and rare metals were weighed by tiny folding scales made of two bronze dishes suspended on bronze chains attached to a cross-bar. The weights were barrel-shaped, of different sizes, marked with from one to five circles or triangles and one cross, or a cross with circles in between the cross-arms. Scales and weights were widely used in the tenth and eleventh centuries. They are usually found in rich men's graves.[9]

During the tenth–twelfth centuries the Balts participated actively in local and international trade with the Russians, the Swedes and western Europe. Trade routes are indicated by numerous huge hoards of Lithuanian silver bars and Baltic silver ornaments, of Arab, Byzantine, Danish, Swedish, German and Anglo-Saxon coins, and of Kievan Russian silver ornaments; also by finds of Viking swords and swords of 'Ulfberth' type imported from the Rhineland in western Germany, and Russian helmets, in the graves of Prussian feudal lords.[10] Truso (Elbing), Samland, the Nemunas estuary (present Klaipéda), the Curonian coasts, the Daugava estuary (present Riga), and the Estonian coasts, were all connected by sea routes with the Swedish commercial centres in Visby (Gotland) and in Birka (central Sweden). The Daugava-Dvina was a river link between Scandinavia and western Europe, the Baltic lands, Russia and Byzantium. Along its banks, hoards containing Arab (Kufian) silver dirhems, Byzantine gold, silver and copper coins, Anglo-Saxon silver denarii, Swedish and Danish coins, Baltic silver bars and silver necklaces, and Russian ornaments abound.[11] It certainly was one of the busiest international routes. From the upper Dvina the continental waterways went north to Novgorod and Ladoga, and south to Kiev and the Black Sea area. The products of Kievan Russia reached the lands of the southern Prussians across Volynia, and the Pripet and Bug rivers. Another important trade route was the River Nemunas and its tributaries. From the Kaunas and Vilnius areas the routes branched out, leading to Semigallia, to Lettigallia, Pskov and Novgorod, and across eastern Lithuania to Polotsk, Smolensk, and Novgorod.

Not amber but furs were now prominent among exports to western Europe, as is vividly described by Adam of Bremen in 1075; 'They [Prussians] have an abundance of strange furs, the odour of which has inoculated our world with the deadly poison of pride. But these furs they regard, indeed, as dung, to our shame, I believe, for right or wrong we hanker after a martenskin robe as much as for supreme happiness. Therefore, they offer their very precious marten furs for the woollen garments called faldones.'[12]

CASTLES, TOWNSHIPS, ADMINISTRA' TIVE UNITS

Almost all excavated earthworks from the tenth to the thirteenth century show considerable enlargement and addi' tional fortifications. The ramparts on the inland side, or en' circling the castle from all sides, became very lofty. The castle of Impiltis near Kretinga in ancient Curonia was surrounded by a rampart up to 10 m. high and nearly 40 m. across. Such

Plate 65

huge ramparts would heighten the steep bank of the promon' tory and from the river or lakeside give the impression of a powerful fort rising to 30 m. or more. Above the ramparts stood wooden fortifications—high fences, towers and log cabins with steep walls on the outer side. In these cabins lived the castle's garrison and craftsmen, who kept animals and grain there. Wooden or stone towers were built at the corners. In the centre or to one side of the level area paved with stones or rectangular logs were the castle buildings, built mainly of wood though stones and clay were also used, and rect' angular in plan. Castles were burnt down and rebuilt, and the excavations have shown consecutive destruction layers, in some cases numbering ten or more in the course of several cen' turies. In historic times they were superseded by brick build' ings, making the reconstruction of earlier wooden castles all but impossible.

The earthwork was protected from two or three sides by rivers and streams, lakes or marshes. A deep ditch filled with water separated it from inland. Access to the castle was by a portcullis, and at the entrance was a wooden gate flanked by small towers, or a tunnel. In the castle of Impiltis the entrance tunnel, built of oak logs, was 8 m. long, 2 m. high and 3 m. wide. Deep wells or water reservoirs were discovered in some earthworks. The excavations in Apuolė revealed rectangular wooden frames for a well, 2 m. deep and 4.5 x 4 m. wide. In some of the earthworks, wells are still filled with water and the present villagers living near by use them. From historic records we know that even during protracted sieges of the castles, the Baltic tribes managed to survive.[13]

In every tribal territory were several principal castles each with an adjoining town, and in addition there were smaller castles, also arranged on heavily fortified earthworks each surrounded by a settlement of smaller dimensions. Of the castle-hills and towns so far excavated the most impressive are: in Curonia, the above-mentioned Apuolė ('Apulia') and Impiltis, the latter with a town extending over at least five hectares (about $12\frac{1}{4}$ acres);[14] in Semigallia, Daugmale on the bank of the River Daugava with an adjoining settlement of more than one hectare (about $2\frac{1}{2}$ acres),[15] Tervete in western Semigallia,[16] and Mežotne on the bank of the River Lielupe, south-east of Riga, surrounded by a town 1 km. across and ending with another, smaller earthwork;[17] in Lettigallia (Latgala), the castle-hill of Jersika on a bank of the upper Daugava, occupying 7,500 sq. m., and the adjacent small town covering an area of 750 by 200 m. In the same tribal area four other important earthworks have been excavated: Dignāja, Asote, Kauguru Pekas Kalns and Raunas Tanīsa Kalns.[18] Others are in eastern Lithuania: the castle-hill of Nemenčinė near Vilnius, covering an area of 2,000 sq. m. within the fortifications and showing foundations of rectangular houses built of stone and clay; and in central Lithuania, Veliuona, set on a steep bank of the River Nemunas which together with the rampart was 33 m. high, its levelled area covering 1,500 sq. m.[19] And there are

Fig. 56

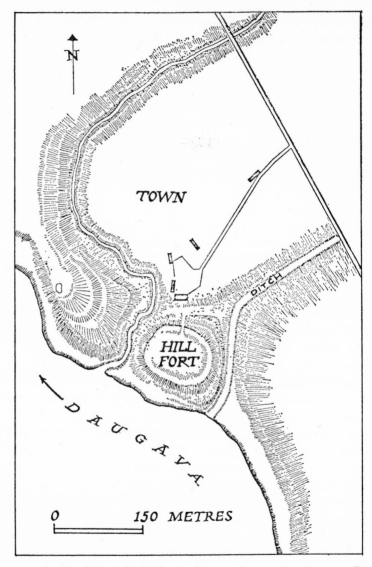

Fig. 56. Plan of the Jersika hill-fort on the River Daugava in ancient Lettigallia (Latgala)

hundreds of other impressive castle-hills which either have been unsystematically excavated or are still completely untouched by the spade.

The largest or the most powerful castle with a town became the military and administrative centre of the tribal district. The ninth-century sources, as mentioned above, found five such 'states' in Curonia; at the beginning of the thirteenth century there were eight 'states', or districts, with their centres in each of which were several villages ('castellatura'). A similar pattern of separate districts pertained to all the other Baltic tribes. The more powerful feudal 'kings' extended their rule over two, three, four, or more districts.

These 'kings', or chieftains, possessed the largest of all the castles. In the earliest written records, the most influential lords who ruled over a large area of the tribe are called 'rex', 'dux', or 'princeps'. Under their control were the rulers of less powerful districts. A strict hierarchical system prevailed within the limits of a tribe as well as within the limits of a smaller tribal district. The chronicles enumerate the names of the chief-tains and even those of their subordinates. The power and the land-ownership were inherited. So, for instance, Viestarts, the lord of Tervete in western Semigallia, was a 'dux' and 'maior natus' and under his rule were all the lands of western Semi-gallia. The ruler of the district of Beverina in Lettigallia at the beginning of the thirteenth century was Tālivaldis, who is described as a rich man having much silver; his three sons were rich also, and possessed many lands. The hierarchical struc-ture of chieftainship is illustrated by the chronicle of Volynia,[20] which tells how 21 Lithuanian dukes came to sign the treaty of 1219 between Lithuania and the Rus' of Halich-Vladimir. Of these, five—the most powerful ones—were 'grand dukes', the other 16 dukes of minor importance. From this we may deduce that Lithuania at that time was ruled by a confederation of the most powerful chieftains. It is quite possible that such a system of government was also in existence in earlier prehistoric centuries.

As is usual in feudal states, there were many wars between the rulers. The power switched from one 'king' to another and stable government was practically impossible. Wulfstan witnessed 'very much war' among the Prussians at the end of the ninth century, and we learn of much warring among the Semigallian, Lettigallian and Lithuanian dukes from the chronicles of the thirteenth century. It was possible to maintain this type of feudalism and government as long as the Balts were surrounded by neighbours whose societies and leadership were based on a similar pattern. After it had lasted for a millennium or so, the situation changed when a vigorous enemy—the Teutonic Order supported by all Europe—appeared on the western border in 1226–30. The Prussians succumbed during the course of the thirteenth century, but the Lithuanians, united under one leadership, not only survived and stopped the Teutonic expansion, but extended their state borders to the east. Mindaugas, one of the five most powerful chieftains of Lithuania mentioned in connection with the treaty of 1219, managed through internal wars and family relations to extend his power over a greater part of Lithuania between 1236 and 1248. Soon thereafter he was crowned as a king, and thus was founded the Lithuanian state.

THE TEUTONIC ORDER The Order of the Teutonic Knights was a monastic and military organization, founded in Palestine during the Crusades. Driven from Asia Minor, they withdrew to Europe and settled in the lower Vistula area (1226–30). The Order immediately began to support the military enterprises of the German colony in Latvia, founded in Riga in the middle of the twelfth century. The chief purpose was to create a German state in the East Baltic area. Christian slogans were used in this war against the last 'pagans' in Europe, or 'the Saracens of the North', as they were called, so that the Order easily enlisted numbers of adventurous kings, princes, and knights with their armies from all Europe to fight for the Order's cause.

In the thirteenth century, the Knights attacked the Prussians by land from the west and the Curonians, Semigallians, Selonians, Lettigallians and Estonians from the Bay of Riga. The Curonians were conquered in 1267; the Prussians resisted the bloody Teutonic onslaught for almost 60 years, from 1231 to 1288. Being divided into many small principalities and unable to organize a united army of all the Prussian people, they could not hold back the increasing numbers of their enemy. Teutonic castles, superior to Prussian ones, covered the whole territory of the Prussian tribes by the end of the thirteenth century.

The 'crusade' (in quotation marks, since it entailed slaughtering of people and a complete devastation of villages and fields) started in the lower Vistula area, and by 1237–38 Pamedė (Pomesania) and Pagudė (Pogesania) were already under the Order's rule. Next, the Teutons pushed on along the Frisches Haff and in 1240 defeated the united Barti, Notangians and Varmians. A Prussian uprising in 1242 held back a further Teuton advance for some time, but by 1260 almost all the western and northern Prussian provinces had been conquered. In 1260, another uprising started which was crushed with the utmost severity in 1274. Nadruvians were slaughtered almost to the last man and their lands became a desert. The last to fall as a result of continuous wars with the Poles (Masurians) and Teutons in the last quarter of the thirteenth century was Sūduva, the land of the Sudovians (Jatvingians). After the loss of nearly two-thirds of the Prussian territory in the south due to Russian and Polish expansion before the thirteenth century, and after a tremendous loss of life in the wars with the Teutons, only some 170,000 ancient Prussians were left; in the Peninsula of Samland, the previously most thickly populated area, their number was reduced to a mere 22,000.

Fig. 57. *The Lithuanian empire in the fourteenth–fifteenth centuries A.D., showing Poland in the fifteenth century*

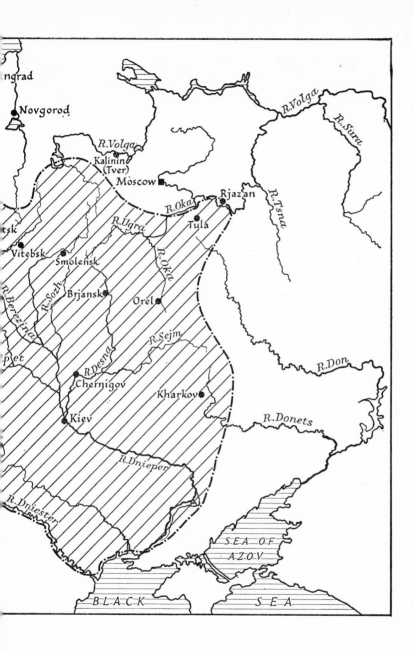

The colonization and Germanization of the Prussian lands began immediately. By 1400, the Teutonic Order could boast 54 towns, 890 villages, and 19,000 farms of new colonists. During the wars the Prussian upper class and the leaders had perished; those remaining yielded to the control of the Order, were baptized, and in striving for social status gradually accepted German customs and language. The lower and the lower-middle classes were underprivileged and peasants were forced into serfdom. The language and customs of the Prussians were preserved by this lower, underprivileged class, and Prussian continued to be spoken for another 400 years. The western provinces were more rapidly Germanized than the peninsula of Samland where the old population lived in compact groups. Catechisms published in Prussian in the sixteenth century show that not everyone understood German. It is known that at the beginning of the seventeenth century sermons were preached with the help of translators, but the Prussian language was living through its last stages at the end of this century. It was only spoken by the old people in villages.[21]

RESISTANCE OF THE LITHUANIAN STATE The thirteenth century was one of the most critical in the history of the Balts. Had it not been for the unification of the Lithuanian state in that century under able leadership, the Teutonic expansion would have proceeded to the east and easily swallowed up all of the remaining Baltic tribes. As soon as the Teutons began building their castles on the River Nemunas, they met well-organized resistance from the Lithuanians. The northern branch of the Teutonic Order was defeated by the Lithuanian king Mindaugas in 1236 at Šiauliai. Throughout the fourteenth and early fifteenth centuries, devastating wars between the Germans and Lithuanians continued to be waged along the Nemunas. Thanks to the clever and energetic leadership of Gediminas (1316–41), Algirdas (1345–77), and Algirdas' heroic brother Kęstutis

(†1382) who spent all his life fighting against Teutons, Lithuania grew into a powerful state instead of succumbing to the German threat.

From the thirteenth century on, the central power in Eastern Europe was the growing Lithuanian state. Lithuania began its very rapid expansion to the east and south through the Russian and Ukrainian lands, to Tartary and the Black Sea. In the period between 1200 and 1263 Lithuanians fell upon Russians seventy-five times. On horseback they conquered Slavic lands. Gediminas occupied nearly all of Byelo-Russia and the north-western Ukraine (Volynia). Algirdas, a son of Gediminas, defeated the Tartars in 1362 near the Blue Waters in Podolia and took from them almost the entire basin of the Dnieper and Dniester. Later, Vytautas the Great (1392–1430), the most powerful of the rulers of Lithuania, annexed the Donets and Oka basins, surrounding Moscow from the west and south, making this area part of the Lithuanian empire.

Fig. 57

This expansion was directed toward lands which for the most part had been possessed by Lithuanians and other East Baltic tribes in the prehistoric period. During its peak period (1362–1569), the empire covered 350,000 square miles. The huge state played an important role in protecting western Europe, as well as its own lands, from being invaded by the Tartars.

However, the Russian territories were not 'Lithuanized'. As from the early sixteenth century, Lithuania began to lose her eastern provinces on the upper Volga, Oka and Donets, to the Russians. The growing threat from Moscow forced Lithu-ania to conclude a political treaty with Poland in 1569 and cede her Ukrainian lands to Poland. Livonia (present Latvia and southern Estonia) became a condominium of Lithuania and Poland. During the following centuries, Lithuania and what was to become Latvia failed to regain either their power or their lost territories. When they emerged as independent states in 1918, after being under the rule of Tsarist Russia and Germany for 123 years (1795 to 1918), Lithuania and Latvia covered the smallest ethnographic territory to which the Baltic-speaking people had ever been reduced.

CHAPTER VIII

Religion

And inasmuch as they [the Prussians] did not
know of [the Christian] God, it so happened that
they worshipped the entire creature-world instead of
God, namely: the sun, moon and stars, the thunder,
birds, even the four-legged animals including toads.
They also had holy groves, sacred fields and waters.
(*Chronicon Prussiae*, by Peter Dusburg, 1326)

IT IS WITH GREAT ASTONISHMENT that the first missionaries in the Baltic lands, the annalists of the Teutonic
Order and many later chroniclers describe all the 'incredibilia'
of the pagan religion: cremation rites; the belief in reincarna-
tion; the veneration of holy groves, trees, fields, waters and fire;
the existence of many gods and spirits; bloody sacrificial offerings and soothsayings. The Teutonic Order carried the
Christian cross to Prussia and to Latvia, but they succeeded
more easily in subduing these people politically than spiritu-
ally. The Prussian villagers remained pagan until their exter-
mination in the seventeenth century, even though officially they
accepted baptism in the thirteenth century and all pagan rites
and customs were strictly forbidden. This was also the case in
western Latvia. Lithuania joined the Christian Church only
in 1387 when the Lithuanian grand duke Jogaila, son of
Algirdas, married the Polish princess Jadwiga and became
king of Poland. Even then, while the Christian faith infiltrated
the palaces of the nobility and cities, the villagers retained the
old religion for many more centuries.

The customs, beliefs, mythological songs and folk art symbolism of the Lithuanians and Latvians are amazingly replete
with antiquity. The Christian stratum is recent and can be
easily detached. For comparative religion, the value of the

Lithuanian and Latvian folklore and folk art is the same as that of the Baltic languages for the reconstruction of the 'mother tongue' of the Indo-Europeans. The pre-Christian stratum is so ancient that it undoubtedly reaches back to prehistoric times— at least to the Iron Age or in the case of some elements even several millennia farther. What the Christian heralds, being foreigners and not understanding native languages, saw and described is usually superficial. The basic source in recon-structing the ancient Baltic religion is folklore, which splen-didly supplements the passages of the recorded history and the archaeological monuments.

'DOMOS SAC-ROS', 'SACRAS VILLAS' AND 'SANCTI VIRI'
Baltic architecture was entirely of wood, as it was in all northern Europe. 'Domos sacros' and 'sacras villas', known from the documents of the fourteenth century,[1] have not sur-vived; and on the sites of the pagan sanctuaries Christian churches arose during the succeeding centuries. It was not until the excavations of 1955–7 that, in the lands of the eastern Balts, remains of a number of wooden temples and large sanctuaries were uncovered. Excavations by Tret'jakov south of Smolensk clearly showed that some of the fortified hill-top villages were not regular habitation sites, but sanctuaries.[2] The uncovered hill-top sanctuaries date from the first century B.C. to about the sixth or seventh centuries A.D., and some of them revealed several successive layers with residues of round wooden temples. These certainly are the predecessors of the 'sacred villas' known to early history. Some of the 'sacred towns' in central and eastern Lithuania, it is said, were important reli-gious centres to which people from several provinces repaired for religious practices.

One of the best excavated sanctuaries is the small hill-fort of Tushemlja, 50 km. south of Smolensk and located on the small River Tushemlja, tributary of the Sozh. Its lowest layer, dating from the fifth to fourth centuries B.C., yielded many post-holes, but it was not possible to reconstruct these earliest

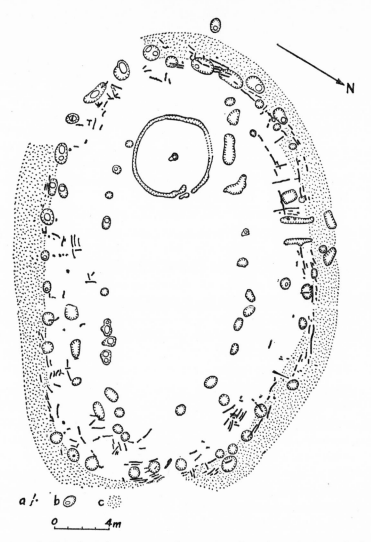

N

Fig. 58. Plan of a Baltic sanctuary with a round temple inside. Tushemlja, south of Smolensk. a, remains of timber structures around the inner side of the rampart; b, pits from timber posts supporting the roof, and from remains of gate and temple; c, sandy rampart along the edges of the hill

buildings and we cannot tell whether the site was already a sanctuary in the Early Iron Age. In the layer from the second– third centuries A.D., traces of a round building 6 m. in diameter appeared. It had timber posts, about 20 cm. thick. Within the area were more post-holes, and in the middle a huge pit, 50 cm. wide and 70 cm. deep, presumed to be the remains of a wooden idol or altar. Superimposed on this layer was a cultural stratum dating from approximately the sixth or seventh centuries, with remains of another round temple, this one within a large structure covering the whole top of the hill-fort, which was surrounded by a sandy rampart 3 m. high. Small wooden rectangular, room-like structures adjoining one another and containing stone hearths encircled the inner side of the rampart. The entire oval structure, measuring 20 x 30 m., is presumed to have been covered by a single roof supported on

Fig. 58

two rows of large posts, the space between the inner and the outer rows being 4.5 m. The posts probably terminated in ver- tical mortises to hold the horizontal beams. Some additional pits and burnt timber beams between the two rows of posts hint at internal walls. It has not been possible to reconstruct the roof itself; the excavator thinks that it was covered over with earth. In the middle of the northern wall was a gate-like entrance. The round temple, 5.5 m. in diameter and standing in the north-eastern end of the sanctuary, had at its centre a large pit, all that remained of what had once been a huge timber post.

At Gorodok, 12 km. from Tushemlja, an almost identical sanctuary was brought to light. Its earliest cultural remains date back to the first century B.C., and its latest are contem- porary with the upper layer of Tushemlja. Here too the re- mains of a round temple were found superimposed on an older one. The temple, 5 m. in diameter, was built of vertical split beams convex on the outside. Within the temple was found the skull of a large bear, apparently associated with the wooden post that stood in the middle. Several other sanctuaries are now known from the area of Smolensk, Mogilev, and Minsk.

What was the purpose of the wooden post inside the temple? It may have been either an image of a god or just a post capped by animal skulls or heads. Until the twentieth century the skull of a horse or bull (or the horns alone) was believed in Lithu-ania to afford protection against the 'evil eye', illness in human beings or animals, hailstorms or other natural perils, and was raised on a high pole wherever the danger threatened. Until very recently, horses' heads, horns, he-goats, rams, cocks and other birds were used as gable decoration on roof-tops.

The presence of priests who performed rites and recited prayers cannot be doubted. In the early historic records they are continually mentioned, as 'sancti viri', 'auguri', 'nigromantici', 'sacerdotes'. In 1075, Adam of Bremen, writing about the Curonians, said: 'All their houses are full of pagan sooth-sayers, diviners, and necromancers, who are even arrayed in a monastic habit. Oracular responses are sought there from all parts of the world, especially by Spaniards and Greeks.'[3] The priests were wise old men chosen by the people and held in greatest respect. Sixteenth-century sources say they were re-garded as divine personages, similar to the Christian bishops.[4] Peter von Dusburg wrote in 1326 that in the Prussian pro-vince of Nadruva, in the place called Romuva, there was a powerful priest named Krivė, whom the people regarded as pope, and whose dominion extended not only over Nadruva, but also over Lithuania, Curonia and Semigallia. The only such 'pope' known to recorded history, Krivė was highly respected by the kings, nobility and common people, and his rule covered almost all the Baltic lands during the wars with the Teutonic Order.[5] It is doubtful whether such powerful priests existed in the earlier periods; the emergence of priestly power in the fourteenth century may have resulted from the old religion being endangered at this particular period by the invasion of Christian enemies. Theocracy is not attested among the Baltic peoples; political power was in the hands of the kings. The pagan religion, however, was universal and profoundly influenced all spheres of life.

THE DEAD   The custom of cremation persisted long after the introduction of Christianity and was abolished only as the result of a fierce struggle against the practice by the Christian missionaries. Lithuanian kings and dukes were cremated with great pomp until the end of the fourteenth century. Algirdas was cremated with 18 horses in 1377 in the forest north of Vilnius. 'He was cremated with the best horses, clothes, resplendent in gold and girdled with a gilted silver belt and was covered with a gown woven of beads and gems.'[6] Algirdas' brother Kęstutis was buried in a similar manner in 1382, 'and splendidly could be seen a deep pit in man's length full of ashes . . . and nothing there escaped death: horses, clothes, weapons, etc., all were cremated; hunting birds and dogs were cremated with him.'[7] The historian Dĺugosz, writing at the beginning of the fifteenth century, mentions that Lithuanians had hearths in holy groves, each family and house its own, where they cremated their relatives and closest friends, along with horses, saddles and costly clothes.[8] A French envoy, Ghillebert de Lanoy, who travelled in Curonia in 1413, noted that there was a sect among the Curonians who still cremated their dead in full dress and with the costliest ornaments on a pyre of pure oak trees in a nearby forest.[9] The sacred groves where the cremation rites were performed were usually on a hill or elevation called 'Alka'. Excavations have revealed large pits and hearths filled with charcoal and ashes, among which were found fragments of animal and human bones, swords and burnt ornaments, tools and weapons.[10]

Without the written records to supplement what we know from cremation graves in barrows or flat graves we could not establish all that was involved in the funeral pomp. The Anglo

Saxon traveller Wulfstan, during his stay in the lands of the
Prussians (Aistians) about 880–90, happened to make ex,
tremely valuable observations about the preservation of the
dead before cremation, and about the funeral races. I shall cite
his text in full:

> And there is a custom among the Aistians that
> when a person dies he lies unburnt surrounded by
> his relatives and friends for a month, sometimes
> two, and the kings and other nobles—the longer the
> more wealthy they are, sometimes for half a year they
> lie unburnt in their houses. And all this time while
> the corpse is in the house, drinking goes on and
> sports are performed until the day on which it is
> cremated. Then the same day they carry it to the
> pyre, they divide his property left after drinking bouts
> and games into five or six parts, or sometimes into
> more which depends on the wealth of the deceased.
> Then they lay the largest part about a mile from the
> town, then another, then a third, so until all his pro,
> perty is laid within the mile; and the least portion
> must be nearest to the town in which the dead man
> lies. Then about five or six miles from the property
> shall be assembled all the men who have the swiftest
> horses in the country. These men all run towards the
> property. He who has the swiftest horse comes first
> to the largest portion, and so one after the other, until
> the whole property is taken, and he takes the least
> portion who takes that which is nearest to the town,
> and then everyone rides away with the property,
> and they may have it all. On this account, swift
> horses are extremely expensive. When the whole
> property is thus dispersed, they carry him out and
> cremate him with his weapons and clothes. Almost
> the whole property of the dead man is spent while
> he is kept so long in the house, and through that
> they lay its part on the way to which the strangers

run for and take away. And it is a custom among
the Aistians that people of every language shall be
cremated; and if anyone finds a bone unconsumed,
compensation must be made [they shall make a
great atonement]. And there is among the Aistians a
tribe that can produce cold, and therefore the dead
whom they freeze can lie so long and do not putrefy.
If anyone sets two vessels full of ale or water, they
contrive that both be frozen, be it summer or be it
winter.[11]

To preserve the dead and keep them unburied for a long
period was a custom deriving from earliest antiquity, probably
universal in all Indo-European groups. We know that the
skeletons from the Kurgan Pit-Grave and Catacomb-Grave
culture before 2000 and in the beginning of the second millennium B.C. north of the Black Sea are often found dismem-
bered, which may be the result of keeping the bodies in the
open for a long time. Signs of fly larvae having fed on the
Bronze Age skeletons of upper-class people in Central Europe
point in a similar direction.[12] Various ways of preserving and
embalming the dead were known to the Baltic tribes during
the whole span of historic times.

For the protracted funeral meals, the Baltic *šermenys* (the
word being connected with 'feeding', *šerti*, to feed), oxen were
slaughtered. Lamentation songs, the *raudos* surviving still in the
villages of Lithuania and Latvia and mentioned in written
records since the thirteenth century, must certainly have been a
part of the funeral wakes at prehistoric burials. Even when at
war, the Balts needed many days to lament the deceased and
cremate them. Thus, in 1210, during the war with the Order
of the Sword, the Curonians at Riga, had to stop the battle for
three days for cremation and lamentation: *et mortuos suos
cremantes fecerunt planctum super eos.*[13] The dead were lamented,
praised and bidden farewell so as to ensure that they would

safely arrive in the kingdom of the dead and stay among parents, brothers, sisters, and other relatives. The lamentation songs were regularly forbidden by the Christian missionaries, and the lamenters were fined; but even so the *raudos* have sur, vived up till modern times, thus preserving beautiful pieces of lyrical and extremely touching folk poetry.

The death of a farmer had to be immediately announced to his horses and cattle, and when a bee,keeper died, the bees had to be told; otherwise, the animals and bees would die out. The horse was not allowed to carry its master to the cemetery; if it did, it would die or fall sick. These beliefs, still held in Lithu, anian villages at the beginning of the twentieth century, are the last traces of the great love that existed between man and animal. In prehistoric times, it was believed that the animals went to the other world to live there with their master. During the first centuries A.D., in Prussia and Lithuania, horses were buried in the standing position and in full attire, ready to be mounted. Dusburg, in speaking of the Prussian religion in 1326, clearly stated that the Notangians, one of the central Prussian tribes, used to be cremated on horseback (*in equo crematus* or *ligatus super equum suum est crematus*).[14] That horses were buried alive is shown by the fact that some of them had their legs bound with ropes, their eyes bandaged, and a nose,bag filled with oat stems attached to the head. From Dusburg we also learn that before the cremation the horse would be driven around as long as it could stand on its feet. Deceased warriors and farmers, it was said, rode their horses through the sky to the realm of the souls, and on horses they usually returned to earth to visit their families and to attend the feast of the dead in October and on many other anniver, saries. Written records of the seventeenth century mention that during the feast of the dead, the intestines and skin of a horse were brought to the grave in order to help the dead come on horseback to the host's house.[15]

During the protracted wars between the Teutons and Lithuanians, the annalists who described the gruesome fights and sieges in Lithuania often expressed shocked surprise at seeing how readily the Lithuanians took their own lives. The most horrifying incident occurred in 1336 in the castle of Pilènai on the River Nemunas. When the Lithuanians perceived they could no longer hold out against the Teuton onslaught, they kindled a huge fire, threw all their possessions and treasures into it, killed their wives and children, and then offered up their necks to their chief, the duke Margiris, for decapitation. During this same siege, an old woman decapitated with an axe 100 men who voluntarily accepted death at her hands; then, when the enemy broke in, she split in two her own head with the same axe. The annalist, Wigand von Marburg, who described this scene in his rhymed chronicle of 1393–4, characterized the spectacle as superhuman and ended with the words: 'However, it is not amazing, since they did that according to their religion and they regarded the death much easier.'[16] After an unsuccessful attack by the Lithuanians in Estonia in 1205, 50 wives of the fallen warriors hanged themselves. 'It is no wonder,' writes Henry of Latvia in his *Chronicon Livoniae*, 'since they believed that very soon they would live together with their husbands.'[17]

In the light of these records, the many 'collective' graves that occur in the Baltic area from the Chalcolithic period to the early centuries of history can be attributed to the obligatory death and burial of the surviving wife, husband, child or children upon the death of a member of the family. When the feudal chief or the king died, not only the members of his family but also his servants and favourite slaves had to follow suit. The practice of burying 'with people' was forbidden by those who brought the Christian faith, but echoes of it are still to be found in some customs and folk songs of the Latvians and Lithuanians. Thus, at the funeral of a betrothed girl or boy, the burial ceremony is more like a wedding: wedding songs are sung, dances are danced, and both the living and the deceased partner are dressed in wedding costume. It was believed that dead relatives and friends also joined in celebra/ ting the wedding. Even in this century the Lithuanian girl has been known to bring a wreath of rue, the symbol of chastity, to the grave of her beloved. The wedding of the dead is not simply connected with belief in the continuity of the earthly life after death, but also with the belief that people who die un/ married and all those who die an unnatural death are a danger to the living since they have not lived through the whole span of life. In the Baltic languages, the word for the devil or the evil spirit, the *velnias*, derives from the dangerous dead who return and threaten the living.

The Baltic *vėlės*—etherealizations of the deceased—go to live their family and village community lives, to 'a sandy hill, a hill of *vėlės*', where they have their houses or chambers, tables and walls, and where they are covered with linen cloths. The 'hill of *vėlės*' has gates through which the *vėlės* enter, and benches on which they sit, and these features recur in descrip/ tions of the after/life in Latvian and Lithuanian folk poetry. The verses would seem to have preserved the image of the ancient burial mounds, the wooden chambers or stone cists. Many passages in the Latvian folk songs speak of a cemetery on a small sandy hill, often so full of graves that there is no more room for new arrivals.[18] They may reflect the communal Bronze Age barrows with hundreds of graves, or the Iron Age barrows with a number of graves of one family.

If the realm of the *vėlės* on 'a high sandy hill' in the neigh/ bourhood of the village reflects the more realistic side of this people's beliefs about life after death, there also exists an imagin/ ary hill, or a steep stone hill, which the dead have to climb, and therefore they need to have good fingernails or the aid of animal claws. On this steep hill *Dievas* (God) resides and summons the *vēlēs*. Here we begin to see the connection between the god's (Lithuanian *Dievas*, Lettish *Dievs*) abode and that of the dead. Further, we learn from the mythological songs that the goal is not the hill, which is the image of the sky, but is the place beyond the hill.

The way to this mystical place is long. The *vēlēs* may ride on horses through the sky, they may rise with the smoke of the fire, or fly like birds through the Milky Way, which in Lithuanian means 'the Birds' Way'; they may also go by boat as does the Sun at night through the waters—the sea, the Daugava or Nemunas rivers—to the west. There the Sun sleeps, there she washes her horses and there appear other gods, *Dievas*, the Thunder god, the Moon, and the deity of the Sea. And somewhere in this remote place are the grey stone and the sun⁄tree, or the iron post, and at the post two horses. These represent the cosmic tree of the Balts, the axis of the sky, having close analogies in Hindu, Roman, Slavic and Germanic mythologies. In folklore it is usually the oak⁄tree or birch⁄tree with silver leaves, copper branches, and iron roots; sometimes it is an enormous linden or an apple⁄tree. It stands on the stone, at the end of 'the way of the Sun'. The Sun hangs her belt on the branches, sleeps in the crown of this tree and, when she rises in the morning, the tree becomes red.[19]

'Beyond the hill is my mother, there where the sun is,' runs the Latvian song. The dead travel to the realm of the gods, to the realm of light, to the end of the visible world. It is still said: 'He is in the realm of *dausos*.' The Lithuanian word *dausos* preserves the meaning of a mysterious realm and cannot be translated either into 'paradise' or into 'heaven'.

The departure of the *vēlē* does not mean the end of the physi⁄cal ties of the dead with the living. Besides the *vēlē*, which is comparable to the Greek *psyche*, there was the *siela*, related to the Roman *anima* or the Greek *pneuma*, meaning a living power which did not depart from the earth. It was reincarnated in trees, flowers, animals, birds. It would leave the body as a breath, a vapour, and immediately find a lodging in plants, animals or birds. Sometimes it would issue directly from the mouth in the shape of a butterfly, a bee, a mouse, a toad, a snake, or grow out of the mouth of a young girl in the shape of a lily. Most frequently, however, it would be reincarnated in trees: men's spirits, in oaks, birches and ash trees; women's, in linden and spruce. The Baltic peoples have extremely intimate relations with these trees. The oak and the linden are basic trees in folklore. At the time of one's birth, a specific tree is assigned to one, and it grows imbued with the same life forces as its human counterpart. If the tree is cut down, the person dies. Trees growing in the old cemeteries of Lithuania are never touched by a pruner's hand, for there is an adage saying that to cut a cemetery tree is to do evil to the deceased. Neither is it permissible to mow the grass: 'From cemetery grass our blood flows,' runs the old proverb. Next after the plants, spirits were most likely to pass into birds—women into a cuckoo or a duck, men into a falcon, a pigeon, a raven, or a cock. Some would also be reincarnated in wolves, bears, dogs, horses and cats. In the Protestant cemeteries of the mid-nineteenth century in Prussian Lithuania (the area of Klaipėda), wooden tomb-stones were found resembling the shapes of toads or other reptiles, combined with motifs of flowers and birds, and other tomb monuments were capped with horses' heads.

Earth is the Great Mother. All life comes from her: humans, plants, animals. In Lettish she is called *Zemes māte*, 'mother earth', in Lithuanian *Žemyna*, from *žemė*, 'earth'. Her anthro-pomorphic image is vague; she is the Earth holding the mys-tery of eternal life. She is called by such picturesque names as 'the blossomer', 'the bud raiser'. Her functions are distributed among the separate minor deities of forest, field, stones, water and animals, who in Latvian folklore acquired the names 'mother of forests', 'mother of fields', 'mother of springs',

'mother of domestic animals', etc. Cardinal Oliver Scholasticus, Bishop of Paderborn, in his description of the Holy Land
written about 1220, refers to Baltic heathens as follows: 'They
honour forest nymphs, forest goddesses, mountain spirits, lowlands, waters, field spirits and forest spirits. They expected
divine assistance from virgin forests, wherein they worshipped
springs and trees, mounds and hills, steep stones and mountains slopes—all of which presumably endowed mankind with
strength and power.'[20]

Man is born of the earth; babies emerge from springs, pools,
swamps, trees or hillocks. As recently as the eighteenth century, Lithuanians offered gifts to *Žemyna* upon the birth of a
child. Earth was to be kissed in the morning and in the evening. Offerings to the might of the earth—ale, bread, grains,
herbs, or a sheaf of rye—were interred, laid in front of stones,
attached to trees or thrown into the sea, rivers, lakes and
springs. According to seventeenth-century records, there were
no festivals in villages during which the earth deity, *Žemyna*,
was not venerated.[21]

During the festival in the month of October, next after
Žemyna the Lithuanians venerated the deity of the homestead,
Žemėpatis or *Žemininkas*, who was considered to be a brother of
Žemyna. The deity of the homestead also appears in Lithuanian
as *Dimstipatis* (from *dimstis*, 'homestead'). Latvians have *Mājas
Kungs*, 'the master of homestead'. A separate deity was the lord
of the fields, the Lithuanian *Laukpatis* (from *laukas*, 'field' and
patis, 'lord') or *Lauksargis*, the 'guardian of the fields' (*sargas*,
'the guardian'), and there were deities or spirits of flowers,
foliage, grass and meadows, rye or flax and hemp fields. The
corn spirit hid in the rye or other grain fields and was believed
to be incarnated in the final sheaf to be reaped. The Lithuanians used to make this sheaf of rye into the shape of a woman;
it is still called *rugių boba*, 'the old one of the rye'. She was
brought home, celebrated at the harvest festival, and then kept

in the house until the next year's harvest. The Prussian corn spirit assumed the shape of a cock, called *Kurke* (known as *Curche* in the Latin text of the treaty between the Teutonic Order and the Prussians of 1249).[22] A cock was offered during the harvest festival, and in the fields some ears of corn were left for the corn spirit.

Trees and flowers, groves and forests, stones and hillocks, and waters were endowed with miraculous life-giving forces. They were thought to bring blessings upon human beings by healing diseases, safeguarding them against misfortunes, and assuring health and fertility. All manifestations of the earth's fecundity were lovingly cared for and protected; the written records from the eleventh–fifteenth centuries repeatedly mention a profound respect for groves, trees and springs, and the 'ignorant ones' (i.e. the Christians) were forbidden access to the sacred forests or groves ('sacrosanctos sylvas'). No one was permitted to cut trees in sacred forests, to fish in sacred springs, or to plough in sacred fields, which were referred to variously as *Alka*, *Alkas* or *Elkas*, and were guarded by 'tabu'. The name itself shows that these reservations of virgin nature were untouchable and protected places: the root *alk-*, *elk-*, is related to Gothic *albs*, Old English *ealh*, Old Saxon *alah*, the 'protected', 'invulnerable'. In the holy *Alkas* votive offerings to the gods were made and human cremations took place. The usual animal offerings were boars and pigs, he-goats, sheep, calves, cocks and hens, as testified by the excavations and the historical records. Here too, by decapitation and cremation, the Baltic heathens offered their enemies to the gods.

Since the holy places were imbued with silence, a number of sacred hills and forests in East Prussia and Lithuania carry names having the root *rom-*, *ram-*, which means 'quiet'; one of these is the sacred hill of *Rambynas* on the north bank of the lower Nemunas near Tilžė (Tilsit), mentioned in records ever since the fourteenth century. A stone with a flat surface formerly crowned this hill and votive offerings were placed on it by newly married couples seeking fertility at home and good crops in the field. The water found up on *Rambynas* was eagerly sought after for drinking and washing. Forests and towns called *Romuva*, *Romainiai* and the like have historic tradi‑ tions going back to the ancient sacred places. The fourteenth century records mention a sacred town ('villa') *Romene* in central Lithuania.[23]

Oak, linden, birch, maple, pine and spruce were prominent among miraculous trees. Particularly the old, mighty, twin‑ boled trees were believed to possess strong healing powers. They were untouchable, none dared cut them down. Historic records since the thirteenth century mention 'sacred oaks', con‑ secrated to the god *Perkūnas*, or 'sacred linden trees', consecrated to *Laima*, the goddess of fate, to which offerings were brought. Such trees were surrounded by a ditch or a stone circle. A stick from an ash tree, a twig of juniper, elder, willow, or southern wood (*artemisia*), or any green bough were regarded as effective weapons against the evil spirits.

Forests had their own goddesses and gods. *Medeinė* (the name comes from *medis*, 'tree') was the Lithuanian forest goddess, attested in the thirteenth century records.[24] Seventeenth‑ and eighteenth‑century sources mention a male god of forests, *Giraitis*. In Latvian folklore we encounter a 'forest mother' and a 'forest father', and there was also a 'mother of shrubs'. A peculiar earth deity living under elderberry bushes was *Puš‑ kaitis*, who ruled over good little subterranean manikins called *Barstukai* (or *Parstukai*) and *Kaukai*. If offerings were made to *Puškaitis*, the little men brought plenty of corn and did the household work. During special feasts for Barstukai, tables laden with bread, meat, cheese and butter were left in barns, where the little men used to come at midnight and eat. In return for this generous treatment the farmers were rewarded with bountiful crops.[25]

In songs trees and flowers are not realistically described, but their essential parts are emphasized, the bud and the crown, their vitality and fecundity. 'A green linden has grown, with nine branchlets and a gorgeous toplet.' A tree is usually three, seven, or nine 'storeys' high. It is a living symbol, guarded in folk art by twin figures or heads of male animals—horses, bulls, stags, he-goats, swans—or it is encircled by suns, moons and stars; or else a bird perches on it. Plants in the folk-songs have golden or silver buds, and the bird atop the tree is a cuckoo, the prophet of human fate.

A peculiar cosmogonical tree of the Baltic peoples was the wooden, roofed pole topped with symbols of sky deities—suns, moons, stars—and guarded by stallions and snakes. Right up to the present century, roofed poles as well as crosses with a sun symbol around the cross-arms could be encountered in Lithuania in front of homesteads, in fields, beside sacred springs, or in the forests. They were erected on the occasion of someone's marriage or illness, during epidemics, or for the purpose of ensuring good crops. Though none of these perishable monuments are more than two hundred years old, their presence in pre-Christian times is attested by historic documents describing them as relics of the old religion. Christian bishops instructed the clergy to destroy the poles and crosses before which the peasants made offerings and observed other pagan rites. The Lithuanian roofed poles and crosses managed to escape destruction because the people fixed some of the Christian symbols to them, and gradually they came under protection of the Catholic Church. They are, nevertheless, monuments stemming from the pre-Christian faith, as well as illustrious examples of Lithuanian folk art, their symbolic and decorative elements manifesting direct ties with the art of the Iron Age.[26]

Old legends cluster about huge stones containing holes or 'footprints'. To drill a round hole into a stone was to fecundate

Plate 79

the earth force which resides in the stone. Rain water falling into these holes acquired magic properties. Until quite recently, Baltic peasant women coming home from work would stop by such stones to cure their aches and pains by washing themselves with the water. Stones found in the Baltic lands were often incised with symbols of suns and snakes, much as they were elsewhere in northern and western Europe from the Bronze Age onward. A huge stone in the shape of a woman's torso, known from Lithuania in the nineteenth century, was believed to possess magical qualities that would bestow fecundity on allegedly barren women. From a description given in 1836 we learn that in Lithuania there were stone monuments—usually about 6 feet high, smoothly cut, and surrounded by a ditch—which were dedicated to goddesses who spent their time at the stones spinning the fates of men. In 1605, a Jesuit reported a stone cult in western Lithuania: 'Huge stones, with flat sur⁄faces, were called goddesses. Such stones were covered with straw and venerated as protectors of crops and animals.'[27]

Great numbers of rivers and lakes are called *Šventa, Šventoji, Šventupė, Šventežeris,* in Lithuania, and *Svētā upe, Svētupe, Svētais ezers* in Latvia, the names coming from the words *švent⁄as, švent⁄a* (Lithuanian) and *svet⁄s, svēt⁄a* (Lettish), that which is 'sacred', 'holy'. Also, there are many rivers called *Alkupė, Alkupis,* all of which were sacred and venerated in antiquity, and some of which are still held in esteem. No one dared soil their life⁄giving water, which had purifying, healing and fertilizing properties. If one gave them holy water, flowers, and trees would blossom bountifully. The fields were sprayed with holy water to ensure good crops, the animals were sprinkled with it to keep them healthy. Washing with clear spring water would heal eye and skin diseases. At the begin⁄ning of summer, during the sun festival (the present St John's night), people would go swimming in the holy waters so that they would be healthy and beautiful and so that young people would soon marry. Holy were those springs and streams which flow toward the east, toward the sun.[28]

Water spirits were beautiful women with long breasts, very long blond hair and a fishtail. They were mute. When people happened to see them, they would stare back silently, spread their wet hair and hide their tails. Historic records mention, and folklore has preserved, the names of separate deities of rivers (Lithuanian *Upinis*), of lakes (Lithuanian *Eźerinis*), and of the sea-storm (Lithuanian *Bangpūtys*, the 'god of waves', who sails over the wild sea in a boat which has a golden anchor). The Latvians had *juŗas māte*, 'mother of the sea'. In sixteenth-century descriptions of Prussian gods we find *Autrimpas*, god of the sea and large lakes; *Patrimpas*, god of rivers and springs; and *Bardoyats*, god of ships.[29] There was also a separate deity of the rain: the Lithuanian *Lytuvonis*, known from sixteenth-century sources.[30] The deities of the waters demanded offerings. To the river god *Upinis*, for example, white sucking-pigs were offered lest the water be not clear and transparent.

Fairies, called *laumes*, peculiar naked women with long hair and long breasts, dwelt in forests, near expanses of water and stones. They were constantly mingling with humans and, yearning for motherhood, frequently used to kidnap infants or small children and dress them in most attractive clothing. They could be extremely good-natured as well as extremely short-tempered. They were the irrational women. They could work fast and spin and launder rapidly, but once angered, they would destroy their handiwork in an instant.

A kind of superior goddess, common to all Balts, was *Laima*, the goddess of fate. She dispensed human happiness and unhappiness as well as determining the length of a person's life. She controlled not only human life but also that of plants and other living things. Her name is inseparable from *laimė*, 'happiness'. Fate usually appears in the shape of this one deity, but recalled in stories are three or even seven goddesses of fate,

analogous to the Greek *moirae* and German *Nornen*. In Lithu⁄
anian songs she is sometimes called by a double name *Laima⁄
Dalia*, 'happiness' and 'fate'. The Latvians also had *Dekla*,
who was very sympathetic to human life, took care of small
children, and grieved over the birth of a baby who was
destined to have an unhappy life. *Laima*, although standing
close to the earthly life, is related in her functions to *Dievas*, the
sky god, and to the Sun.[31]

The earth's great impulse for giving birth was matched by
the dynamism of the sky and the male element in nature,
endowed with the life⁄stimulating and evil⁄combating powers.
The animate and dynamic forces of the heavenly bodies—the
sun, moon and stars—and phenomena such as thunder,
lightning, fire and the rainbow; male animals like the stag, bull,
stallion, he⁄goat, ram, cock, swan and other birds; and such
reptiles as snakes and toads were all believed to exercise a great
influence on the development of plants and of animal and
human life. The divine significance of the life⁄ and light⁄
bringing powers inspired the personification of the sun, moon,
morning and evening stars, thunder and bright sky, giving rise
to the images of sky deities. Male animals and birds and reptiles,
because of their sexual nature or their ability to prophesy a
change in the weather and the regular awakening of nature,
became inseparable associates of the sky deities.

The Baltic pantheon of sky gods is very closely related to that
of all other Indo⁄European groups. To it belong *Dievas* (proto⁄
Baltic *Deivas*), the god of the shining sky, related to Old Indic
Dyaus, Greek *Zeus*, Roman *Deus*; the Thunder god, Lithu⁄
anian *Perkūnas*, Latvian *Pērkons*, Prussian *Perkonis*, in name
and function closely associated with the Slavic *Perun*, Hittite
Peruna, Old Indic *Parjānya*, Celtic *Hercynia*, as well as to Scan⁄
dinavian *Thor*, German *Donnar* and Roman *Jupiter* (the oak,
the tree of *Perkūnas*, in Latin is *quercus* which comes from *per⁄
cus*); *Saule*, the Sun, very closely related to Vedic *Surya* and

Savitar, the early Greek *Helios*, and the other Indo-European sun-gods, though the Baltic *Saule* is of a feminine gender; Lithuanian *Mėnuo*, Latvian *Mēness*, the Moon god; Latvian *Auseklis*, Lithuanian *Aušrinė*, the morning star and goddess of the Dawn, related to the Vedic *Ushas*, and its counterpart, the Lithuanian *Vakarinė*, the evening star, both being personifications of the planet Venus. Among the sky gods there was also the divine smith, called simply *Kalvis*, 'smith', or in diminutive form, *Kalvelis* and *Kalvaitis*. Most prominent among the divine animals was the horse, the escort of *Dievas* and *Saule*. In mythological songs, the horse (Lithuanian *žirgas*, Latvian *zirgs*) is so intimately related to *Saule*, the Sun, that sometimes it seems to stand as a symbol for the sun. Next in importance was the he-goat (Lithuanian *ožys*) escort of the Thunder god, a symbol of virile power and a weather-prophesying animal.

Common Indo-European roots of these gods and their associates are incontestable, especially in that the Baltic gods preserved very ancient traits in not loosening their ties with natural phenomena, the sky, the sun, the moon, the stars, the thunder. Except for *Dievas* and *Perkūnas*, the anthropomorphic images of the gods were not very strongly developed.

The name of the god *Dievas* is directly connected with 'the sky'. The Lithuanian *dievas* and Lettish *dievs* still have preserved the meaning 'the sky' as in Sanskrit. The etymology of the god's name is made clear through the Sanskrit verb *dyut*, 'to shine', 'to beam', and the adjective *deiyos*, 'of the sky'. *Dievas* is represented as an extremely handsome man, dressed in a silver gown, a cap, his clothes adorned with pendants, and with a belt and a sword attached. This image undoubtedly goes back to the Late Iron Age, being very much akin to the appearance of a Baltic king. He is inseparable from his horses, one, two, three, five, nine or more, in silver harness, with golden saddle and golden stirrups. His large fenced homestead recalls a castle, having three silver gates and comprising manor, farmhouses and vapour bath, with a garden and forest trees around. It is located beyond the sky; beyond the stone, silver, gold or amber hill. From this hill *Dievas* rides on horseback, or in a chariot or sleigh of gold or copper, holding golden reins ending in golden tassels. He approaches the earth very slowly, extremely carefully, lest he shake off the dew drops and snow‑ball tree blossoms, lest he stop the growth of shoots, lest he hinder the work of sower and ploughman. He raises up the rye, he steps on weed‑grass. In Latvian mythological songs he appears sowing rye or barley from a silver container and, among other things, hunts and brews ale. *Dievas* is the guardian and stimulator of crops. In these functions he is closely related to the Sun, Moon and Venus. He is endowed, too, with the power to control human destiny and the whole order of the world. On his account, the sun and moon and the day are bright. With *Laima*, the goddess of human fate, he determines the life span and the fortune of man. Although *Dievas* possessed higher powers than other gods, he was not considered to be the supreme god and to rule others. In the pantheon of the sky, *Dievas* was friendly and democratic. His homestead and his sons, Latvian *Dieva dēli*, Lithuanian *Dievo sūneliai*, were par‑ticularly closely associated with *Saule*, the Sun, and her daughters, who also had a castle with silver gates beyond the hill in the valley or at the end of the water.[32]

Saule's anthropomorphic image is vague, but more import‑ant is her journey over the stone or silver hill in a chariot with copper wheels drawn by fiery steeds, who are never tired, never sweat and never rest on the way. Toward evening she washes her horses in the sea, after which she sits on top of the hill holding the golden reins, or goes down to the apple orchard, in nine chariots drawn by a hundred steeds. She also sails in a golden boat, or is herself a boat which sinks into the sea. The ball of the setting Sun is picturesquely portrayed as a sinking crown, or a ring, or a red apple falling from the tree into the water. The falling apple makes the Sun cry and the red berries on the hill are her tears. The sun's sphere is also a jug or a ladle, since the light of the sun is conceived as a fluid substance. In the even‚ ing, *Saule's* daughters wash the jug in the sea and disappear into the water. The daughters may have signified the light the sun sheds at dusk and at dawn, and may have been connected with the morning and evening stars. During the midsummer festival on June 24, the rising sun was thought to be adorned with a wreath of braided red‚fern blossoms and she 'danced on the silver hill wearing silver shoes'. In songs, *Saule* is 'rolling', 'swaying', 'hopping'. The Latvian solar songs have the refrain *līgo* (*līgot* means 'to sway) or *rotā* (from *rotāt* 'to roll', 'to hop'). In art the sun is depicted as a ring, a wheel, a circle, a circle with rays, a rosette or a daisy (in Lithuanian called *saulutė*, 'little sun', or *ratilas*, 'wheel'), the flower of the Sun. The dynamic vigour of the sun, the regularity of its daily journey, its influence on verdant life and on human happiness was a great source of inspiration for countless pieces of ancient Baltic poetry and Baltic works of art. Spring and midsummer fes‚ tivals (present Easter and St John's Day) were festivals of joy, of the resurrection of nature, during which sun symbolism played the central role. The farmer's life was regularly patterned by prayers to *Saule* at sunrise and at sunset, for all fieldwork was entirely dependent on the sun's beneficence. Prayers to *Saule* had to be said with one's head uncovered.[33]

Mènuo or *Mēness*, the Moon god, was a very close associate of *Saule's*. Like the periodical appearance of the sun, the moon's disappearance and renewal in the form of a young moon brought well‚being, light and health. It is still believed that flowers must be planted either at new or full moon. Prayers were especially useful to the young moon. The Moon god (of masculine gender) wore a gown of starry night and was drawn by grey horses. Frequently he was at the silver gates of *Saule's* castle, courting her daughters (in Latvian mythology); he even married *Saule* herself, but being unstable, fell in love with *Aušrinė* (Lithuanian, 'morning star'); this angered *Saule*, and the Thunder god *Perkūnas* broke him in two (Lithuanian mythology). He finally married the weaver of the star-canopy, and while counting the stars found that all were there except *Auseklis* (Latvian, 'morning star').[34] The Prussian mythology knows another god of light, who in the records of the sixteenth century appears as *Swayxtix* or *Suaixtis*, which in present Lithuanian will be *Žvaigždys*, from *žvaigždė*, 'the star'.[35]

Kalvaitis, the heavenly smith, hammers at the end of the waters or in the sky a ring or a crown for the Dawn and a silver belt and golden stirrups for *Dievas'* sons. Every morning he hammers a new sun ('a ring', 'a crown'), When he hammers in the clouds, silver pieces fall down upon the waters. In Baltic mythology, *Kalvaitis* or *Kalvelis* is a figure similar to *Hephaistos* in the Greek, *Volundr*, *Wêlant* in the Scandinavian, and *Ilmarinen* in the Finnish mythologies.[36] His hammer was gigantic; Jerome of Prague, a missionary in Lithuania, noted in 1431 that Lithuanians honoured not only the sun, but also the iron hammer of rare size, by whose aid the sun was said to have been freed from imprisonment.[37]

Perkūnas, the Thunder god, ruler of the air, is a vigorous man with a copper beard holding an axe in one hand. He traverses the sky with great noise in a fiery two-wheeled chariot, drawn by a he-goat. When thunder is heard, a proverb says, 'God is coming—the wheels are striking fire.' His castle is on the high hill (in the sky). *Perkūnas* is very just, but restless and impatient; he is the great enemy of evil spirits, devils, and unjust or evil men. He seeks out the devil and smites him with lightning. He throws his axe at evil people or tosses lightning bolts at their homes. He does not tolerate liars, thieves, or selfish and vain persons. The tree or stone that has been struck by lightning gives protection from evil spirits and cures maladies, especially the toothache, fever and fright. The stone axes dropped by *Perkūnas* possess a peculiar power of fecundity. They are still called 'the bullets of Perkūnas'. (Stone or bronze axes, 'battle⁄axes', were frequently ornamented in prehistory by zig⁄zags, the symbol of lightning, and by circles, the sun symbols. Miniature axes of bronze were worn as amulets up to the last epoch of the prehistoric era.) *Perkūnas* also purifies the Earth by exorcising evil winter spirits. The first thunder in the spring moves the earth to action; the grass begins to grow rapidly, grains take root, trees turn green.[38]

In addition to horse and he⁄goat, the bull, the stag and the swan were symbols of virile, life⁄bringing power, but the harm⁄less green snake, the Lithuanian *Žaltys*, played a prominent part in the sexual sphere. It was a blessing to have a *Žaltys* in one's home, under the bed or in some corner, or even in a place of honour at the table. He was thought to bring happiness and prosperity, to ensure fertility of the soil and an increase in the family. Encountering a snake meant either marriage or birth. This mystically endowed creature is known to Lithuanian folklore as 'the sentinel of the gods'. *Žaltys* is loved by the Sun, and to kill it is a crime. 'The sight of a dead *Žaltys* causes the Sun to cry,' says the proverb. The very name for 'snake' in Lithuanian, *gyvatė*, shows association with *gyvybė*, *gyvata*, 'life', 'viability'. Another mysterious, wealth⁄bringing crea⁄ture, known from the early records as well as folklore, is *Aitvaras*. He sometimes has the head of a *Žaltys* and a long tail which emits light as he flies through the air. Sometimes he is a golden cock.[39]

The Balts were great venerators of fire. *Lituani sacrum colebat ignem eumque perpetuum appellabat.*[40] Fire was sacred and eternal. Tribes had official sanctuaries on high hills and on river banks where fire was kept, guarded by priests,[41] and in each house was the sacred hearth in which fire was never extinguished. Only once a year, on the eve of the midsummer festival, was it symbolically extinguished, and then kindled again. Fire was a goddess, who required offerings. She was fed and carefully guarded and covered over at night by the mother of the family. The Latvians call this flame 'mother of the fire', *uguns māte*; in Lithuanian it is *Gabija* (from the verb *gaubti*, 'to cover'); in Prussian *Panike*, 'the little fire'. Fire was the purifying element and the symbol of happiness. Legends relate that fire was transferred to earth by *Perkūnas* in a storm, or that it was brought by a bird, usually a swallow, who burned itself while bringing it.[42]

This is not the place to present in more detail all the 'incredibilia' seen by Christian missionaries in the Baltic lands, or to portray the folk religion which still lives in folklore in surprisingly pure elements going back to earliest antiquity; but from this short survey I hope the reader will have gained a general impression of their character. The Baltic religion has faithfully preserved the basic elements of ancient history, which relate it closely to the early recorded religions of the Indo-European peoples, particularly to that of the Indo-Iranians, as seen in the cult of the dead, the burial rituals, the cures of the sky and air deity, as well as the sun, snake, horse, water and fire cults; at the same time, it has remained true to the peasant's perception of the real world and to his rich natural environment, sustaining his profound veneration for the living land—forests, trees and flowers—and his intimate relationship with animals and birds. In speaking of the legacy of Baltic prehistory, we mean above all the ancient religion, which is incarnate in the cosmic and lyrical conception of the world of present-day Lithuanians and Latvians, and is an unceasing inspiration to their poets, painters and musicians.

Notes

[1] Tacitus (90), XLV.

[2] Orosius (87).

[3] Adam of Bremen (82), 199.

[4] G. Gerullis, *Die altpreussischen Ortsnamen*, Berlin-Leipzig, 1922; A Salys, 'Prūsai', *Lietuvių Enciklopedija*, XXIV (Boston), pp. 146-57.

[5] L. Kilian, 'Baltische Ortsnamen westlich der Weichsel', *Altpreussen*, IV, 3 (1939), pp. 67-68; H. Krahe, 'Baltische Ortsnamen westlich der Weichsel?', *Altpreussen*, 1943: 1, pp. 11-12.

[6] V. N. Toporov, 'Dve zametki iz oblasti baltijskoj tomonimii', *Rakstu krājums veltījums audd. J. Endzelīnam*, Riga, 1959, pp. 251-66.

[7] A. Kamiński, *Jaćwież, Terytorium, ludność, stosunki gospodarcze i społeczne* (*Jatvingia. Territory, population, economy and social structure*), Łódź, Societas Scientiarum Lodziensis, sectio II, No. 14, 1953.

[8] *Polnoe sobranie russkikh letopisej*, I, 1, Petersburg, 1908.

[9] Būga (1).

[10] Vasmer (6).

[11] The etymology of *Volga* as proposed by the linguist Trubetzkoy—in his lectures at the University of Vienna—was as follows: in primitive eastern Slavic, unrounded front vowels changed into rounded back vowels before a tauto-syllabic *l*, so that *jilga* must have changed to *julga*; the initial *j* was lost before rounded vowels in eastern Slavic, and the initial *u* acquired an obligatory prothetic *v*. Thus the form *vulga* arose, and short *u* changed in the 12th-13th centuries into *o*. So through a long series of changes *Jilga* became *Volga*. (Oral information by Roman Jakobson.)

[12] Thomsen (4).

[13] B. A. Serebrennikov, 'O nekotorykh sledakh izcheznuvshego indoevro-pejskogo jazyka v centre Evropejskoj chasti SSSR, blizkogo k baltijskim jazykam' (Traces of an extinct Indo-European language related to the Baltic in the centre of the European part of the USSR), *Lietuvių Mokslų Akademijos Darbai* (*Trudy AN Litovskoj SSR*), serija A, vyp. 1 (2), Vilnius, 1957.

[14] M. Vasmer, 'Die alten Bevölkerungsverhältnisse Russlands im Lichte der Sprachforschung', *Vorträge und Schriften der Preussischen Akademie*, No. 5, 1941.

CHAPTER II

¹ Mark (3), pp. 15, 22; M. V. Vitov, K. Ju. Mark and N. N. Chebok/
sarov, 'Etnicheskaja antropologija vostochnoj pribaltiki' (Physical anthropology
of the East Baltic area), *Trudy Pribaltijskoj Objedinennoj Kompleksnoj Ekspeditsii*,
2, ed. by H. A. Moora, B. A. Rybakov, S. P. Tolstov and N. N. Chebok/
sarov. Moscow, 1959.

² Gimbutas (23), pp. 140–76 (including bibliography); Kilian (29);
A. Äyräpää, 'Über Streitaxtkulturen in Russland', *ESA*, VIII (1933).

³ J. Żurek, 'Osada neolityczna w Rzucewie w pow. wejherowskim' (Le
village néolithique de Rzucewo, distr. de Wejherowo), *Fontes Archaeologici
Posnanienses*, vol. IV, 1954.

⁴ B. Ehrlich (20), 'Succase, eine steinzeitliche Siedlung der Schnurker/
amiker', *Elbinger Jahrbuch*, Bd. XII/XIII (1936).

⁵ I. Heydeck, 'Zwei Steinzeitskelette (liegende Hocker) in dem Prussia/
Museum', *Prussia*, 18, pp. 46–60.

CHAPTER III

¹ *Odyssey*, XVIII, 294–5; Spekke (47), p. 18.

² O. Helm, 'Mitteilungen über Bernstein', *Schriften der Naturforschenden
Gesellschaft Danzig*, VI, 2 (1885); L. Jonas, 'Bernsteinperlen aus einem myken/
ischen Kuppelgrabe und die Identifizierung ihrer Substanz mit Succinit',
Physisch-Oekonom. Gesellschaft, Konigsberg i. Pr., 49, pp. 35 ff. (1908).

³ A. Bezzenberger and E. F. Peiser, 'Die Bronzefigur von Schernen', *Prussia*,
22 (1909), pp. 424–44; J. Wiesner, 'Die Bronzefigur von Schernen, Kr.
Memel', *Altpreussen*, 1941: 2, pp. 19–22.

⁴ W. Gaerte, 'Die ostbaltische Erdhacke mit Schlangenkopf und ihre
europäischen Beziehungen', *Prussia*, 30–31 (1933), pp. 241–54.

⁵ A. Gardawski, J. Dąbrowski and R. Miklaszewska, 'Kraal z wczesnej
epoki brązu w Biskupinie pow. Żnin' (with résumé in Russian and English),
WA, 24 (1957), pp. 189–208.

⁶ J. Kostrzewski, 'Od mezolitu do okresu Wędrówek ludów', *Prehistoria
Ziem Polskich: Encyklopedia Polska*, IV, 1, 197–200.

⁷ Gardawski (22).

⁸ Gimbutas (25).

⁹ Engel (21); E. Šturms, *Regionale Unterschiede in den Beziehungen zwischen
dem Ostbaltikum und Skandinavien in der Bronzezeit*, Contributions of Baltic
University of Pinneberg, No. 53 (1947).

¹⁰ Engel (21); Šturms (31).

[11] Engel (21); W. Gaerte, 'Das Hügelgrab von Workeim, Kreis Heilsberg', *Prussia*, 27, pp. 279–81.

[12] Vankina (32), pp. 66–68; Moora (14), pp. 47–49.

[13] Reports in: *Prussia*, 15 (1890), pp. 125–7, 139–53; 23 (1914), pp. 85–159, 459–68; 29 (1931), pp. 47 ff. Also Gaerte (10); Engel (21).

[14] G. Bujack, 'Das Hügelgräberfeld vorchristlicher Zeit in dem Drusker Forst', *Prussia*, 15, pp. 139–53.

[15] H. J. Eggers, 'Hausurnen in Pommern', *Mitteilungen aus dem vorg. Seminar der Universität Greifswald* (1940); J. Antoniewicz, 'The origin and chronology of the Pomeranian hut urns', *PA*, VII, 1 (1946), pp. 93–98; F. Oelmann, 'Pfahlhausurnen', *Germania*, 37 (1959), pp. 205–23.

[16] W. La Baume and H. Seger, 'Gesichtsurnenkultur', *Reallexicon*, Bd. IV, 1926.

[17] W. La Baume, 'Die Anfangsstufe der ostgermanischen Gesichtsurnen-kultur', *Prussia*, 32 (1939), pp. 215–74 (German scholars in the twenties and during the Nazi period held the 'Face-urn culture' to be 'East Germanic').

[18] W. La Baume, 'Der Moorleichenfund von Dröbnitz, Kr. Osterode, Ostpreussen', *Altpreussen*, V, 2, 1940.

[19] K. O. Rossius, 'Die sogenannten Pfahlbauten Ostpreussens', *PZ*, Bd. 24, 1933.

[20] Antoniewicz (19); also J. Dąbrowski in *WA*, 26 (1960), pp. 226–72.

[21] Heym (26).

[22] E. Petersen, 'Die frühgermanische Kultur in Ostdeutschland und Polen', *Vorgeschichtliche Forschungen*, Bd. II, 2, 1929.

[23] So far no monographs exist on Pot-covered urn culture. Reports are in: *Światowit*, 13 (1929), pp. 95–148; 15 (1938), pp. 3113–332; *WA*, 7 (1922), pp. 98–106; 9 (1924/5), pp. 246–60; 12 (1933), pp. 43–100; 20 (1954), pp. 134–71; 23 (1956), pp. 297–308; *PA*, 8 (1948), pp. 55–59; *Biblioteka Prehistoryczna*, 1 (1930), pp. 241–65; *Fontes Archaeologici Posnanienses*, 5 (1955), pp. 49–59; 7 (1957), pp. 144–53; 8–9 (1958), pp. 150–78; *M St* 1 (1956), pp. 135–47.

[24] T. Sulimirski, 'Die Kisten- und die Glockenbecherkulturen in Südost-polen' (Kultura grobów skrzynkowych i podkloszowych w Malopolsce Wschodniej), *Światowit*, tom XV, 1932/33. Yu.V. Kukharenko, 'Pam'jatniki zheleznogo veka na territorii Poles'ja' (Iron Age sites in Polesie), *Arkheologija SSSR, Svod Arkheologicheskikh Istochnikov*, vyp. D1–29, Moscow, 1961.

[25] J. Eggers, 'Die Mittel-Latènezeit in Mittelpommern', *Baltische Studien*, 43 (1955), pp. 13–16; R. Wolągiewicz, 'Uwagi do zagadnienia stosunków kultur-owych w okresie lateńskim na Pomorzu Zachodnim', *Materialy Zachodnio-Pomorskie*, 5 (1959), pp. 121–43.

26 W. Antoniewicz, 'Zagadnienie Gotów i Gepidów na ziemiach polskich w okresie rzymskim' (A contribution to the question of Goths and Gepids in Poland in the Roman period), *Przegląd Zachodni*, No. 5/7, 1951. Z. Kmieciński, 'Wedrówka gotów', *Z Otchłani Wieków*, 25 (1959), pp. 8–16.
27 Reports in: *Prussia*, 22 (1909), pp. 376–453; *Altpreussen*, 1940: 3.

CHAPTER IV

1 Bader (33).
2 Merpert (36).
3 Kulikauskas, Kulikauskienė and Tautavičius (12), pp. 113–28; P. F. Tarasenko, 'Gorodishcha Litvy' (Hill-forts of Lithuania), *KSIIMK*, vyp. 42, 1952. A. G. Mitrofanov, 'K istorii naselenija srednej Belorusii v epokhu rannego zheleza', Avtoreferat, Leningrad University, 1955.
4 O. N. Mel'nikovskaja, 'Drevnejshie gorodishcha juzhnoj Belorussii' (The earliest hill-forts in southern Byelo-Russia), *KSIIMK*, vyp. 70, 1957. The Milograd group was revealed in the last decade, but its sites already total 140; Yu. V. Kukharenko, 'Pam'jatniki zheleznogo veka na territorii Poles'ja' (Iron Age sites in Polesie), *Arkheologija SSSR, Svod Arkheologicheskikh Istoch-nikov*, vyp. D1–29, Moscow, 1961.
5 S. S. Berezanskaja, 'Novye pam'jatniki epokhi bronzy i rannego zheleza v bassejne Sejma' (New Bronze and early Iron Age finds in the basin of R. Sejm), *KSIIMK*, 67, 1957; S. S. Berezanskaja, 'Pam'jatki periodu serednoj bronzy na Desni ta Sejmi' (Middle Bronze Age finds in the basins of the Desna and Sejm rivers), *Arkheologija*, tom XI, 1957; Ilinskaja (34); Levenok (35); M. V. Voevodskij, 'Gorodishcha verkhnej Desny' (Hill-forts in the basin of Upper Desna), *KSIIMK*, vyp. 24, 1949; Nikol'skaja (37), pp. 14–36.
6 Herodotus (85).
7 A. A. Shakhmatov, *Russkaja istoricheskaja dialektologija*, St Petersburg, 1910/11, mimeographed, 144 pp.
8 Pliny (88), IV, 12, 88; Ammianus Marcellinus, XXII, 8, 40.
9 Nikol'skaja (37), pp. 32–35.
10 J. V. Kukharenko, 'K voprosu proiskhozhdenii zarubinetskoj kul'tury', *SA*, 1960-1, pp. 289–300; P. N. Tret'jakov (ed.), 'Pam'jatniki zarubineckoj kul'tury', *MIA*, 70 (1959).

CHAPTER V

[1] Engel (43); Gimbutienė (11); Moora (45), II, pp. 21–56.

[2] J. Antoniewicz, 'Odkrycie grobu rolnika jaćwieckiego z narzędziami produkcji z okresu rzymskiego' (Discovery of the Jatwingian farmer's grave from the Roman period), *Rocznik Białostocki*, III, 1962.

[3] L. Krzywicki, 'Grodziska górno-litewskie' (The earthworks of Upper Lithuania), *Pamiętnik Fizyograficzny*, vol. XXIV, Warsaw, 1917.

[4] Stankevich (48), pp. 89–90.

[5] Stankevich (48), pp. 90–91.

[6] Pliny (88), pp. 397–404.

[7] Tacitus (90), XLV, pp. 340–3.

[8] Pliny (88), VI, chapter 11.

[9] Pliny (88), VI, chapter 12.

[10] Sculptures reproduced in Spekke (47).

[11] M. Cary, *The Geographic Background of Greek and Roman History*, Oxford 1949 (map of amber routes in Noricum, Pannonia and Dacia).

[12] R. E. M. Wheeler, *Rome beyond the Imperial Frontiers*, London, 1954, p. 14.

[13] Bolin (41).

[14] Moora (45), II, pp. 578 ff.

[15] A. Brinkmann, 'Funde von Terra sigillata in Ostpreussen', *Prussia*, 21, pp. 71–77; W. Gaerte, 'Römische Importwaren aus ostpreussischen Gräbern', *Prussia*, 28, pp. 372–4; V. Ģinters, 'Romas imports Latvijā', *Senatne un Māksla*, 1936: 2, pp. 47–61; Moora (45), II, pp. 586–92; J. Puzinas, 'Die Flügelfibel in Litauen', *Festschrift Wahle*, Heidelberg, 1950, pp. 189–99.

[16] Moora (45), II, pp. 586–89.

[17] Moora (45), II; basic source of information on the forms, origin, and chronology of ornaments and other objects of the period from 0 to A.D. 500.

[18] H. Moora, 'Zur Frage nach der Herkunft des ostbaltischen emailverzierten Schmucks', *SMYA*, 40, pp. 75–90; P. Kulikauskas, 'Emaliuotieji dirbiniai Lietuvoje' (Enamelled ornaments in Lithuania), *Vytauto D. Kultūros Muziejaus Metraštis*, I, Kaunas, 1941, pp. 43 ff.

[19] J. Baye, 'Les bronzes émaillés de Mostchina gouvernement de Kaluga (Russie)', Paris, 1891; Boulitchov (42); A. A. Spicyn, 'Drevnosti basejnov riek Oki i Kamy', *Materialy op Arkheologii Rossii*, 25, St Petersburg, 1901; A. M. Tallgren, 'Enameled ornaments in the valley of the Desna', *ESA*, II (1937), pp. 147–56.

[20] Distribution of the Baltic enamelled ornaments in eastern Europe: Moora (15), p. 27.

[21] J. Antoniewicz, M. Kaczyński and J. Okulicz, 'Wyniki badań prze-prowadzonych w 1956 roku na cmentarzysku kurhanowym w miejsc. Szwaj-caria, pow. Suwałki' (Results of the 1956 excavations of barrows in Szwajcaria, district of Suwałki), *WA*, tom. XXV, 1-2, 1958; J. Antoniewicz, 'Badania kurhanów z okresu rzymskiego dokonane w 1957 r. w miejscowości Szwaj-caria pow. Suwałki' (The 1957 excavations of the barrows in Szwajcaria, district of Suwałki, dating from the Roman period), *WA*, vol. XXVII, 1, 1961; J. Antoniewicz, 'Several imported objects from the Roman period found in the Sudovian tribal territory', *Światowit*, vol. XXIV, 1962.

[22] J. Okulicz, *WA*, XXVII, 1, 1961, pp. 82-90; J. Jaskanis, *WA*, XXV, 1-2, 1958, pp. 75-98, and *Rocznik Białostocki*, I, Białystok, 1961, pp. 131-91; D. and J. Jaskanis, *WA*, XXVII, 1, 1961, pp. 27-49; W. Ziemlińska-Odojowa, *Rocznik Białostocki*, I, Białystok, 1961, pp. 193-221; T. Żurowski, *WA*, XXVII, 1, 1961, pp. 58-82.

[23] Kulikauskas, Kulikauskienė and Tautavičius (12), pp. 300-2.

CHAPTER VI

[1] S. Nosek, 'Zabytki brązowe z Niewiadomej w powiecie sokołowskim na Podlasiu', *MA*, II, 1960, pp. 333-47; also: cemetery of Virtki in Polesie north of the River Pripet, dating from the 6th-7th centuries and having very close analogies in the eastern Lithuanian cemeteries.

[2] Puzinas (16), pp. 120-3.

[3] Kulikauskas, Kulikauskienė and Tautavičius (12), p. 273.

[4] Ginters (51); Balodis (54), pp. 37 ff.; Balodis (8), pp. 84, 89.

[5] Orosius (87), pp. 53, 54.

[6] Rimbert (89), p. 232.

[7] B. Ehrlich, 'Elbing, Benkenstein und Meislatein. Ein neuer Beitrag zur Trusoforschung', *Mannus Z.*, Bd 24, 1932; Ebert (50).

[8] O. Kleemann, 'Die vorgeschichtlichen Funde bei Cranz und die Siedlung von Wiskiauten', *Prussia*, Bd XXXIII, 1939.

[9] E. Petersen, 'Fragen der germanischen Besiedlung im Raume zwischen Oder und Weichsel in der Völkerwanderungszeit', *Mannus*, XXVIII, pp. 19-65; also Engel-La Baume, 1937, pp. 175 ff.

[10] Engel-La Baume (9), p. 166.

[11] The letter of Theodoricus was written by his secretary Roman F. Magnus Aurelius Cassiodorus and is found in his work *Variae*, Book V, published in 537: Hodgins (86), p. 546.

[12] Ju. V. Kukharenko, 'Pam'jatniki prazhskogo tipa na territorii pridne-prov'ja', *Slavia antiqua*, VII (1960), pp. 111-24; I. I. Ljapushkin, 'Mesto

romensko-borshevskikh pam'jatnikov sredi slavjanskikh drevnostej', *Vestnik Leningradskogo Universiteta*, 20, p. 58.

[13] Barrows and hill-forts of Svinukhovo, Ogubskoe and Vorotyncevo on the River Oka and its tributary the River Zusha: Nikol'skaja (37), pp. 37–57.

[14] V. V. Sedov, 'Krivichi', *SA*, 1960: 1, pp. 46–63.

[15] K. Būga, *Lietuvių kalbos žodynas* (The dictionary of the Lithuanian language). Introduction. Kaunas, 1924.

[16] Sedov, *ibid.*, pp. 56–58.

[17] *Ibid.*, p. 59.

[18] *Ibid.*, pp. 47–48, 60; barrows from the excavations by A. A. Spicyn at the end of the 19th century.

[19] Cemeteries and hill-forts on the small rivers Snopot and Serena: Boulit-chov (42), pp. 39–42, 58–61, 63, 67–78.

[20] G. Vernadsky, *The Origins of Russia*, Oxford, 1959, p. 266.

[21] Nerman (53).

[22] Rimbert (89), pp. 232 ff.

CHAPTER VII

[1] Snorri Sturluson, *Heimskringla*, III, 116, ed. W. Morris, E. Magnusson, London, 1893–1905.

[2] Snorre Sturleson, Ynglinga-saga, ed. F. Jónsson, *Samfund til Udgivelse of gammel nordisk Literatur*, No. 23, Kopenhagen, 1893–1900, I, 73 ff.

[3] Heinrici Chronicon Livoniae, *Scriptores Rerum Germanicarum Monumentis Germaniae Historicis*, ed. L. Arbusow and A. Bauer, Hanover, 1955.

[4] B. Nerman (64), pp. 165–80; Nerman, 'Einige auf Gotland gefundene ostbaltische Gegenstände der jüngeren Eisenzeit', *Verhandlungen*, vol. 30, 2, 1938.

[5] Eddison (84), pp. 87–90.

[6] Kulikauskas, Kulikauskienė and Tautavičius (12), p. 514; also Nagevičius (63); Hoffmann (57).

[7] Johansen (58), pp. 263–4.

[8] Puzinas (16), pp. 115–20, pls. 47–51; Kulikauskienė (60).

[9] Kulikauskas, Kulikauskienė and Tautavičius (12), pp. 413, 510; Balodis (8), pp. 160, 173.

[10] J. Antoniewicz, 'Kontakty Słowiansko-pruskie', *WA*, XXII, 3–4, pp. 233–77.

[11] Balodis (8), pp. 160–76.

[12] Adam of Bremen (82), p. 199.

[13] Dusburg (83).

[14] Puzinas (16), pp. 120–5.

[15] Ģinters (51); Moora (14), pp. 144–5.
[16] Brivkalne (55).
[17] Ģinters (56).
[18] Balodis (54); Moora (14), pp. 155 ff.; Shnore (66); Shnore (65).
[19] Kulikauskas, Kulikauskienė and Tautavičius (12), pp. 369–76.
[20] Volynian (or Hypatios) chronicle of 1201–92: 'Lietopis' po ipatskomu spisku', Petersburg, 1871, II, p. 187.
[21] A. Salys, 'Prūsai', *Lietuvių Enciklopedija*, 24, 1961.

CHAPTER VIII

[1] Mannhardt (75), pp. 122, 130.
[2] Tret'jakov (81).
[3] Adam of Bremen (82), p. 197.
[4] *Sudauerbüchlein*: Mannhardt (75), p. 244.
[5] Mannhardt (75), p. 88.
[6] *Historia Poloniae*, by Długosz (1413–18): Mannhardt (75), p. 142.
[7] Hermann de Wartberge, *Chronicum Livoniae*, Leipzig, 1863. Mannhardt (75), p. 124.
[8] Mannhardt (75), p. 141.
[9] *Ibid.*, p. 175.
[10] Šturms (79).
[11] Orosius (87), pp. 54–56.
[12] Gimbutas (23), p. 82; R. Feustel, 'Bronzezeitliche Hügelgräberkultur im Gebiet von Schwarza, Südthüringen', *Veröffentlichungen des Museums für Ur- und Frühgeschichte Thüringens*, 1.
[13] Heinrici Chronicon Livoniae, 1225/27, *Scriptores Rerum Germanicarum Monumentis Germaniae Historicis*, ed. L. Arbusow and A. Bauer, Hanover, 1955; Mannhardt (75), p. 33.
[14] Mannhardt (75), p. 85.
[15] J. Kleijntjenss, *Fontes historiae Latviae Societatis Jesu*, I, Riga, 1940, p. 479.
[16] Mannhardt (75), p. 120.
[17] *Ibid.*, p. 30.
[18] Straubergs (77), p. 132.
[19] Straubergs (77).
[20] Mannhardt (75), p. 17.
[21] Praetorius' Deliciae Prussicae *c.* 1684: Mannhardt (75), pp. 570 ff.
[22] Mannhardt (75), p. 41.
[23] Peter Dusburg in 1326 (83); Mannhardt (75), p. 103.
[24] By Volynian Chronicle in 1252: Mannhardt (75), p. 51.

[25] M. Stryjkowski, 'Kronika polska, litewska', 1582: Mannhardt (75), p. 332.

[26] Gimbutas (73).

[27] *Ibid.*, pp. 94, 95.

[28] Balys (68), pp. 32–42.

[29] Mannhardt (75), pp. 228 ff.

[30] *Ibid.*, p. 331.

[31] Biezais (71); Balys (68), pp. 76–89.

[32] Biezais (72).

[33] Mannhardt (74); Gimbutas (73).

[34] *Ibid.*; Balys (68), pp. 42–51.

[35] Mannhardt (75), pp. 570 ff.

[36] Mannhardt (74).

[37] Mannhardt (75), p. 135.

[38] Balys (68), pp. 7–15; Gimbutas (73), pp. 47, 102; E. Zicāns, *Der altlettische Gott Pērkons*, Riga, 1938.

[39] Gimbutas (73), pp. 25–36; Balys (68), pp. 65–76.

[40] Eneo Silvio, beginning of the 15th century: Mannhardt (75), p. 135.

[41] J. Długosz, 1455–80: Mannhardt (75), p. 139.

[42] Balys (68), pp. 25–32.

The numbers in brackets refer to the bibliography where full details of the publications will be found.

Bibliography

Abbreviations

AN   *Akademija Nauk SSSR,* Moscow.

Congressus   *Congressus Secundus Archaeologorum Balticorum Rigae 1930.*

ESA   *Eurasia Septentrionalis Antiqua. Zeitschrift für Erforschung der osteuropäischen und nord-asiatischen Archäologie und Ethnographie.* Helsinki.

KSIA   *Kratkie Soobschenija Instituta Arkheologii,* Kiiv (Kiev).

KSIIMK   *Kratkie Soobshchenija o Dokladakh i Polevykh Issledovanijakh Instituta Istorii Material'noj Kul'tury,* Moscow.

MA   *Materiały Archeologiczne,* Kraków (Cracow) *Zakład Archeologii Polski* of the Polish Academy of Sciences.

MIA   *Materialy i Issledovanija po Arkheologii SSSR,* Moscow.

MSt   *Materiały Starożytne,* Warsaw, *Państwowe Muzeum Archeologiczne.*

PA   *Przegląd Archeologiczny,* Poznań, *Muzeum Archeologiczne.*

Prussia   *Sitzungsberichte der Altertumsgesellschaft Prussia, Königsberg in Preussen.*

PZ   *Prähistorische Zeitschrift,* Berlin, *Akademie der Wissenschaften.*

Reallexicon	*Reallexicon der Vorgeschichte.* Ed. by Max Ebert, Berlin, 1924–32.
SA	*Sovetskaja Arkheologija,* Moscow, *Akademija Nauk SSSR.*
Trudy POKE	*Trudy Pribaltijskoj Ob'edinennoj Kompleksnoj Ekspedicii,* ed. by H. A. Moora, B. A. Rybakov, S. P. Tolstov and N. N. Chebok-sarov, Moscow, *Akademija Nauk SSSR* (including Academies of Sciences of Estonia, Latvia, Lithuania and Byelo-Russia).
Verhandlungen	*Verhandlungen der Gelehrten Estnischen Gesell-schaft. Øpetatud Eesti Seltsi Toimetused, Tartu.*
WA	*Wiadomości Archeologiczne. Bulletin Archéolo-gique Polonais,* Warsaw.

Baltic tribes (linguistic, physical anthropological data)

1 BŪGA, K., 'Die Vorgeschichte der aistischen (baltischen) Stämme im Lichte der Ortsnamenforschung', *Streitberg-Festgabe,* Leipzig, 1924.

2 Letten, die, *Die Letten. Aufsätze über Geschichte, Sprache und Kultur der alten Letten.* (Articles by: Adamovičs, Fr.; Adamovičs, L.; Balodis, F.; Blese, E.; Endzelins, J.; Plākis, J.; Spekke, A.; Straubergs, K.; Schmidt, P.; Tentelis, A.; Wipper, R.). Riga, 1930.

3 MARK, K., 'Zur Entstehung der gegenwärtigen Rassentypen im Ost-baltikum', *SMYA,* vol. 59, 4 (1958).

4 THOMSEN, V., *Beröringer mellem de finske og de baltiske (litauisk-lettiske) sprog,* Kopenhagen, Vidensk. Selsk. Skrifter, 6. Histori.-philos. I, 1, 1890.

5 TOPOROV, V. N. and TRUBACHEV, O. N., *Lingvisticheskij analiz gidronimov verkhnego podneprov'ja.* (Linguistic analysis of river names of the upper Dnieper basin.) *AN,* Moscow, 1962.

6 VASMER, M., 'Über die Ostgrenze der baltischen Stämme. Beiträge zur historischen Völkerkunde Osteuropas', *Sitzungsberichte der Preuss. Akad. Berlin. Phil.-Hist. Klasse*, 1932.

Archaeology, general (all periods)

7 BALODIS, F. (ed.), *Latvijas archaiologija* (*Archaeology of Latvia*; articles by Tallgren, A.M.; Šturms, E.; Moora, H.; Schmiedehelme, M.; Balodis, F.; Kundziņš, P.; Šmits, P.); Riga, 1926.

8 BALODIS, F., *Det äldsta Lettland* (Swedish translation by W. W. Freij), Uppsala, 1940.

9 ENGEL, C. and LA BAUME, W., *Kulturen und Völker der Frühzeit im Preussenlande*, Königsberg Pr., 1937.

10 GAERTE, W., *Urgeschichte von Ostpreussen*, Königsberg Pr., 1929.

11 GIMBUTIENĖ, ALSEIKAITĖ, M., *Die Bestattung in Litauen in der vorgeschichtlichen Zeit*, Tübingen, 1946.

12 KULIKAUSKAS, P., KULIKAUSKIENĖ, R. and TAUTAVIČIUS, A., *Lietuvos archeologijos bruožai* (*An outline of the archaeology in Lithuania*), Lietuvos TSR Mokslų Akademija, Istorijos Institutas, Vilnius, 1961.

13 KULIKAUSKIENĖ, R. and RIMANTIENĖ, R., 'Senovės lietuvių papuošalai. Ukrashenija drevnikh litovcev (Ornaments of ancient Lithuanians)', I. *Lietuvių Liaudies Menas, Vilnius*, 1958 (601 plates).

14 MOORA, H., *Pirmatnējā kopienas iekārta un agrā feodalā sabiedrība Latvijas PSR teritorijā* (*Clan and early feudal society in the Latvian SSR*), Riga, 1952.

15 MOORA, H., 'O drevnej territorii rasselenija baltijskikh plemen' (A contribution to the question of the ancient Baltic territory)' *SA*, 1958: 2.

16 PUZINAS, J., 'Naujausių proistorinių tyrinėjimų duomenys (Results of archaeological excavations in Lithuania from 1918 to 1938)', *Senovė*, IV, 1938.

17 TARAKANOVA, S. A. and TERENT'EVA, L. N. (ed.), 'Voprosy etnicheskoj istorii narodov pribaltiki (Problems of the ethnogenesis of the East Baltic peoples)', *Trudy POKE*, I, 1959.

18 TAUTAVIČIUS, A. Z., 'Vostochnolitovskie kurgany (East Lithuanian barrows)', *Trudy POKE*, I, 1959.

Chalcolithic, Bronze and Early Iron Ages in the East Baltic area

19 ANTONIEWICZ, J., 'Zagadnienie wczesnożelaznych osiedli obronnych na wschód od dolnej Wisły i w dorzeczu rzeki Pregoły (The Early Iron Age defensive settlements to the east of the lower Vistula and in the Pregoła basin)', *WA*, tom XX, 4 (1954).

20 EHRLICH, B., 'Ein jungsteinzeitliches Dorf der Schnurkeramiker in Succase, Kr. Elbing', *Altschlesien*, Bd V (1934).

21 ENGEL, C., *Vorgeschichte der altpreussischen Stämme. Untersuchungen über Siedlungsstetigkeit und Kulturgruppen im vorgeschichtlichen Ostpreussen*, Königsberg Pr., 1935.

22 GARDAWSKI, A., 'Plemiona kultury trzcinieckiej w Polsce (The Trzciniec people in Poland)', *M St*, tom V, 1959.

23 GIMBUTAS, M., *The Prehistory of Eastern Europe. Part I. Mesolithic, Neolithic, and Copper Age cultures in Russia and the Baltic area*, Peabody Museum, Harvard University, Bulletin No. 20, 1956.

24 GIMBUTAS, M., 'A Survey of the Bronze Age culture in the south-eastern Baltic Area', *Światowit*, tom XXIII, 1960.

25 GIMBUTAS, M., *Bronze Age cultures in eastern and central Europe* (in print).

26 HEYM, W., 'Eine baltische Siedlung der frühen Eisenzeit am Kleinen See bei Kl. Stärkenau (Westpreussen)', *Mannus Z.*, 29, 1937.

27 JANITS, L. Ju., 'K voprosu ob etnicheskoj pridnadlezhnosti neoliticheskogo naselenija territorii Estonskoj SSR (A contribution to the question of the ethnogenesis of the neolithic people in Estonia)', *Voprosy etnicheskoj istorii Estonskogo naroda*, 1956.

28 KERSTEN, K., 'Die Funde der älteren Bronzezeit in Pommern', 7. Bei' *heft zum Atlas der Urgeschichte*, Hamburgisches Museum für Völker' kunde und Vorgegeschichte, 1958.

29 KILIAN, L., *Haffküstenkultur und Ursprung der Balten*, Bonn, 1955.

30 ŠTURMS, E., 'Die bronzezeitlichen Funde in Lettland', *Congressus*, Riga, 1931.

31 ŠTURMS, E., 'Die ältere Bronzezeit im Ostbaltikum', *Vorgeschichtliche Forschungen*, Heft 10, 1936.

32 VANKINA, L. V., 'Arkheologicheskie pam'jatniki I tysjacheletija do nashej ery na territorii Latvijskoj SSR (Archaeological finds of the first millennium B.C. in Latvia)', *KSIIMK*, vyp. 42, 1952.

Bronze and Early Iron Age in Byelo-Russia and central Russia

33 BADER, O. N., 'Balanovskaja kul'tura', *SA*, 1961: 4.

34 ILINSKAJA, V. A., 'Bondarikhinskaja kul'tura bronzovogo veka (The Bondarikha culture of the Bronze Age)', *SA*, 1960: 1.

35 LEVENOK, V. P., 'Gorodishcha Jukhnovskoj kul'tury (Hill-forts of the Jukhnovo culture)', *KSIA*, vyp. 7, 1957.

36 MERPERT, N. JA. (ed.), 'Abashevskaja kul'tura v srednem Povolzh'e (The Abashevo culture in the Middle Volga basin)', *MIA*, No. 97, 1961.

37 NIKOL'SKAJA, T. N., 'Kul'tura plemen' bassejna verkhnej Oki v I tys' jacheletii n.e. (The culture of the tribes in the basin of Upper Oka in the 1st millennium A.D.)', *MIA*, No. 72, 1959.

Golden Age, A.D. c. 100–400

38 ANTONIEWICZ, J., 'The mysterious Sudovian people', *Archaeology*, II, 3, 1958.

39 ANTONIEWICZ, J., *The Sudovians*, Białystok, 1962.

40 BEZZENBERGER, A., 'Litauische Gräberfelder. Das Gräberfeld bei Schernen, Kr. Memel', *Prussia*, Bd. 17, 1892.

41 BOLIN, S., 'Die Funde römischer und byzantinischer Münzen in Ost‑preussen', *Prussia*, Bd. 26, 1926.

42 BOULITCHOV, N. DE, *Kourgans et gorodietz. Fouillés de la Russie Centrale. Recherches archéologique sur la ligne de partage des eaux de la Volga et du Dnieper*, Moscow, 1900.

43 ENGEL, C., 'Die kaiserzeitlichen Kulturgruppen zwischen Weichsel und finnischem Meerbusen und ihr Verhältnis zueinander', *Prussia*, Bd. 30, Teil I, 1933.

44 GUREVICH, F. D., 'Das Samland als altbaltisches Kulturzentrum und seine vorgeschichtliche Beziehungen zu den Nachbargebieten', *Alt‑preussische Beiträge*, Königsberg Pr., 1933.

45 MOORA, H., 'Die Eisenzeit in Lettland', *Verhandlungen*, Teil I, 1929; Teil II, 1938.

46 MOORA, H., 'Arkheologicheskie pam'jatniki I–IV vv. v Pribaltike (Archaeological finds of the 1st–4th centuries A.D. in the East Baltic area)', *KSIIMK*, vyp, 53, 1954.

47 SPEKKE, A., *The ancient amber routes and the geographical discovery of the eastern Baltic*, Stockholm, 1957.

48 STANKEVICH, J. and V., 'K istorii naselenija verkhnego podvin'ja I i nachale II tysjacheletija n.e. (A contribution to the history of settlement in the basin of Upper Dvina in the 1st and beginning of the 2nd mil‑lennia A.D.)', *MIA*, No. 76, 1960.

Middle Iron Age, Slavic Expansion, Wars with the Scandinavians, 400 – end of the ninth century A.D.

49 ÅBERG, N., *Ostpreussen in der Völkerwanderungszeit*, Uppsala, 1919.

50 EBERT, M., *Truso*, Königsberg Pr., 1926.

51 ĢINTERS, V., 'Daugmales pilskalna 1935 gada izrakumi (1935 excava/ tions of the hill-fort of Daugmale)', *Senatne un Māksla*, Riga, 1936: 1; 'Daugmales pilskalna 1936 gada izrakumi (1936 excavations of the hill-fort of Daugmale)', *Senatne un Māksla*, Riga, 1936: 4.

52 LINCKE, B., *Eine baltische Halsringform der Völkerwanderungszeit*, Berlin, 1937.

53 NERMAN, B., *Grobin-Seeburg Ausgrabungen und Funde*, Kungl. Vitterhets Historie och Antikvitets Akademien, Stockholm, 1958.

Balts before the Dawn of History, end of the ninth century – A.D. 1200

54 BALODIS, F., *Jersika un tai 1939 gadā izdarītie izrakumi (Jersika, excavations of 1939)*, Riga, 1940.

55 BRIVKALNE, E. P., 'Gorodishche Tervete i ego istoricheskoe znachenie (The earthwork of Tervete and its historical significance)', *Trudy POKE*, I, 1959.

56 ĢINTERS, V., 'Senā Mežotne. 1939 g. izrakumi (Ancient Mežotne. Excavations of 1939)', *Senatne un Māksla*, 1938–42; 'Senā Mežotne. 1938. g. izrakumi (Ancient Mežotne Excavations of 1938)', *Senatne un Māksla*, 1939.

57 HOFFMANN, J., *Die spätheidnische Kultur des Memellandes*, Königsberg Pr., 1941.

58 JOHANSEN, P., 'Kurlands Bewohner zu Anfang der historischen Zeit', *Baltische Lande*, Bd I, 1939.

59 KULIKAUSKIENĖ, R., 'Pogrebal'nye pam'jatniki Litvy konca I—
nachala II tys'jacheletii nashej ery (The cemeteries of Lithuania dating
from the end of the 1st and beginning of the 2nd millennia A.D.)',
KSIIMK, vyp. 42, 1952.

60 KULIKAUSKIENĖ, R., 'Progrebenija s koniami u drevnikh litovcev
(Burials with horses of ancient Lithuanians)', *SA*, tom 16, 1953.

61 LA BAUME, W., 'Ein spätpreussisches Reitergrab mit Helm und ver-
zierten Lanzen aus Ekritten, Kr. Samland', *Altpreussen*, IV, 4, 1940.

62 LA BAUME, W., 'Zur Technik der Verzierung ostpreussischer Waffen',
Altpreussen, VI, 2, 1941.

63 NAGEVIČIUS, V., 'Mūsų pajūrio medžiaginė kultūra (The material
culture along the Baltic coast in Lithuania)', *Senovė*, I, Kaunas,
1935.

64 NERMAN, B., *Die Verbindungen zwischen Skandinavien und dem Ostbaltikum
in der jüngeren Eisenzeit*, Stockholm, 1929.

65 SHNORE, E., 'Gorodishcha drevnikh Latgalov (Earthworks of the
ancient Lettigallians)', *Trudy POKE*, I, 1959.

66 SHNORE, E., 'Dignājas pilskalns (The hill-fort of Dignāja)', *Senatne un
Māksla*, 1939: 4,

67 SPICYN, A. A., *Ljucinskij mogil'nik*, St Petersburg, 1893.

Religion

68 BALYS, J., *Lietuvių tautosakos skaitymai. Lesebuch der litauischen Volkskunde*,
I–II, Tübingen, 1948.

69 BALYS, J., 'Lithuanian mythology', *The Standard Dictionary of Folklore,
Mythology and Legend*, ed. M. Leach, II, New York, 1950.

70 BIEZAIS, H., *Die Religionsquellen der baltischen Völker und die Ergebnisse der
bisherigen Forschungen*, Uppsala, 1954.

71 BIEZAIS, H., *Die Hauptgöttinnen der alten Letten*, Uppsala, 1955.

72 BIEZAIS, H., *Die Gottesgestalt der lettischen Volksreligion*, Stockholm⸝ Göteborg⸝Uppsala (Almquist⸝Wiksell), 1961.

73 GIMBUTAS, M., 'Ancient Symbolism in Lithuanian Folk Art', *Ameri⸝ can Folklore Society, Memoir Series*, vol. 49, Philadelphia, 1958.

74 Mannhardt, W., 'Die Lettischen Sonnenmythen', *Zeitschrift für Ethno⸝ logie*, Bd 7, 1875.

75 Mannhardt, W., 'Letto⸝preussische Götterlehre', *Lettisch⸝Literarische Gesellschaft*, Bd 21, Riga, 1936.

76 STRAUBERGS, K., 'Latvju mītologija. Lettische Mythologie', *Latviešu Konversācijas vardnīca*, Riga, 1934.

77 STRAUBERGS, K., 'Lettisk folkro om de döda', *Nordiska Museets Hand⸝ lingar*, 32, Stockholm, 1949.

78 STRAUBERGS, K., 'Zur Jenseitstopographie', *ARV (Journal of Scandi⸝ navian Folklore)*, vol. 13, 1957.

79 ŠTURMS, E., 'Baltische Alkhügel', *Conventus primus historicorum Balti⸝ corum Rigae*, 1938.

80 TÖPPEN, M., 'Geschichte des Heidenthums in Preussen. Die letzten Spuren des Heidenthums in Preussen', *Neue Preuss. Prov.⸝Blätter*, I, II, 1846.

81 TRET'JAKOV, P. N., 'Gorodishcha—svjatilishcha levoberezhnoj Smo⸝ lenshchiny (Hill⸝fort sanctuaries in the area of Smolensk, west of the Upper Dnieper)', *SA*, 1958: 4.

Historic Records

82 ADAM OF BREMEN, *History of the Archbishops of Hamburg⸝Bremen*. Trans⸝ lated by Francis J. Tschan, New York, 1959.

83 DUSBURG (PETRI DE DUSBURG), *Chronicon Prussiae*, ed. Chr. Hart⸝ knoch, Jena, 1879.

84 EDDISON, E. R., *Egil's saga*, Cambridge, 1930.

85   *Herodotus*, translated by J. E. Powell, vol. I, 1949.

86   HODGINS, T., *The letters of Cassiodorus*, London, 1886.

87   *Orosius*, King Alfred's Anglo-Saxon version of the compendious history of the world, London, 1959.

88   *Pliny, The National History of Pliny*, Book IV, Bohn's Library.

89   *Rimbert:* 'Vita sancti Anscharii per s. Rembertum', *Scriptores Rerum Svevicarum*, vol. II, Uppsala, 1828.

90   *Tacitus, Tacitus' Germania*, Everyman's Library.

Sources of Illustrations

FIGURES. *Fig. 4*, after Mark (3). *Fig. 5*, pots from the villages of Succase (*a, b*), Kuršių Neringa (*c, d*), and Wiek–Luisenthal (*e*). Reproduced from Kilian (29). *Fig. 6*, reproduced from Kilian (29). *Fig. 7*, barrow from Kaup, excavated in 1893 by Heydeck. Reproduced from Kilian (29). *Fig. 9*, hoe from Lapmiežciems near Riga, reproduced from Moora (14). *Fig. 12*, after Šturms (31). *Figs. 13, 14*, from A. Bezzenberger, *Analysen vorgeschichtlicher Bronzen Ostpreussens*, 1904. *Figs. 15, 16*, from J. Puzinas, *Ankstyvojo geležies amžiaus kapas Kurmaičiuose, Vytauto D. Metraštis*, I, 1941. *Fig. 17*, La Baume, *Archiv für Anthropologie*, 23. *Fig. 18*, Face–urns: *a*, from Kl. Borkow, in Prähistorische Staatssammlung, Berlin; *b*, Oliwa near Danzig (Gdańsk), Prehistoric Museum, Danzig; *c*, Samland, formerly in Prussia Museum, Königsberg; *a* and *b*, drawings made after La Baume– Seger, 'Gesichsturnenkultur', *Reallexicon*, IV, 1926; *c*, after Engel (21). *Fig. 19*, necklace from Merowin near Poznań. Drawing after Engel–La Baume (9). *Fig. 21*, from the cemetery of Kehrwalde, eastern Pomerania, drawing after La Baume, 'Bildliche Darstellungen', *Ipek*, 3, 1928. *Fig. 22*, after La Baume, *Altpreussen*, V, 2. *Fig. 23*, drawing after Heym (26). *Fig. 25*, Łochyńsko, Pomerania. Reproduced from Ossowski, *Prusy Królewskie*, 1888. *Fig. 26, a*, Pomerania; *b*, Piotrkosice near Milicz. Drawing after J. Kostrzewski, *Związki Śląska*, 1961. *Fig. 27*, Grünwalde, distr. of Eylau, former E. Prussia (present Zielenica near Górowo Iławeckie). Drawing after Gaerte (10). *Fig. 28*, urns from: *a*, Grünwalde; *b–d*, Bärwalde near Fischhausen; *e, f*, Preussisch–Mark, Mohrungen– Morąg, n. Masuria. After Engel (21). *Fig. 29*, urns from: *a, c*, Craam; *b*, Tikrenen (Tikrėnai), near Fischhausen (Primorsk), Samland. Draw– ings after Bezzenberger, *Analysen*, 1904. *Fig. 30*, Balanovo pot reproduced from O. N. Bader, *Kulturen der Bronzezeit*, 1958. *Fig. 31*, Bronze Age pots of 'Studenok' type. Drawings after D. Ja. Telegin, 'Oskolskaja ekspedi– cija', *KSIA*, vyp. 8, 1959; 'Bondarikha' pots from the site on R. Oskol, tributary of R. Donets, after Ilinskaja (34) and 'Jukhnovo' pots from the hill–forts in the R. Desna basin, after Levenok (35). *Figs. 32–35*, after Nikol'skaja (37) (*Fig. 35*, objects from the hill–forts of Svinukhovo on R. Ugra and Nadezhda at the confluence of R. Oka with R. Orlik).

Fig. 37, excavations by Heydeck and nineteenth-century drawing after *Prussia,* XXII. *Fig. 38,* by courtesy of J. Antoniewicz, Warsaw. *Fig. 39,* reproduced from Moora (14). *Fig. 40,* reproduction based on: *a,* finds from the cemeteries of Paviekiai and Sargėnai, central Lithuania; *b,* grave finds in the cemetery of Sargėnai, suburb of Kaunas; *c* (upper), finds from the cemetery of Kurmaičiai near Kretinga. Istorinis Muziejus, Kaunas; *c* (lower), woollen cap decorated with convex round bronze plates and double-spiral pendants from the cemetery of Šernai near Klaipėda, western Lithuania. Prussia Museum, Königsberg. *Figs. 41, 42, 44, 45,* redrawn from Kulikauskienė and Rimantienė (13). *Fig. 43, a,* drawing after Gaerte (10); *Fig. 43, b,* drawing after the photograph in Istorinis Muziejus, Kaunas. *Fig. 46,* Cemetery of Moythienen, east Masuria (ancient Sudovia), after E. Hollack and F. E. Peiser, *Das Gräberfeld von Moythienen,* Königsberg, 1904. *Figs. 47, 48,* after Åberg (49). *Figs. 49, 51, 52, 54,* Vēstures Muzejs, Riga, after Ebert, *Führer durch die Sammlung, Dommuseum,* Riga, 1914. *Fig. 53,* Istorinis Muziejus, Kaunas, author's drawings after Nagevičius (63). *Fig. 55,* after Moora (14). *Fig. 56,* after Balodis (54). *Fig. 58,* after Tret'jakov (81). The maps (Figs. 1–4, 8, 10, 11, 24, 36, 50, 57) were drawn by H. A. Shelley.

PLATES. Original photographs for the plates were supplied by the Kansalismuseo (National Museum) in Helsinki: *2, 3;* Istorinis Muziejus in Kaunas (Historical Museum, which, in independent Lithuania, was called 'The Cultural Museum of Vytautas the Great'): *4–7, 17, 18, 19a, 21–25, 41, 45, 47–50, 55, 57, 58, 60–62, 66, 67, 70–78;* Lietuvos TSR Mokslų Akademijos Istorijos-Etnografijos Muziejus (History-Ethno-graphy Museum of the Academy of Sciences of the Lithuanian SSR, Vilnius): *19b, 20, 46, 52–54, 56, 59, 63;* Latvijas TSR Valsts Vēstures Muzejs, Riga (State Historical Museum of the Latvian SSR, Riga) by courtesy of V. Ģinters, Stockholm: *51, 64, 65;* Muzeum Archeologiczne in Poznań: *10, 12, 14, 15;* Muzeum Archeologiczne in Warsaw: *26–31, 44.*
Plate *1,* reproduced from T. Dobrzeniecki, *Drzwi Gnieznienskie,* Cracow, 1953; *11, 13,* from La Baume and Seger, 'Gesichtsurnenkultur', *Reallexicon,* IV; *16,* from La Baume, 'Der Moorleichenfund', *Altpreussen,* V, 2 (1940); *32–40,* from Kulikauskienė and Rimantienė (13); *42, 43,* from Boulichov (42); *68, 69,* from La Baume, 'Zur Technik der Ver-zierung ostpreussischen Waffen', *Altpreussen,* 1941.

THE PLATES

1

2

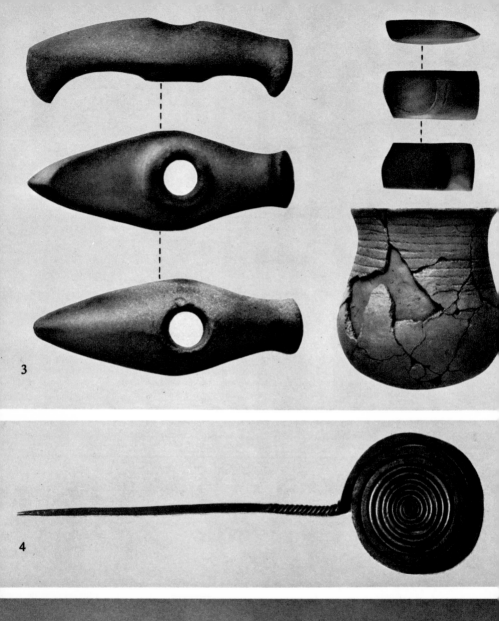

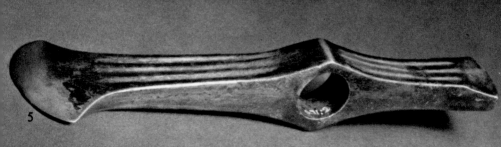

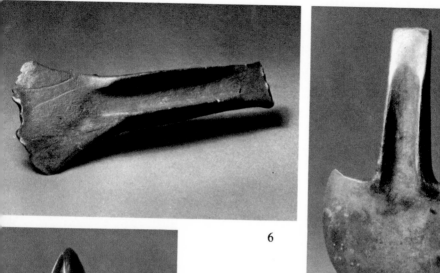

6

8　　　　　7

9

10

11

12

13

14

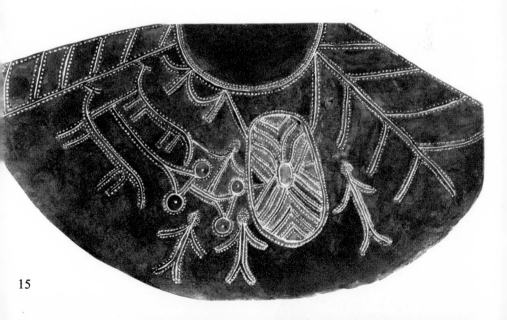

15

17

18

a

b

19

20

21

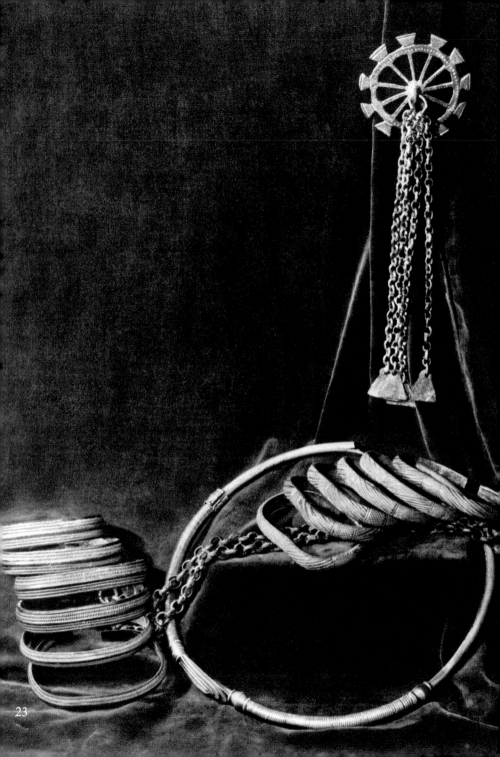

25

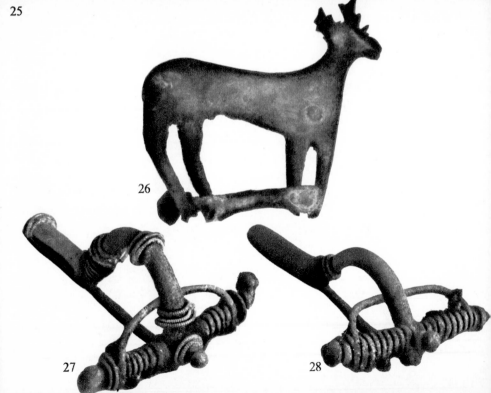

26

27　　　　　　　　　　28

29

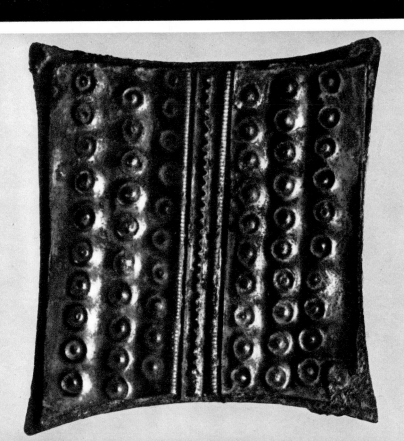

30

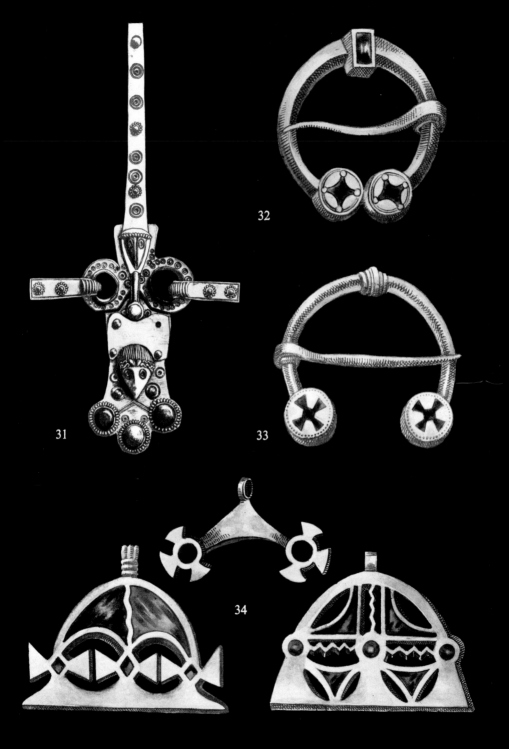

31

32

33

34

35

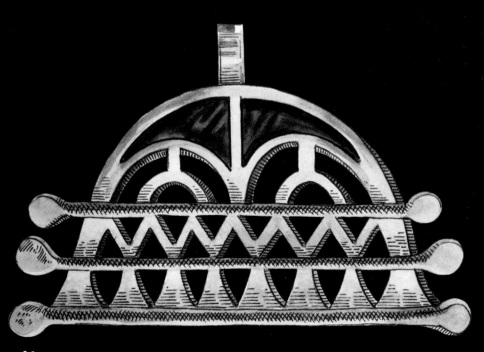

36

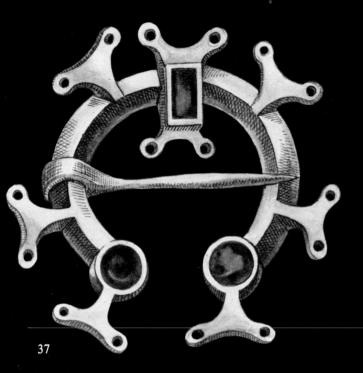

37

38

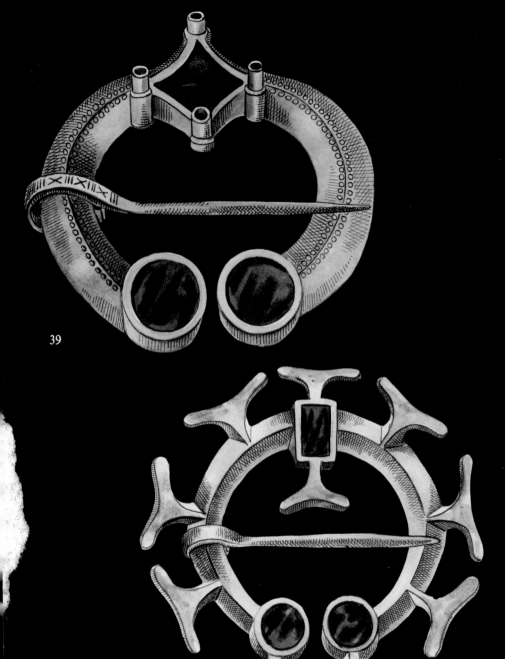

39

40

41

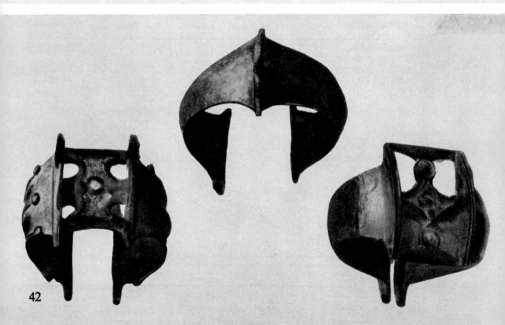

42

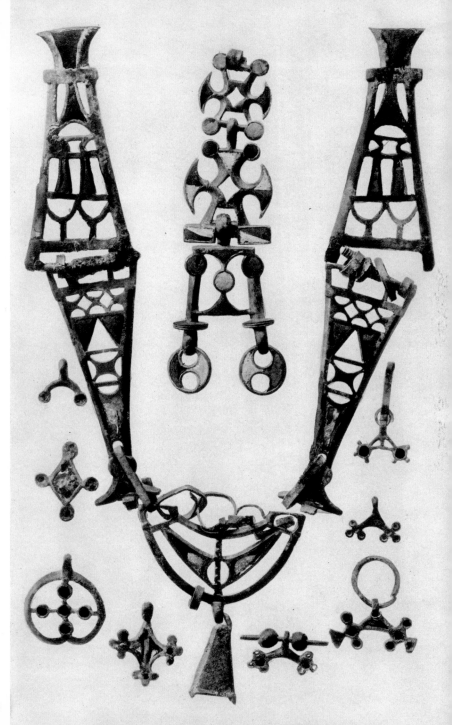

44

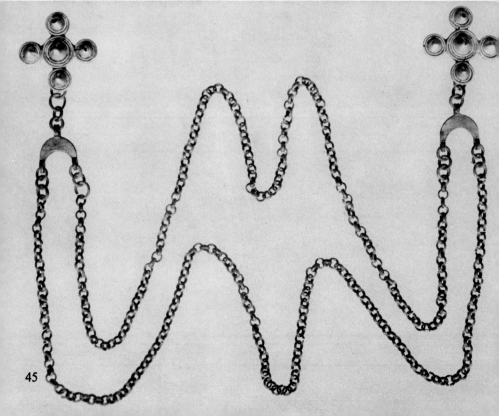

45

47

48

49

50

51

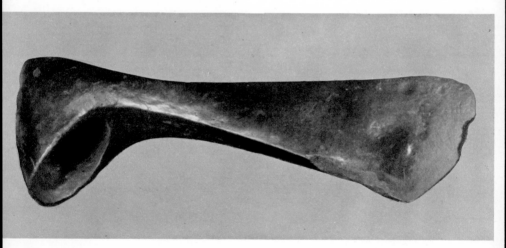

52

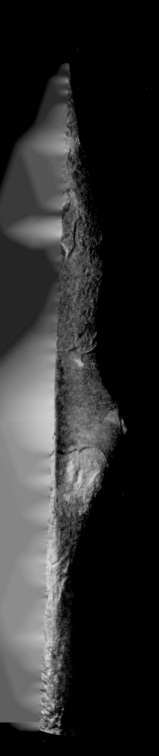

54

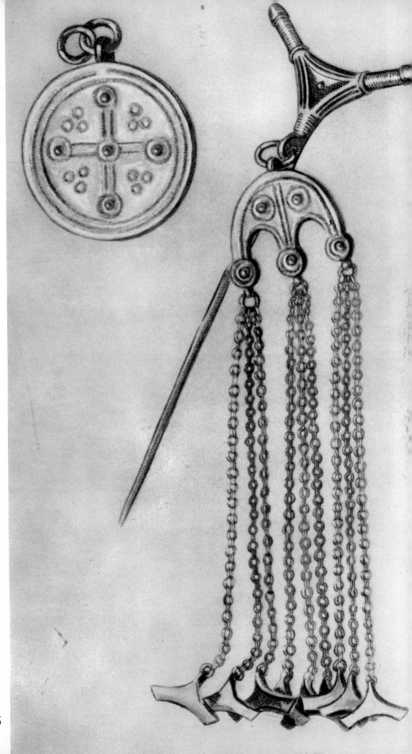

60

61

62

63

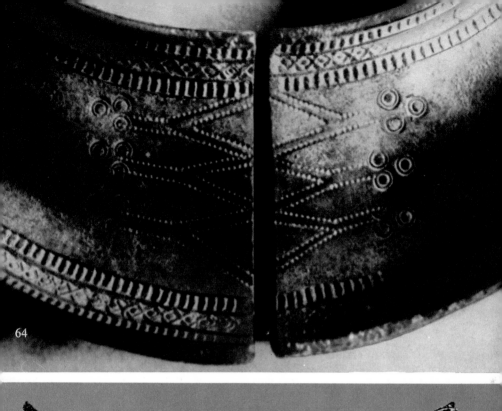

64

5

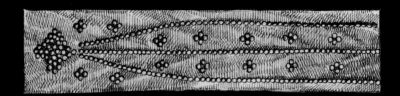

a

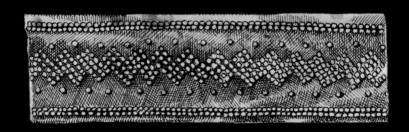

b

c

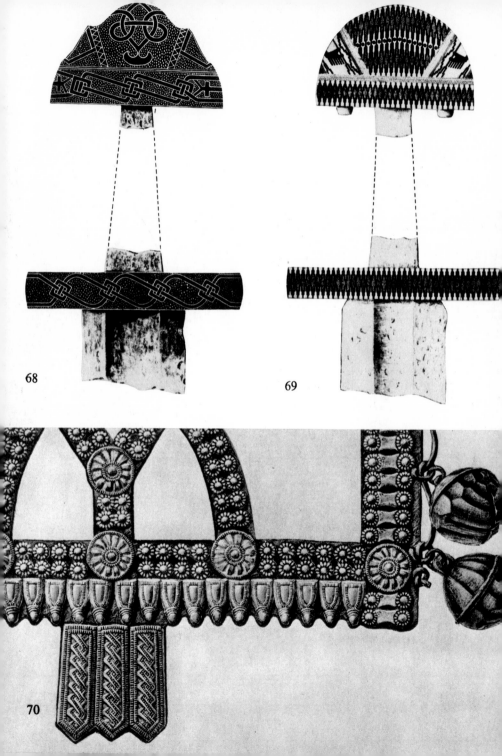

68

69

70

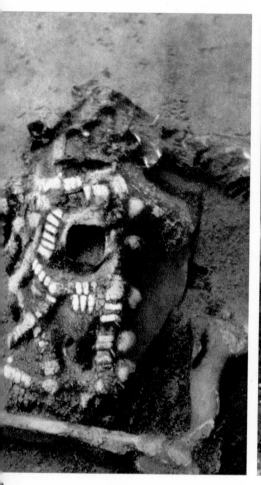

72

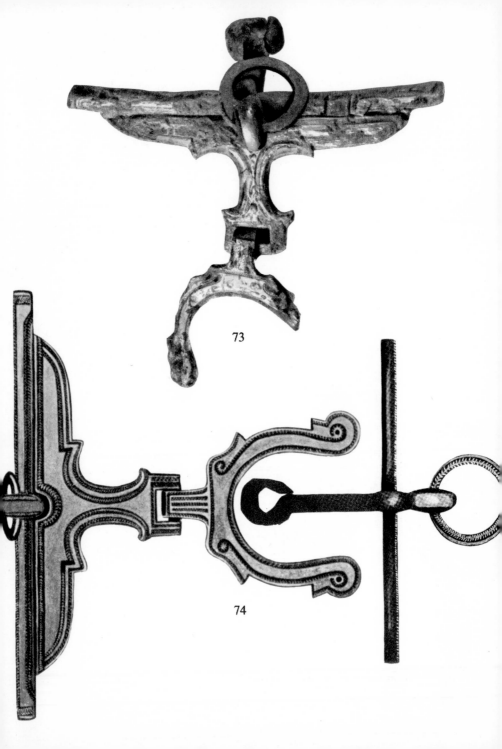

73

74

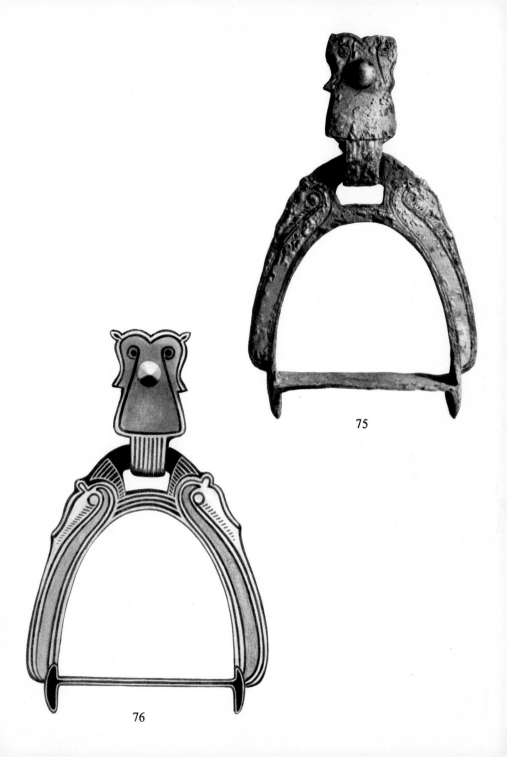

75

76

77

78

79

Notes on the Plates

1 Ancient Prussians (right) equipped with shields, spears, and swords meet the first missionary, Bishop Adalbert in 997. Bas-relief on bronze door of the cathedral of Gniezno, twelfth century.

2 Corded and pinched pottery from south-western Finland, *c.* 2000 B.C. Grave at Pozvoon maalaiskunta. Kansallismuseo, Helsinki.

3 Grave goods of the Corded or Battle-Axe culture: stone boat-axe (three views), stone celt (three views) and corded pot. Cemetery of Lempääla, Aimalankangas, south-western Finland. Kansallismuseo, Helsinki.

4, 5 Bronze pin and axe. Classical Baltic Bronze Age, *c.* thirteenth century B.C. Bog find from Rešketa-Virvyčia, district of Telsiai, Lithuania. Pin 18 cm. long, axe 14·5 cm. long. Istorinis Muziejus, Kaunas.

6 Bronze flanged axe, *c.* thirteenth century B.C. Streménai, central Lithuania. 12·2 cm. long. Istorinis Muziejus, Kaunas.

7 Bronze axe with a semicircular edge, *c.* twelfth–eleventh centuries B.C. Lauménai, district of Šiauliai. 13·7 cm. long. Istorinis Muziejus, Kaunas.

8 Late Bronze Age spearhead from Alytus, southern Lithuania. 13·9 cm. long. Istorinis Muziejus, Kaunas.

9 Late Bronze Age socketed axe. Žygaičiai near Tauragé, Lithuania. 21·3 cm. long. Istorinis Muziejus, Kaunas.

10 Urn adorned with a necklace in relief. Fifth century B.C. Ciążen near Słupca, N. Poland. Muzeum Archeologiczne in Poznań.

11 Face-urn with three pairs of amber bead ear-rings. Fifth century B.C, Vistula mouth area. Archaeological Museum, Danzig (Gdańsk).

12 Face on an urn from Rzadkowo near Chodzież, N. Poland. Fifth century B.C. Muzeum Archeologiczne in Poznań.

13 Urn with engraved horse and stela with a sun symbol at the top. Fifth century B.C. Starogard, lower Vistula area. Archaeological Museum. Danzig (Gdańsk).

14, 15 Urn from Grabowo near Starogard, west of the lower Vistula. 15, Symbolic scene on the urn (detail). Fifth century B.C. Muzeum Archeologiczne in Poznań.

16 Sheepskin coat (two sides), found in Dröbnitz bog near Ostróda (Osterode), Masuria, *c.* fifth century B.C. Formerly in Prussia Museum, Königsberg.

17 Hill-fort dating from the first centuries A.D. Paukščiai near Jieznas, southern Lithuania.

18 Man's grave goods: iron socketed axe, scythe, two spearheads, miniature pot, bracelet, and a Roman coin in a small birch-bark box (within the bracelet), *c.* A.D. 300. Rūdaičiai near Kretinga, western Lithuania. Inset, Roman coins from the same cemetery. Istorinis Muziejus, Kaunas.

19 *a.* Bronze bead necklace from Akmena near Kelmė, central Lithuania. Second or third century A.D. Istorinis Muziejus Kaunas; *b.* Necklace made of bronze spirals and solar pendants from eastern Lithuania. Third or fourth century A.D. Istorijos-etnografijos Muziejus, Vilnius.

20 Fretworked belt separator composed of two rows of stylized human figures and two birds above. Bronze, coated with silver plate. Fourth century A.D. Stragna near Priekulė. Istorijos-etnografijos Muziejus, Vilnius.

21 Fretworked fibula. Bronze, originally coated with silver. 5 cm. wide. Fourth century A.D. Istorinis Muziejus, Kaunas.

22 Woman's grave goods from *c.* A.D. 300: gold-plated silver fibula, bronze 'step' fibulae, a bronze pin, bronze chains with fretworked chain-holders, and a neck-ring with conical ends. Noruišiai near Kelmė, western Lithuania. Istorinis Muziejus, Kaunas.

23 Silver fibula with pendants, bronze bracelets, silver neck-ring with spoon-shaped end and a chain of bronze. Woman's grave goods from a double grave of the fourth century A.D. Upytė, district of Panevėžys, northern Lithuania. Istorinis Muziejus, Kaunas.

24 Woman's grave goods from the double grave (plate 25) of Veršvai, fourth century A.D.; neck-rings, bracelets, glass-bead necklace, chest ornaments with chains and pendants attached, and a Roman bronze vase. Istorinis Muziejus, Kaunas.

25 A double grave (husband and wife?). The man is equipped with an iron axe and a bronze pin; the woman, with an enormous quantity of orna-ments and a Roman bronze vase (plate 24). Fourth century A.D. Veršvai, a suburb of Kaunas. Istorinis Muziejus, Kaunas.

26 Elk in silver-plated bronze, found among the grave goods of a chieftain's burial (barrow 2) of the fourth century A.D. at Szwajcaria near Suwałki (Suvalkai). Muzeum Archeologiczne, Warsaw.

27, 28 Silver-plated bronze fibulae from the chieftain's grave at Szwajcaria (see note to Plate 26).

29 Gold-plated plaques from the chieftain's grave at Szwajcaria (see note to Plate 26).

30 Silver-plated plaque from the chieftain's grave at Szwajcaria (see note to Plate 26).

31 Details of horse's head-gear from the chieftain's grave at Szwajcaria (see note to Plate 26). 5 cm. broad.

32 Bronze fibula with incrustation of green (top) and red enamel (ends). Second century A.D. Sargėnai, suburb of Kaunas. Istorinis Muziejus, Kaunas.

33 Bronze fibula decorated with red enamel inlay (cross pattern on circular ends). Second century A.D. Istorinis Muziejus, Kaunas.

34 Pendants decorated with red and green enamel inlay. End of third–fourth centuries A.D. Mėžionys near Švenčionys, eastern Lithuania.

35, 36 Bronze pendants incrusted with red and green enamel over the upper part. 10·6 cm. long. End of fourth–beginning of fifth century A.D. Dusetos, eastern Lithuania. Istorinis Muziejus, Kaunas.

37, 38 Fibulae with red enamel inlay. 37, Žadavainiai. 10·5 cm. wide. Fifth century A.D.; 38, Velikuškės. 9·1 cm. wide. Fourth to fifth century A.D. Near Dusetos, E. Lithuania. Istorinis Muziejus, Kaunas.

39, 40 Fibulae with enamel inlay (39, square incrusted with green; the rest with red). Fifth century A.D. 39, Voropniškiai at Nemenčinė near Vilnius; 40, Rakėnai near Dūkštas, eastern Lithuania. Istorinis Muziejus, Kaunas.

41 Bronze bracelet decorated with red enamel inlay (black stripes in net pattern) and iron ribs. Second or beginning of third century A.D. Paulaičiai near Priekulė, district of Klaipėda, western Lithuania. Istorinis Muziejus, Kaunas. 7·8 cm. wide.

42 Bronze bracelets with red, green and orange enamel inlay. Fourth century A.D. Moshchiny, central Russia. Gos. Istoricheskij Muzej, Moscow.

43 Enamelled ornaments, pendants and attachments to drinking horns (dark shades represent either red, light-green or blue). Fourth century A.D. Moshchiny hill-fort at Popolta river, tributary of R. Ugra, central Russia. Gos. Istoricheskij Muzej, Moscow.

44 Silver fibula with a bronze spring and an enamelled plaque from chieftain's grave (barrow 25) in Szwajcaria near Suwałki (Suvalkai). Early fifth century A.D. Muzeum Archeologiczne, Warsaw.

45 Chest ornament: bronze chains attached to semi-lunar pendants and pins with cross-shaped heads decorated with conical silver plates and striated rings. Woman's grave from the fifth century A.D., which also yielded a silver necklace, silver bracelets, glass beads and bronze finger-rings. Veršvai, suburb of Kaunas. Istorinis Muziejus, Kaunas.

46 Chest ornament: bronze chains, 80 cm. long, attached to a bronze pin and a silver bow-fibula. Seventh century A.D. Pašušvis near Radviliškis, northern Lithuania. Istorijos-etnografijos Muziejus, Vilnius.

47 Silver bow-fibula ornamented with silver rings and gold plates with a net pattern. Sixth century A.D. 8 cm. long. Užpelkiai near Salantai, western Lithuania. Istorinis Muziejus, Kaunas.

48 Silver bracelet. Sixth century A.D. Dvelaičiai near Žagarė, northern Lithuania. Istorinis Muziejus, Kaunas.

49 Silver necklace, *c.* A.D. 500. Lyduvėnai near Tytuvėnai, central Lithu‍ania. Istorinis Muziejus, Kaunas.

50 Silver neck‍ring. Sixth century A.D. Akmenė near Tytuvėnai, central Lithuania. Istorinis Muziejus, Kaunas.

51 Snake‍headed silver fibula. Seventh century A.D. Grobiņa near Liepāja, western Latvia. Vēstures Muzejs, Riga.

52–54 Shaft‍hole axe, Podmonteikiai, actual size (52); spearhead, Dukštas, north‍eastern Lithuania, 21·2 cm. long (53); iron umbo of wooden shield, Ignalina, 23 cm. diam. Sixth–seventh centuries A.D. Istorijos‍etnografijos Muziejus, Vilnius.

55 Grave goods from man's burial: bronze fibulae, neck‍ring, bracelets, ring, iron spearheads, axe, scythes, bridle‍bits, ring for bridle, and spurs. Sixth century A.D. Reketė, grave 33, near Salantai, western Lithuania. Istorinis Muziejus, Kaunas.

56 Silver‍coated bronze pendant and a bronze pin with chains and a silver‍coated chain holder. Ninth century A.D. Pin 22·5 cm. long. Laiviai, district of Salantai, western Lithuania. Istorijos‍etnografijos Muziejus, Vilnius.

57 Woman's grave goods; pins with silver‍plated head, and chain‍holders, neck‍rings, fibulae, spiral arm‍ring and finger‍rings, glass bead, and iron knife. Tenth century A.D. Paluknys near Tytuvėnai, central Lithuania. Istorinis Muziejus, Kaunas.

58 Cross‍shaped bronze pins with chains. Woman's chest ornament. Pins 15·4 cm. long. Vėžlaukis near Tytuvėnai, central Lithuania. Istorinis Muziejus, Kaunas.

59 Bronze necklace with flat overlapping ends and pendants attached. Eleventh century A.D. Peršiukštai near Švenčionys, eastern Lithuania. Istorijos‍etnografijos Muziejus, Vilnius.

60 Silver neck‍ring with conical ends. Tenth century A.D. Dvarčėnai near Daugai, eastern Lithuania. Istorinis Muziejus, Kaunas.

61 Bronze horseshoe fibula. Eleventh century A.D. Stačiūnai near Pakruojus, central Lithuania. Istorinis Muziejus, Kaunas.

62 Horseshoe fibula. Bronze, tenth century A.D. Slepsniai near Joniškis, northern Lithuania, 10·2 cm. diam. Istorinis Muziejus, Kaunas.

63 Massive bronze bracelet, triangular in cross-cut. Tenth century A.D. Švėkšna near Priekulė, western Lithuania. Istorijos-ethnografijos Muzie-jus, Vilnius.

64 Man's bracelet. Eleventh century A.D. Madliena near Ėrgļi, Latgale (Latvia). Vēstures Muzejs, Riga.

65 Kerchief (reconstruction) of indigo-blue wool. Ornament made of bronze rings. Eleventh-century woman's grave from Ainava near Kārļi, Vidzeme, Vēstures Muzejs, Riga.

66 Parts of leather belts, and a belt decorated with bronze plates (reconstruc-tion). Ninth–tenth centuries A.D. *a, b,* Mažeikiai, northern Lithuania; *c,* Laiviai near Salantai, western Lithuania. Width, *a,* 2·6 cm.; *b,* 3·4 cm.; *c,* 2·5 cm. Istorinis Muziejus, Kaunas.

67 Instruments for girdle twisting in a birch-bark box found in a woman's cremation grave of the tenth or eleventh century in the cemetery of Jazdai near Kretinga, western Lithuania, *c.* 1 : 1. Istorinis Muziejus, Kaunas.

68, 69 Swords of Viking type. Iron hilts with silver inlay (white tone). 72, Lin-kūnai near Klaipėda; 73, Viskiautai (Wiskiauten) near Fischhausen. Formerly Prussia Museum, Königsberg.

70 Horse bridle: lead and silver plates and bronze jingle bells, *c.* twelfth century. Cemetery of Veršvai, suburb of Kaunas. Istorinis Muziejus, Kaunas.

71, 72 Details of horses' graves from the cemetery of Veršvai, suburb of Kaunas. Istorinis Muziejus, Kaunas.

73, 74 Silver-plated iron bridle (photograph and reconstruction). Twelfth century A.D. Rimaisai near Ramygala, central Lithuania. Istorinis Muzie-jus, Kaunas.

75, 76 Silver-plated iron stirrup (photograph and reconstruction). Twelfth century A.D. Rimaisai near Ramygala, central Lithuania. Istorinis Muzie-jus, Kaunas.

77, 78   Hill-fort of Impiltis near Skuodas, western Lithuania; 77, viewed from the river; 78, air photograph taken during the excavations.

79   Roofed poles topped with iron sun and moon symbols in the nineteenth-century cemetery of eastern Lithuania.

Abalus, isle, 118, 119
Abashevo culture, 62, 93
Adalbert, Bishop, 25, 26
Adam of Bremen, 25, 168, 183
Adriatic Sea, 118, 119, 121
Aestii, Aisti, Aistians, 21, 22, 25, 119, 144, 185
Agathyrsi, 98, 102
agriculture: Bronze Age, 60; cereals, 40, 104, 115, 116, 166; flax, 117; 'Golden Age', 113; hoes, 59, 60, 64, 114; Kurgan, 40, 49; scythe, 115–6, 166; sickles, 64, 104, 107, 114, 115; slash-and-burn, 115, 116; two-field system, 166
Aismarės, *see* Frisches Haff
Aizezari near Sakstagals, cemetery, 160
ale, 25
Algirdas, Lithuanian grand duke, 176, 177, 184
Alka, sacred grove, hills, 84, 193
Alkupė, Alkupis, 196
amber, 55, Bronze Age, 55–9; Chalcolithic, 49; Early Iron Age, 69–74; Gothic times, 144–5; offerings, 52; Roman times, 109, 118–21, 129; sources of, 56, 57; statuette of Assurnasirpal, 65; trade routes, Bronze Age, 58–59; trade routes, Early Iron Age, 71, 72, 74
Anatolia, 38, 41, 59
Androphagi (Mordvins), 83, 98, 99, 101, 102

Ansgar, archbishop of the Bremen-Hamburg diocese, 143, 153
Antoniewicz, J., 11, 19, 138
Apulia (Apuolė), 143, 153, 154, 169
Aquileia, 121
Armenian language, 40, 41, 43
Asote, earthwork, 169
Austeravia, 119
Auseklis, Latvian morning star, 199, 202
Aušrinė, Lithuanian morning star, 199, 202
Autrimpas, Prussian god of the sea, 197
Avars, 148
Avestan language, 40, 41, 42
axe: Baltic, Nortycken, 62, 64, 65; battle-, 44, 49, 157, 164; boat-, 49; flanged, 59, 64; in cult, 68, 202; socketed, 115, 157

Balanovo, culture, 62, 92, 93
Balt, name, 21
Barta, Barthi, Barti, Prussian tribe and province, 23, 173
Basilia, 118, 119
battle-axe, *see* axe
Battle-axe culture, 44
Bell Beaker culture, 44
Bell-grave (lamp-shade) culture, 83, 85
belts, leather, 162–4
Berzha, R., 32
Bezzenberger, A., 17
Bilogrudovka, culture, 62, 99
Bilopotok, culture, 62

Black Sea, 68, 97, 177
Blue Waters, 177
Boat-axe culture, East Baltic, 46, 49
bog burial, 79
Bohemia, 58, 74, 145, 149
Bondarikha, culture, 95, 96
Borshevo, hill-forts, 149
Boters, near Gerum, cemetery, 156
bridle, 145, 147, 165
Brushed Pottery culture, 83, 95, 150
Budini, 98, 101
Bug, Western, R., 27, 167
Būga, K., 28–9
Buj II, site, 93
burial rites: animal bones in graves, 53, 68;
    barrows, 52–3, 65, 72–3, 112, 142;
    Bronze Age, 52–3, 65–7; cremation, 65,
    141–2, 184; coffins, 61, 65–6, 112, 157;
    Curonian, 157; Early Iron Age, 72–3;
    funeral meals, 186; funeral races, 185;
    funeral wedding, 189; 'Golden Age',
    112; horse sacrifice, graves, 66, 164, 187;
    Middle Iron Age, 142; obligatory death,
    double-graves, suttee, 42, 137, 188;
    preservation by freezing, 186; royal
    graves, 66, 138–9, 184
Byelo-Russia, 13, 27, 28, 43, 48, 95, 100,
    102, 150, 152, 177

caps, woollen, 126–7, 145, 163
Carnuntum, 119, 121
castle (acropolis), 41, feudal, 157, 165,
    168 ff.
Caucasus, Caucasian elements, 68–9, 70
Celts, Celtic, 19, 54, 68, 108, 117, 166
Chernjakovo culture, 109–11
Chernoleska culture, 99, 108

Christianity, introduction of, 179
Cimmerians, 20, 54, 68, 69, 97
climate, 13
coffins, tree trunk, 61, 65–6, 112, 157
coins: Anglo-Saxon, 156, 167; Arab, 156,
    167; Byzantine, 156, 167; Danish, 156,
    167; German, 156, 167; Roman, 116,
    123–4, 128; Roman-Byzantine, 144;
    Swedish, 167
Comb-marked and Pitted-ware, people, 44
copper: sources of, W. Carpathian, 54, E.
    Alpine, 54, S. Ural, 55, 93; industry,
    central Europe, 54
Corded Pottery, proto-Baltic, culture, 50
Corded Ware culture, 44
corn spirit, 192, 193
costumes, garments, 161–3
Courish Lagoon, 50, 143–4
cremation, 65, 68, 142, 184
Crusades, 172–3
Curonia (Kurland), 24, 123, 153–4,
    157–8, 160, 168–9, 184
Curonians (Chori, Cori), tribe, 21, 24,
    83, 112, 124, 126, 141–3, 146–8,
    152–3, 155–9, 167, 171, 173, 183–4
currency, 166
Czechoslovakia, 68, 80

daina, the song, 15
Danzig, *see* Gdańsk
Daugava (Düna, Dvina), R., 13, 100,
    112, 116–17, 150, 152, 158, 167, 169,
    170
Daugmale, earthwork, 169
Danes (Vikings), 148, 153, 158
Danube, R., 61, 121
Darius, Persian king, 97

Dekla, Latvian deity of fate, 198
Denmark, 74, 155
Desna, R., 33, 95–6, 100, 136, 148–9, 151
Dievas, sky god, 189, 190, 198–9, 200
Dignāja, hill-fort, 169
Djakovo, hill-forts, 150
Dlugosz, 184
Dnieper, R., basin, 32, 95, 99, 100, 101–2, 107, 122, 136, 149, 177
Dniester, R., 86, 99
Don, R., 95, 149
Dorotowo (Darethen), site, 123
Dröbnitz, bog, 79, 80
Drusken (Druskiai), site, 73
Dusburg, P., 22, 179, 183

Earth, deity, veneration, 191–2
earthworks, 168
East Prussia, 13, 17–19, 48, 51–2, 54, 64–5, 70, 71, 73, 76, 79, 80, 85
Egil's-saga, 157
Einhard, 22
Elbe–Saale region, 74
elektron (amber), 55
Elbing (Truso), town, trading centre, 143, 153
enamel, enamelled ornaments, 135–7
engravings, 77
Estonia, Estonians, 21, 48, 57, 149, 158, 167, 173, 177, 188
Europoid skulls, 46
Eylau (Bagratinovsk), town, 89

Face-urn culture, 83, 85
face-urns, 75 ff.
Fat'janovo, culture, 34, 45–6, 49, 62, 91–3
Fennoscandia, 55

feudal system, 139, 171
Finland, 48, 132
Finno-Ugrian, lands, tribes, 20, 21, 27–9, 36, 54, 97, 109, 111, 122, 148, 150, 154
fire, in religion, 203
Fischhausen (Primorsk), town, 52, 64, 67
fishing, 105, 106
flint mines, 49
folklore, 15; folk art, 181
Frisches Haff, 25, 50, 51, 143–4, 173
Frische Nehrung, 56
funeral rites, *see* burial rites
Funnel-Beaker, culture, 40, 44, 49
furs, trade in, 168

Gabrieliskiai near Girkalnis, site, 116
Galinda, Galindians, Prussian province and tribe, 22–3, 27, 83, 88, 122, 136, 144
Galindians (*Goljad'*), eastern Baltic tribe, 28, 151
Gediminas, Lithuanian grand duke, 177, 178
Gelehrte Estnische Gesellschaft, Tartu, 16
Gdańsk (Danzig), 77
Germany, 48, 62, 64, 69, 85, 167, 178
Germanic: expansion, 87; Jastorf culture, 86; Northern Area culture, 19, 20, 117; ornaments, 64–5, 71, 125; people, tribes, 25, 86, 122
Ghillebert de Lanoy, 184
girdles (*juostos*), 163
glaesum, glesum (amber), 119
glass industry, 128, 165
Globular Amphora culture, 44
Gniezno, cathedral, 26

gold, 55, 57, 125, 137–8, 165

Gorodok, sanctuary, 182

Goths, 19, 87–8, 111, 118, 122, 141, 145, 148

Gothic: cemeteries, 109–11; fibulae, 145; kingdom, 144, 148; language, 40–2

Gotland, 152–3, 155–6, 167

Grabowo urn, 78–9

graves, *see* burial rites

Greek language, 40–3

Grewingk, C., 18

Grobin (Grobiņa), Swedish colony in Curonia, 152–4, 158

groves and forests, holy, 193

Grünwalde (Zielenica), barrow, 87, 89

Haesti, *see* Aesti

Haffküstenkultur, 49

Halich-Vladimir, Rus' of, 171

Hallstatt culture, 19, 69, 75, 95

hammer, in religion, 202

Harald hildetand, Swedish king, 153

harness, horse, 164

harrows, 114

head cloth, 126–7, 161

Helladic culture, 56

helmet, 164, 167

Henry of Latvia, 188

Herodotus, 22, 97–9, 101–2

Hervarar saga, 153

hill-forts, hill-top villages, 16, 102–3, 113, 148, 150

hills, sacred, 193

Hittite deity, 59

hoes: iron, 114; snake-headed of stone, 59, 60, 64

holy rivers and lakes, 196

horse, 41, 49, 78, 92, 105, 117, 164, 187

house: Chalcolithic, 51; Early Iron Age, 80, 81, 104; Indo-European words, for, 42; Late Iron Age, 157; house-urns, 74

Hugleifs near Silte, Gotland, 155–6

human sacrifice, 52, 193

Hungary, 68–9

Huns, 109–111, 122, 148

Hylae(a), place, 98–9

Hypatius, chronicle, 151

Ibrāhīm-ibn-Jakūb, 24

Icelandic sagas, 153

Illyrian, Illyrians, 43, 54

Impiltis, earthwork, 143, 168–9

Indo-European: common words, 40–2; expansion to Europe, 38–9; groups, 19, 21, 43; languages, 37

iron smelting, 106, 117

Ivar vidfamne, Swedish king, 153

Iwno, pottery type, 60

Jastorf culture, 86–7

Jerome of Prague, 202

Jersika, earthwork and town, 169, 170

Jordanes, 22

Jotvingai, Jatwiagi, *see* Sudovians

Jukhnovo culture, 95–6

Julianus, knight in Nero's reign, 120, 122

Juodkrantė, site, 57

juostos, see girdles

Jutland, 56–7

jūšė (iūs, juxá, yuh), meal of meat, 41

Kaluga, town, 100, 150, 152

Kalvis, Kalvelis, Kalvaitis, Lithuanian heavenly smith, 199, 202

kanklės, the zither, 35
Kapsēda, town, 124
Kaukai, subterranean manikins, 194
Kauguru Pekas Kalns, earthwork, 169
Kaunas, town, 57, 129, 135, 167
Kaup (Viskiautai), barrow, 52–3
Kazan, town, 93
kerchief, 161–3
Kęstutis, Lithuanian duke, 116, 184
key, of iron, 158
Kiev, area, town, 107, 136, 149, 167
Kirghizian steppes, 122
Klaipėda (Memel), town, 59, 122, 152, 156, 167
Komarov culture, 62, 99
Kretinga, town, 73, 127–8, 156–7, 161, 168
Krikštonys, cemetery, 139
Krivė, priest, 183
Krivichi, eastern Slavic tribe, 109–11, 150–2
Kurgan (Corded, Battle-axe) culture, 38–44; acropolises, 41; burial rites, 42; houses, 42; metallurgy, 41; proto-Baltic branch, 48; vehicles, 41; villages, 42
Kurland, *see* Curonia
Kurmaičiai, cemeteries, 72–3, 127–8
Kuršių Nerija (Kurische Nehrung), 56, 57

Labotakiai, cemetery, 130
Laima, goddess of fate, 194, 197–8
Laiviai, cemetery, 157
lamentation songs (*raudos*), 186–7
Langobardic fibulae, 144
language relationships, 40–3
La Tène culture, 86, 90, 95, 108, 125, 131

Latgala, *see* Lettigallia
Latin 40–2
Latvia, 13, 18, 48, 54, 57, 65, 95, 100, 123–4, 132–3, 141, 149, 151–2, 156, 158–9, 165, 172, 177, 179, 181
Laumes, fairies, 197
Laurentius, chronicle, 151
Lausitz culture, *see* Lusatian
leather working, 165
Lettigallia, Lettigallians (Latgallians, Letts), 24, 83, 112, 142, 147, 150, 162, 167, 169–73
Lettish language, 21, 40–2
Lithuania, 13, 18, 48, 54, 57, 71–3, 100, 114, 116, 123, 126, 128, 130–3, 135, 156, 159, 161, 164, 169, 171–2, 188
Lithuanian empire, 174–5, 177
Lithuanian language, 37, 40–2
Lithuanian state, 19, 155, 172, 177
Lithuanians, people, tribe, 21, 24, 83, 112, 117, 126, 141–3, 147, 171–2, 184
Littausdorf hoard, 64
loan words, Baltic in Finno-Ugrian, 33–6, 91
Lusatian culture, 27, 62, 64, 69, 71, 80

Mājas kungs, Lettish deity of homestead, 192
Mälar Valley, 153
mare's milk, 25
Margiris, Lithuanian duke, 188
Mari, Merja, Volga Finnic tribe, 34, 83
Maskatuži, cemetery, 116
Masuria, province, 13, 77, 79, 116
Masurian lakes, 136
mead, 25
Melanchlaeni, 98, 101–2

Mėnuo, Meness, moon god, 190, 199, 201
metallurgy, 41, 54–5, 94, 117, 165
Mežotne, earthwork, 169
Milky Way, 190
Milograd group, 83, 95, 107
Mindaugas, Lithuanian king, 172, 176
Minsk, town, 102, 123
Montelius, O., 18
Moravia, 58, 121, 145, 149
Mordvins, Mordva, Volga–Finnic tribe, 34, 83, 99
Moscow, 97, 100, 150, 152, 177
Moshchiny hoard, 136
Mycenae, Mycenaean Greece, 55, 56, 59, 65

Nadruva, Nadruvians, Prussian province and people, 23, 173, 183
Nara, R., 32, 102
Narew (Naruve), R., 27, 32
Nemenčinė, earthwork, 169
Nemunas (Niemen, Memel), R., 13, 27–8, 38, 83, 102, 122, 139, 143, 150, 158, 167, 169, 176, 188, 193
Nerman, Birger, 152
Neroma, east Baltic province, 100
Neuri, 22, 83, 97–101
Nikolo–Lenivets, village, 103–4, 106
Nikol'skaja, T. N., 103
Noricum, 121, 124
Norsemen, 152, 154
Northern Area culture, 19
Norwegian sagas, 153
Notanga, Notangia, Notangians, Prussian province and people, 22–3, 88, 116, 173
Novgorod, town, 149, 152, 167

Nydam, Jutland, 139

oak, sacred, 194
Oder, R., 48, 55, 61, 71–2, 121
Odyssey, 55
offerings: human, 52, 193; goat, sheep, 53, 193; oxen, horse, 68, 193; pig, 193, 197; cock, hen, 193
Oka, R., 32, 91, 93, 97, 102, 136–7, 148–9, 177
Oksywia culture, 87
Öland, 156
Oliver Scholasticus, Bishop of Paderborn, 192
Olov, Swedish king, 153
Olsztyn (Allenstein), town, 27, 123
Order of the Sword, 186
ornaments, art, 125–37, 159–63; bracelets, 71, 135, 137, 160–1; chains, 129, 130, 145; diadems, 128, 145; fibulae, 128–9, 131, 134–5, 145–7, 156, 159; neck-rings, 70, 128–9, 131–2, 145, 159; pendant, 69, 70, 129, 130, 133; pins, 64, 70, 71, 106, 129, 130–1, 156, 159; teeth, 164; temple, 73, 126–7
Ostróda (Osterode), town, 123
Ostrogoths, 144
Ostrówka, town, 27

Pagudė, Pogesania, Prussian province and people, 22–3, 173
Painted Pottery culture, 40
Pamedė, Pomesania, Prussian province and people, 22–3, 173
Pannonia, 121, 124
Perkūnas, Perkonis, Perkons, Baltic god of the air, 194, 198, 199, 202

Persante (Parsęta), R., 86
Persians, 102
Petersen, E., 85
physical type, 46–7
Pilėnai, castle, 188
pincers, 164
Pitted Ware culture, 92
Plain Pottery culture or group, 83, 95, 97, 108
Plavniekkalns, cemetery, 146
Pleškučiai, cemetery, 133
Pliny, 88, 118–21
plough-shares, 114, 115, 166
Poland, 53, 54, 60, 86, 174, 177
Poljane, eastern Slavic tribe, 149, 151
Polotsk, 117, 150, 152
Pomerania, eastern, 19, 27, 56, 62, 65, 71–7, 84–7
Pomponius Mela, 118
Pot-covered Urn (Bell-grave) culture, 84, 108
potter's wheel, 166
'Povest Vremennykh Let', 28
Poznań, town, 76
Pregel, Prėglius, R., 32, 116
preservation by freezing, 186
Preussisch-Görlitz, town, 123
Priekulė, town, 131, 133
priests, 183
Protva, R., 27, 151
Prussia Museum, 17, 130
Prussia, Prussians, western Balts, 22, 24, 26, 88–9, 141, 160, 173, 179
Prussian language, 21, 26, 40–2, 176
Pryšmantai, cemetery, 161
Pskov, town, 149, 150, 167
Ptolemy, 28, 88

Puškaitis, Lithuanian earth god, 194
Pytheas, 118

Radimichi, eastern Slavic tribe, 152
Rambynas, sacred hill, 193
Rantau, cemetery, 66–7
Raunas Tanīsa Kalns, earthwork, 169
Ravenna, 144
Rezne, barrow, 66, 68
Rhineland, 124, 167
Riga, Bay of, 62, 173
Riga, city, 66, 169, 172
Rimbert, Bishop, 143, 153
river names, Baltic, 28 ff.
Roman: coins, 116, 123–4, 128, 144; empire, 109–11; fibulae, 124; glass, 124, 127–8; oil lamp, 124; terra sigillata, 124
Romainiai, Romene, sacred town, 194
Romny, hill-forts, 149
Romuva, sacred place, 183, 194
roofed poles, 195
Rucava, town, 148
Rumania, 68
Russia: Greater, 43, 45, 49, 105, 136; north-western, 113
Russian Archaeological Congresses, 17, 18
Russian chronicle, 151
Rzucewo: culture, 49; village, 51, 52

sacred towns, Lithuania, 180
saddle, 165
Saeborg, Curonian town, 143, 154
Sakstagals, cemetery, 160
Samland, Semba, Prussian province and people, 23, 25, 52–3, 55–6, 62, 64, 66–7, 69, 71, 73, 77, 80, 83, 88–90, 112, 116, 119, 121–3, 129, 158, 167, 173, 176

sanctuaries, 180–2
Sanskrit, 37, 40–2
Saule, deity of the sun, 198, 200, 201, 203
Sauslaukas, Swedish colony, 153
scales, 158, 166, 167
Scandinavia, Scandinavian, 20, 77, 139, 146, 154, 158
Schlakalken, cemetery, 71
Schleicher, A., 37
Schleswig-Holstein, 74
scythe, 115–16, 166
Scythia, 88, 99–102
Scythian, Scythians, 18–20, 54, 68–9, 80, 82–3, 93–4, 97–102, 164
seal hunting, 49
Selian, Selians, Selonians, east Baltic tribe, 21, 83, 173
Semigallia, Semigallians, east Baltic province and tribe, 21, 24, 83, 112, 142, 159, 162, 167, 169, 171–3
Serebrennikov, B. A., 34
Šernai, Hittite figurine in Lithuania, 59
shield, 78, 112, 147–8, 164
Siberian steppes, 38
sickle, 104, 107, 114–15, 166
Silesia, 58, 61, 69, 85–6, 121
silver, 125, 131–2, 134, 137–8, 145, 147, 158, 161–3, 165–7, 171
Slavic, expansion, language, lands, 20, 40, 54, 87, 97, 107, 141, 145, 148–52, 154
Smolensk, town, 32, 102, 117, 150, 152, 167, 180–2
Snorre Sturleson, 155
songs: Baltic, 15; solar, 201
spear, spearhead, 62, 78, 112, 147, 157, 164
springs, holy, 193
spurs, 164

Starogard urn, 78
Starzykowe Małe, fortified village, 81–2
State Historic Museum, Riga, 17–18
steel, 117
stirrups, 147, 165
stock-breeding, domestic animals, 40, 41, 60, 117, 166
stone cult, 196
stones, footprints on, 195
Strabo, 88, 118
Stragna, cemetery, 131
Strobjenen, bracelet, 144
Studenok culture, 96
Succase (Suchacz), village, 51–2
Sudovian, Sūduva, Prussian people and province, 19, 22–3, 83, 112, 126, 139, 141, 147, 159
Suevian ocean, 119
Susz (Rosenberg), town, 82
Svein Estrithson, Danish king, 158
Svinukhovo, hill-fort, 104–6
Swayxtix, Suaixtis, Prussian god of stars, 202
Sweden, Swedish, 74, 143, 148, 152–3, 154, 158, 167
sword, 138–9, 147, 164, 167

Tacitus, 21, 25, 55, 88, 113–14, 122, 144
Talivaldis, duke of Lettigallia, 171
Tervete, province of Semigallia, 169, 171
Teutonic Order, Knights, 141, 155, 172–3, 177, 179, 183, 193
theocracy, 184
Theodoric, Gothic king, 144
Thomsen, V., 33
Thorolf, Viking, 157
Tilžė, 32, 71, 122, 193

Timaeus, 118
Timber-grave culture, 62, 94, 97
Tira, bog, 148
Tiryns, 59
Tokharians, 38, 41–3
Tolzha, R., 32
Tomashek, 99
toponymy, Baltic, 28 ff.
Toporov, V. N., 29
townships, 168 ff.
trade, Baltic: amber, *see* amber; furs, 168;
  Phoenician, 65; with central Europe,
  56–8, 62, 64, 69; with Goths, 144; with
  Finno-Ugrians, 109–11, 148; with free
  Germany, 122, 124–5; with Mycenaean
  Greece, 56–7, 59; with Roman empire,
  118, 121, 123–4; with Russians, 167;
  with Sweden, 167; with western Europe,
  167–8
Transylvania, 61
tree, in religion, 191, 194, 195
Tret'jakov, P. N., 180
Trubachev, O. N., 29
Trulick, cemetery, 70
Truso, trading town, 143, 153, 158, 167
Trzciniec culture, 61
Tsna (Cna), R., 32
Turaida, cemetery, 162
Turko-Tartar peoples, 148
Tushemlja, sanctuary, 180–2
Tyszkiewicz, E., 17

Udmurtian, Finno-Ugric language, 34–5
Ugra, R., 32, 102, 136
Ukraine, 48, 86, 177
Únětice culture, 56, 58, 60, 92
Únětice-Tumulus-Urnfield culture, 19, 62

Upa, R., 102
Uppland, 156
Upinis, Lithuanian river spirit, 197
Upytė, cemetery, 137
Uralic race, 46
Urals, Mts, 93, 136
Ushas, Vedic morning star, 199

Vakarinė, Lithuanian evening star, 199
Varmė, Varmians, Prussian province and
  people, 22–3, 173
Vasmer, M., 29
vegetation, 14
vehicle, 41, 78
vėlės, in folklore, 189, 190
Velikaja, R., 113, 148–50
Velikie Luki, town, 117
Veliuona, town, earthwork, 57, 169
Veneti, 119, 121
Veršvai, cemetery, 131, 137
Viestarts, duke of Semigallia, 171
Vikings, 24, 141, 143, 154, 156–8, 160
Vilkumuiža, cemetery, 165
village: Chalcolithic, 51; Early Iron Age,
  80, 81, 102–3, 107; Golden Age, 113;
  Middle Iron Age, 142; Slavic, 149
Vilnius, city, 135, 167, 169, 184
Visby, trading centre, 167
Vistula, R., 27, 38, 48, 51, 55, 57, 61, 69,
  75, 78, 80, 82, 87, 112, 121, 122, 132,
  144, 158, 172–3
Vitebsk, town, 102, 117, 152
Vjatichi, eastern Slavic tribe, 149, 151
Volga, R., 33, 38, 91–2, 177
Volga-Finnic, tribes, languages, 27, 33–6,
  137
Volosovo culture, 92

Volynia, 48–9, 61, 107, 149, 171
Voronezh, town, 149
Votyaks, Volga-Finnic tribe, 101
Vysocko culture, 62, 108
Vytautas, grand duke of Lithuania, 177

wagon, 78
Warta, R., 58, 121
water, holy, spirits, 196, 197
weapons, armament: bridle, 69, 145, 147–148, 165; bow and arrow, 49, 154, 164; halberd, 57; helmet, 164, 167; knife, warrior's, 161–2, 164; shield, 78, 117, 147–8, 164; spear, spearhead, 62, 64, 78, 112, 147–8, 157, 164; spur, 117, 147–8; stirrup, 147, 165; sword, 138–9, 147, 167
weights, 166
Wheeler, R. E. M., 122

Wiekau, cemetery, 112
Wigand von Marburg, 188
Wiskiauten (Viskiautai), trading centre, 143, 158
Workeim, barrow, 66
writing, 26
Wulfstan, 25, 142–3, 172, 185

Xenophon of Lampracus, 119

Ynglingasaga, 155

Zaltys, green snake, in Lithuanian folk-lore, 203
Zarubincy, Zarubinec culture, 107–11
Zhizdra, R., 32, 102, 150
žirgas, zirgs, riding horse, 164, 199
Złota, culture, 49, 53